Better Homes and Gardens®

THE BEST OF
WOOD®
BOOK 2

WE CARE!

All of us at Meredith® Books are dedicated to giving you the
information and ideas you need to create beautiful and useful
woodworking projects. We guarantee your satisfaction with this book
for as long as you own it. We also welcome your comments and
suggestions. Please write us at Meredith® Books, RW-240,
1716 Locust St., Des Moines, IA 50309-3023.

A **WOOD**® BOOK
Published by Meredith® Books

MEREDITH® **BOOKS**
President, Book Group: Joseph J. Ward
Vice President and Editorial Director: Elizabeth P. Rice
Managing Editor: Christopher Cavanaugh
Art Director: Ernest Shelton

WOOD® **MAGAZINE**
President, Magazine Group: William T. Kerr
Editor: Larry Clayton

THE BEST OF WOOD® **BOOK 2**
Produced by Roundtable Press, Inc.
Directors: Susan E. Meyer, Marsha Melnick
Senior Editor: Marisa Bulzone
Managing Editor: Ross L. Horowitz
Graphic Designer: Leslie Goldman
Design Assistant: Betty Lew
Art Assistant: Polly King
Proofreader: Amy Handy

For Meredith® **Books**
Editorial Project Manager/Associate Art Director: Tom Wegner
Contributing How-To Editors: Marlen Kemmet, Larry Johnston
Contributing Techniques Editor: Bill Krier
Production Manager: Doug Johnston

On the front cover: Fun-in-the-Sun Furniture, pages 7–11
On the back cover: Worth-Every-Minute Wall Clock, pages 45–48;
    Wheat-Motif Bread Box, pages 134–135; Keep-on-Recycling Toy Box,
    pages 99–103; The One-and-Only Teddy Bear Chair, pages 89–95

Meredith Corporation Corporate Officers:
Chairman of the Executive Committee: E. T. Meredith III
Chairman of the Board, President and Chief Executive Officer: Jack D. Rehm
Group Presidents: Joseph J. Ward, Books; William T. Kerr, Magazines;
    Philip A. Jones, Broadcasting; Allen L. Sabbag, Real Estate
Vice Presidents: Leo R. Armatis, Corporate Relations;
    Thomas G. Fisher, General Counsel and Secretary;
    Larry D. Hartsook, Finance; Michael A. Sell, Treasurer;
    Kathleen J. Zehr, Controller and Assistant Secretary

Throughout each year, WOOD® Magazine publishes instructions for building a wonderful array of woodworking projects. These projects are designed to help craftspeople of every skill level create pieces that will be appreciated for years to come. In this special collection, we invite you to look back on some of our best from 1993.

Contents

Projects for the Outdoors

6

Fun-in-the-Sun Furniture • 7
Lazy-Days Porch Rocker • 12
Leafy Lodging Birdhouse • 18
Seeds-and-Such Snack Shop • 20
Craftsman-Style Wall Lantern • 24
Plant Hanger from Paradise • 28

Fine Furnishings for the Home

30

Elegant Oak Dining Table • 31
Elegant Oak Dining Chairs • 38
Worth-Every-Minute Wall Clock • 45

Leaded-Glass Panels • 49
Woven-Wood Hamper • 56
The Safe-and-Simple Thin-Strip Ripper • 63
Bow-Front Table • 65
Pocket-Hole Drill Guide • 69
Down-to-Business Oak Desk • 70
High-Styled Raised Panels and Frames • 76
High-and-Mighty Tablesaw Jig • 82
Wild Kingdom Coatrack • 84

For the Very Young   88

The One-and-Only Teddy Bear Chair • 89
Little Red Tote Barn • 96
Keep-on-Recycling Toy Box • 99
Dresser-Top Dragon • 104
Choo-Choo to Go • 106
Smiley the Rocking Snail • 108
Baby's First Bed • 112

Special Mementos and Gifts   118

Autumn Leaves • 119
Echoes of Antiquity • 122
A Welcome Sign That Says It All • 126
Olympian Display • 128
A Picture-Book Box • 130
One-Stop Chopping • 132
Wheat-Motif Bread Box • 134
Lamination Sensation • 136
Down-Under Desk Clock • 140
Projects with Porpoise • 142
Ring Around the Wrist Watch • 146
Jewel of a Vial • 149
One Sweetheart of a Jewelry Box • 151
Country-Time Plate Rack • 155
A Stirring Display • 158

Acknowledgments   160

Enlarging Patterns • 160
Metric Equivalents • 160

Projects for the Outdoors

Out of the workshop and into the yard! Whether you're looking for a way to light up the night, a fantastic feeder for your feathered friends, a colorful hanging home for a favorite plant, or a way to sit back and relax on the front porch— here are projects to help you put the "great" into your outdoors.

Fun-in-the-Sun Furniture

Sit back and relax with this matching set

Perk up your patio or deck with this handsome furniture grouping that includes a table and chair along with the porch rocker shown on *page 12*. Build a patio-full of furniture that'll be the envy of the neighborhood, and at a price that won't break the bank.

Note: *Because of space limitations, we can't provide full-sized patterns for this project. However, to enable you to build the project, we've included gridded patterns. To enlarge these patterns, see the instructions on page 160.*

LET'S BEGIN WITH THE LEGS, RAILS, AND ARMRESTS

1 From 1¹⁄₁₆" genuine mahogany (not Philippine mahogany, which is not a true mahogany), cut the legs (A, B) to size plus 1" in length. Miter-cut the top end of each leg at 4° to cut the legs to the finished length stated in the Bill of Materials on *page 8* and shown on the End Frame Assembly drawing on *page 9*.

2 From ¾" genuine mahogany, cut the rails (C) to size.

3 Using the dimensions on the End Frame Assembly drawing, carefully mark the mortise and ¼" hole center-points on each leg (A, B). Following the four-step procedure on the Forming the Mortises drawing on *page 9*, drill and chisel the mortises through the legs.

4 Drill and countersink a ¼" hole in each front leg (A) and two in each back leg (B).

5 Mark the tenon locations on the ends of each rail (C). (See the Tenon detail on the End Frame Assembly drawing.) Then, cut tenons on both ends of each rail.

6 Cut two armrest blanks (D) to 3¼ x21¼" from ¾"-thick white oak. Using the Armrest drawing for reference, transfer the outline to one of the blanks. Tape the armrest blanks together (we used double-faced tape), with the edges and ends flush. Bandsaw the armrests to shape, sand the edges smooth, separate the armrests, and remove the tape.

7 Mark (but don't drill) the center-points for two pair of screw mounting holes on the top of each armrest.

CONSTRUCTING THE END FRAME ASSEMBLIES COMES NEXT

Note: *Construct your chair using Titebond II water-resistant glue, slow-set epoxy, or resorcinol glue so it can stand up to the elements.*

1 Rout ⅛" and ¼" round-overs on parts A, B, C, and D where shown on the End Frame Assembly and Exploded View drawings.

2 Glue and clamp a rail (C) between a front and back leg. Using a framing square, check that the legs are square to the rail.

3 Clamp an armrest on the top of each end frame assembly (A, B, C). Verify that the marked mounting holes are located on the top of the legs. Re-mark if necessary.

4 Drill the mounting holes through the armrests and into the top ends of the legs. Screw the armrests to the leg tops, plug the holes, and sand the plugs flush.

NOW, ADD THE STRETCHERS, AND JOIN THE END ASSEMBLIES

1 Cut the stretchers (E) to size. Cut 1¹⁄₁₆"-long tenons on the ends of each stretcher.

2 Rout ⅛" round-overs along the edges of each stretcher.

3 Glue the pair of stretchers between the end frames. (To ensure that the end assemblies would stay square to the stretchers, we clamped square corner braces in place and left them there until the glue dried.) Sand the chair frame.

LET'S MAKE THE SLAT-SUPPORT ASSEMBLIES

1 Cut two pieces of 1¹⁄₁₆" mahogany to 4¾x21" for the bottom-slat supports (F) and two pieces to 3x23" for back-slat supports (G).

2 Using the Slat Support drawing for reference, mark the location of a half-lap joint on one end of each slat support (F, G).

3 Mount a ¾"-wide dado blade to your tablesaw and an auxiliary wooden fence to your miter gauge. Elevate the blade to cut exactly half the thickness of your stock. (We used scrap the same thickness as the supports, and made test cuts to verify blade height.) Angle the miter gauge 20° from center, and clamp a stop to your auxiliary miter-gauge fence. Cut a half-lap on one end of each of the four slat supports where dimensioned on the drawing on *page 10*.

continued

Fun-in-the-Sun Furniture

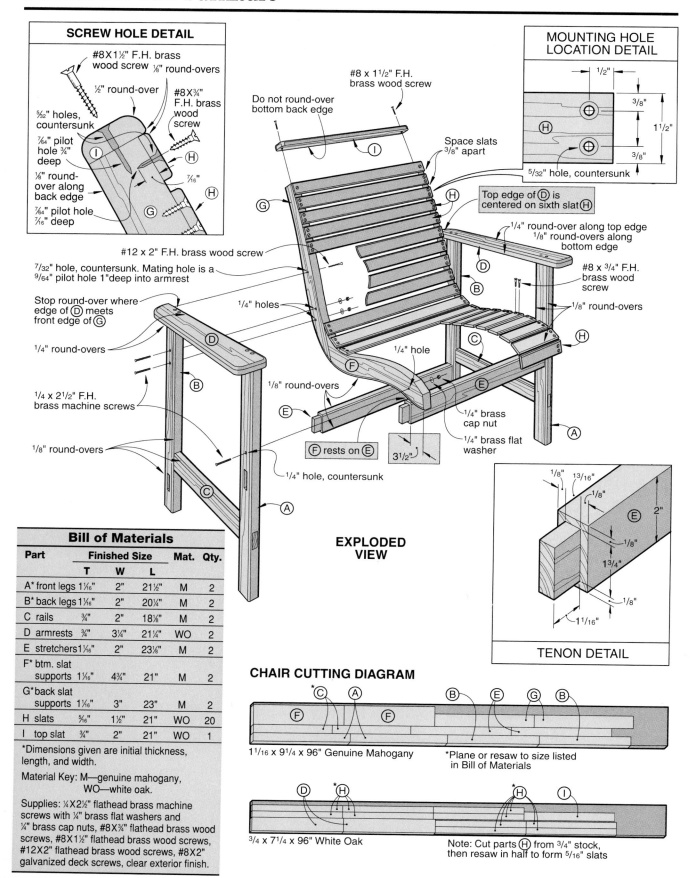

SCREW HOLE DETAIL

#8X1½" F.H. brass wood screw ⅛" round-overs

½" round-over

#8X¾" F.H. wood screw

⁵⁄₃₂" holes, countersunk

⁷⁄₆₄" pilot hole ¾" deep

⅛" round-over along back edge

⁷⁄₆₄" pilot hole ⁷⁄₁₆" deep

⁷⁄₁₆"

MOUNTING HOLE LOCATION DETAIL

½"   ⅜"   1½"   ⅜"

⁵⁄₃₂" hole, countersunk

#8 x 1½" F.H. brass wood screw

Do not round-over bottom back edge

Space slats ⅜" apart

Top edge of D is centered on sixth slat H

¼" round-over along top edge
⅛" round-overs along bottom edge

#8 x ¾" F.H. brass wood screw

⅛" round-overs

#12 x 2" F.H. brass wood screw

⁷⁄₃₂" hole, countersunk. Mating hole is a ⁹⁄₆₄" pilot hole 1"deep into armrest

¼" holes

Stop round-over where edge of D meets front edge of G

¼" round-overs

¼ x 2½" F.H. brass machine screws

⅛" round-overs

¼" hole

⅛" round-overs

F rests on E

3½"

¼" hole, countersunk

¼" brass cap nut

¼" brass flat washer

EXPLODED VIEW

TENON DETAIL

⅛" ¹³⁄₁₆" ⅛" 2" ⅛" 1¾" ⅛" 1¹⁄₁₆"

Bill of Materials

Part	Finished Size			Mat.	Qty.
	T	W	L		
A* front legs	1¹⁄₁₆"	2"	21½"	M	2
B* back legs	1¹⁄₁₆"	2"	20¼"	M	2
C rails	¾"	2"	18⅛"	M	2
D armrests	¾"	3¼"	21¼"	WO	2
E stretchers	1¹⁄₁₆"	2"	23⅛"	M	2
F* btm. slat supports	1¹⁄₁₆"	4¾"	21"	M	2
G* back slat supports	1¹⁄₁₆"	3"	23"	M	2
H slats	⁵⁄₁₆"	1½"	21"	WO	20
I top slat	¾"	2"	21"	WO	1

*Dimensions given are initial thickness, length, and width.

Material Key: M—genuine mahogany, WO—white oak.

Supplies: ¼X2½" flathead brass machine screws with ¼" brass flat washers and ¼" brass cap nuts, #8X¾" flathead brass wood screws, #8X1½" flathead brass wood screws, #12X2" flathead brass wood screws, #8X2" galvanized deck screws, clear exterior finish.

CHAIR CUTTING DIAGRAM

1¹⁄₁₆ x 9¼ x 96" Genuine Mahogany

*Plane or resaw to size listed in Bill of Materials

¾ x 7¼ x 96" White Oak

Note: Cut parts H from ¾" stock, then resaw in half to form ⁵⁄₁₆" slats

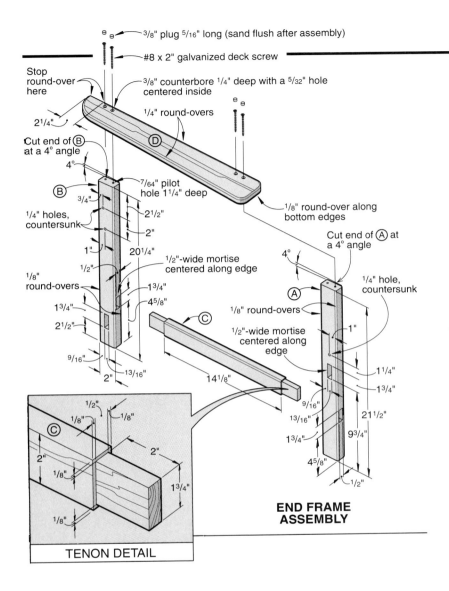

3/8" plug 5/16" long (sand flush after assembly)

#8 x 2" galvanized deck screw

Stop round-over here

3/8" counterbore 1/4" deep with a 5/32" hole centered inside

1/4" round-overs

2 1/4"

Cut end of (B) at a 4° angle

4°

(B)

3/4"

7/64" pilot hole 1 1/4" deep

1/4" holes, countersunk

2 1/2"

2"

1"

20 1/4"

1/2"

1/8" round-overs

1 3/4"

1 3/4"

4 5/8"

2 1/2"

9/16"

2"

13/16"

1/2"-wide mortise centered along edge

1/8" round-over along bottom edges

Cut end of (A) at a 4° angle

4°

(A)

1/4" hole, countersunk

1/8" round-overs

1/2"-wide mortise centered along edge

(C)

14 1/8"

1"

1 1/4"

1 3/4"

9/16"

13/16"

13/16"

1 3/4"

21 1/2"

9 3/4"

4 5/8"

1/2"

END FRAME ASSEMBLY

1/2"

1/8"

1/8"

(C)

2"

1/8"

2"

1/8"

1 3/4"

1/8"

TENON DETAIL

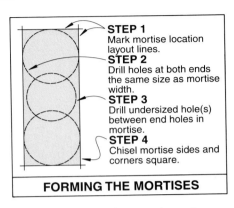

STEP 1
Mark mortise location layout lines.
STEP 2
Drill holes at both ends the same size as mortise width.
STEP 3
Drill undersized hole(s) between end holes in mortise.
STEP 4
Chisel mortise sides and corners square.

FORMING THE MORTISES

6 Rout ⅛" round-overs along the bottom and back edges of each slat support where shown on the Exploded View drawing *opposite*.

FASTEN THE SLATS TO THE SLAT SUPPORTS

1 From ⁵⁄₁₆"-thick white oak (we planed thicker stock to size), cut 20 seat slats (H) to 1½x21". From ¾" stock, cut the top slat (I) to size.

2 Rout a ⅛" round-over along the top edges and ends of each ⁵⁄₁₆" slat (H) and a ½" round-over along the top edges and ends of the top slat (I). See the Exploded View and accompanying Screw Hole detail for reference. Next, rout a ⅛" round-over along the bottom front edge of the top slat.

3 Drill countersunk screw holes in each slat where dimensioned on the Exploded View drawing and accompanying Mounting Hole Location detail. Note that the bottom and top two slats have only one hole per end. (We clamped a fence and a stopblock to our drill-press table to consistently position the holes from slat to slat.)

4 Place the two slat supports on your benchtop. Clamp a large handscrew clamp to each to hold them upright.

5 Screw the top slat (I) to the slat supports. Fasten one of the ⁵⁄₁₆" slats (H) to the opposite bottom end of the assembly. Following the layout marks on the slat supports, fasten the remaining seat slats (H). Check that the slats are square to the supports.

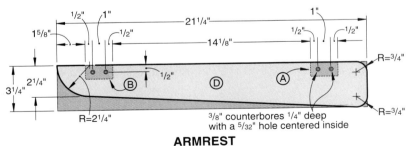

1/2"

1"

21 1/4"

1"

1 5/8"

1/2"

1/2"

14 1/8"

1/2"

1/2"

1/2"

R=3/4"

3 1/4"

2 1/4"

1/2"

(B)

(D)

(A)

R=3/4"

R=2 1/4"

3/8" counterbores 1/4" deep with a 5/32" hole centered inside

ARMREST

4 Dry-clamp the two supports (one F and one G per support) to check the fit. Glue and clamp each of the two slat supports.

5 Following the method described to form the matching armrests, tape the slat supports (F, G) together, transfer the pattern outlines to the slat supports, cut the supports to shape, and sand the edges smooth. Then, using a try square, transfer the slat (H) locations to the top front edge of each slat support. Pry the pieces apart, remove the double-faced tape, and finish-sand the slat supports, being careful not to sand away the slat location lines.

continued

Fun-in-the-Sun Furniture

continued

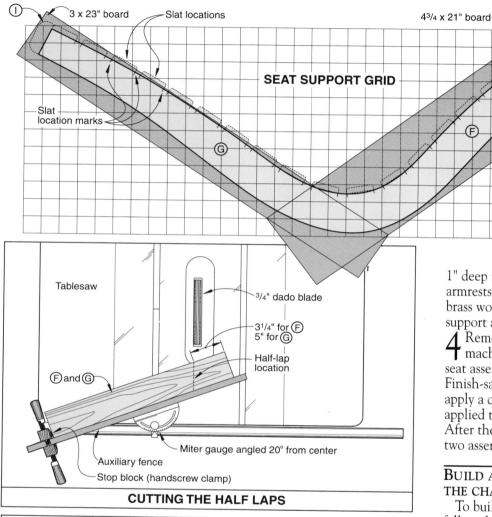

SEAT SUPPORT GRID

ⓘ   3 x 23" board ——— Slat locations

4³/₄ x 21" board ———

Front end

Slat location marks

Ⓖ

Ⓕ

Each square=1"

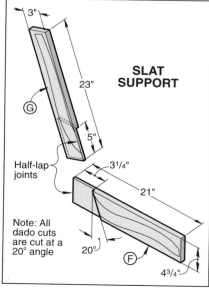

Tablesaw

³/₄" dado blade

3¹/₄" for Ⓕ
5" for Ⓖ

Half-lap location

Ⓕ and Ⓖ

Miter gauge angled 20° from center

Auxiliary fence

Stop block (handscrew clamp)

CUTTING THE HALF LAPS

SLAT SUPPORT

3"

23"

Ⓖ

5"

Half-lap joints

3¹/₄"

21"

Note: All dado cuts are cut at a 20° angle

20°

Ⓕ

4³/₄"

1" deep into the inside edge of the armrests. Drive a #12x2" flathead brass wood screw through each support and into the armrests.

4 Remove the wood screws and machine screws to separate the seat assembly from the chair frame. Finish-sand both assemblies and apply a quality exterior finish. (We applied three coats of spar varnish.) After the finish has dried, fasten the two assemblies back together.

BUILD A TABLE TO MATCH THE CHAIR

To build the matching table, follow the same construction procedure used to build the chair, and refer to the Table Exploded View drawing and the Bill of Materials for the table *opposite*.

ATTACH THE SEAT ASSEMBLY TO THE CHAIR FRAME

1 With a helper, position the seat assembly on the chair frame where dimensioned in the tinted boxes on the Exploded View drawing. Once positioned, firmly clamp the seat to the frame.

2 Using the previously drilled ¼" holes in the front and rear legs as guides, drill ¼" holes through the supports. Using ¼" brass machine screws, flat washers, and cap nuts, connect the two assemblies.

3 Working from the back of the chair, drill a ⁷/₃₂" countersunk shank hole through the back seat supports (G) and a ⁹/₆₄" pilot hole

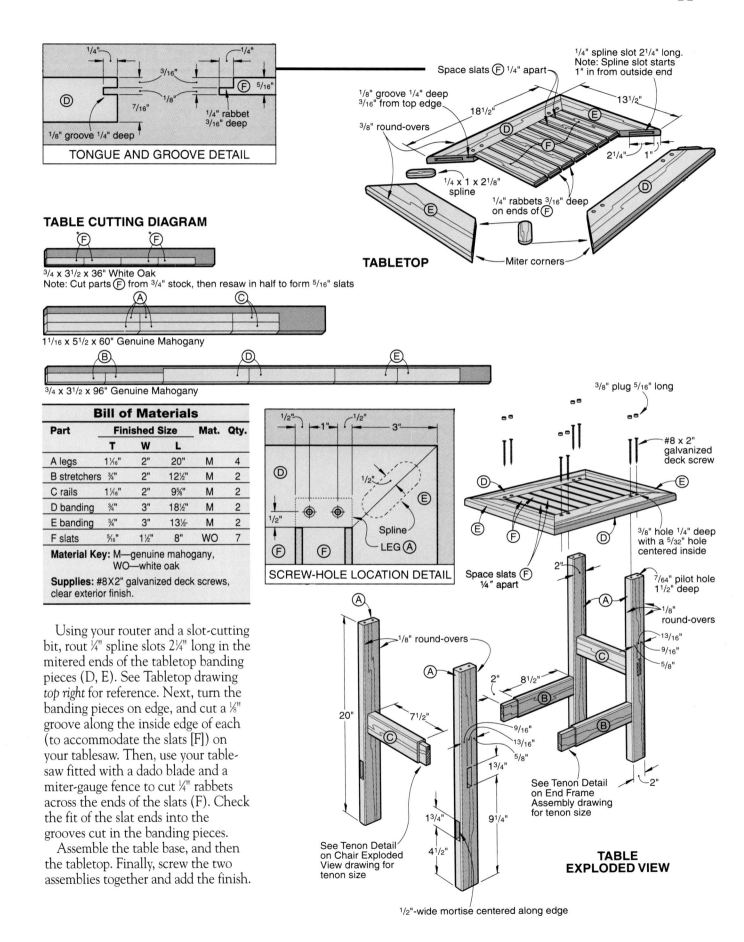

TONGUE AND GROOVE DETAIL

- 1/4"
- 3/16"
- 1/4"
- 5/16"
- 1/8"
- 7/16"
- 1/4" rabbet 3/16" deep
- 1/8" groove 1/4" deep

(D) (F)

TABLETOP

1/4" spline slot 2 1/4" long.
Note: Spline slot starts
1" in from outside end

Space slats (F) 1/4" apart

1/8" groove 1/4" deep
3/16" from top edge

3/8" round-overs

18 1/2"

13 1/2"

(D) (E)

(F)

2 1/4" 1"

(D)

1/4 x 1 x 2 1/8"
spline

(E)

1/4" rabbets 3/16" deep
on ends of (F)

Miter corners

TABLE CUTTING DIAGRAM

(F) (F)

3/4 x 3 1/2 x 36" White Oak
Note: Cut parts (F) from 3/4" stock, then resaw in half to form 5/16" slats

(A) (C)

1 1/16 x 5 1/2 x 60" Genuine Mahogany

(B) (D) (E)

3/4 x 3 1/2 x 96" Genuine Mahogany

Bill of Materials

Part	Finished Size			Mat.	Qty.
	T	W	L		
A legs	1 1/16"	2"	20"	M	4
B stretchers	3/4"	2"	12 1/2"	M	2
C rails	1 1/16"	2"	9 5/8"	M	2
D banding	3/4"	3"	18 1/2"	M	2
E banding	3/4"	3"	13 1/2"	M	2
F slats	5/16"	1 1/2"	8"	WO	7

Material Key: M—genuine mahogany,
WO—white oak

Supplies: #8X2" galvanized deck screws,
clear exterior finish.

SCREW-HOLE LOCATION DETAIL

1/2" 1" 1/2" 3"

(D)

1/2"

1/2"

(F) (F)

Spline
LEG (A)

(E)

3/8" plug 5/16" long

#8 x 2"
galvanized
deck screw

(D) (E)

(E) (F) (D)

3/8" hole 1/4" deep
with a 5/32" hole
centered inside

7/64" pilot hole
1 1/2" deep

1/8"
round-overs

13/16"
9/16"
5/8"

Space slats (F)
1/4" apart

2"

(A) (A)

(C)

9/16"
13/16"
5/8"

See Tenon Detail
on End Frame
Assembly drawing
for tenon size

2"

**TABLE
EXPLODED VIEW**

1/8" round-overs

(A) (A)

2" 8 1/2"

(B)

(B)

20"

7 1/2"

(C)

1 3/4"

9 1/4"

1 3/4"

4 1/2"

See Tenon Detail
on Chair Exploded
View drawing for
tenon size

1/2"-wide mortise centered along edge

Using your router and a slot-cutting bit, rout 1/4" spline slots 2 1/4" long in the mitered ends of the tabletop banding pieces (D, E). See Tabletop drawing *top right* for reference. Next, turn the banding pieces on edge, and cut a 1/8" groove along the inside edge of each (to accommodate the slats [F]) on your tablesaw. Then, use your tablesaw fitted with a dado blade and a miter-gauge fence to cut 1/4" rabbets across the ends of the slats (F). Check the fit of the slat ends into the grooves cut in the banding pieces.

Assemble the table base, and then the tabletop. Finally, screw the two assemblies together and add the finish.

Lazy-Days Porch Rocker

More fun-in-the-sun furniture

After a hard day's work, what could be more relaxing than sitting back with a tall glass of lemonade in this sturdy, attractive porch rocker? We contoured the seat and back for maximum comfort. For the wood parts, we chose weather-resistant white oak and mahogany so the rocker can be used outdoors.

Note: *Because of space limitations, we can't provide full-sized patterns for this project. However, to enable you to build the project, we've included gridded patterns. To enlarge these patterns, see the instructions on page 160.*

LET'S BEGIN WITH THE ROCKER

1 Cut four pieces of ¾" white oak to 6¼" wide by 32" long for the rocker blanks (A). Plane or resaw each piece to ⅝" thick.

2 Using the dimensions on the Rocker Lamination Drawing *opposite*, mark the dado locations on each rocker blank. Cut the dadoes. (We attached a wooden auxiliary fence to our miter gauge, and clamped a stop to the fence to ensure the dadoes were consistently positioned from blank to blank.)
Note: *For joints that will stand up to the extremes of Mother Nature, use Titebond II water-resistant glue, slow-set epoxy, or resorcinol glue.*

3 Glue the mating rocker blanks (A) face-to-face, with the dadoes aligned and the ends and edges flush. Immediately remove glue squeeze-out from the mortises.

4 Using double-faced tape, stick the two rocker blanks together face-to-face, with the edges and ends flush.

5 Enlarge the rocker pattern. See the Cutting Diagram on *page 14* for how we laid out the patterns. Using spray adhesive, adhere the full-sized rocker pattern to one of the rocker laminations, aligning the dadoes on the pattern with those cut in the wood.

6 Bandsaw the taped-together rocker laminations to shape. Sand the rocker edges flush. Separate the rockers, and remove the tape.

NEXT, COMPLETE THE END FRAME ASSEMBLIES

1 From 1¹⁄₁₆" Honduras mahogany, cut the legs (B, C) to size. From ¾" mahogany, cut the rails (D) to size.

2 Using the dimensions on the End Frame Assembly drawing *opposite* and the drawings titled Forming the Mortises and Forming the Tenons
continued

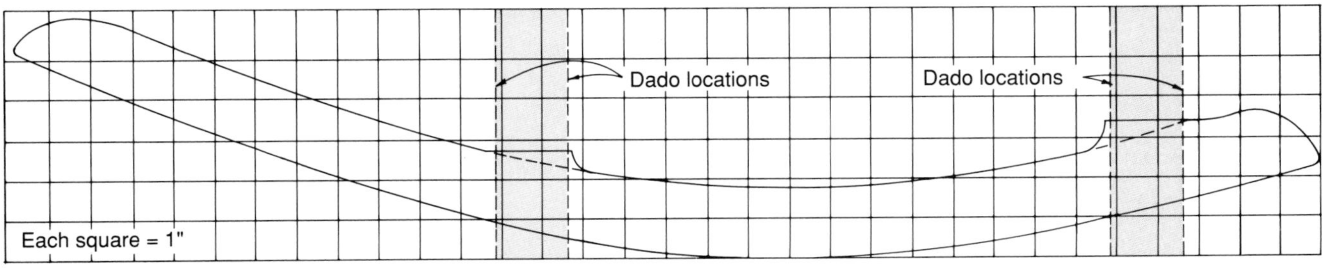
Dado locations
Dado locations
Each square = 1"

ROCKER GRID

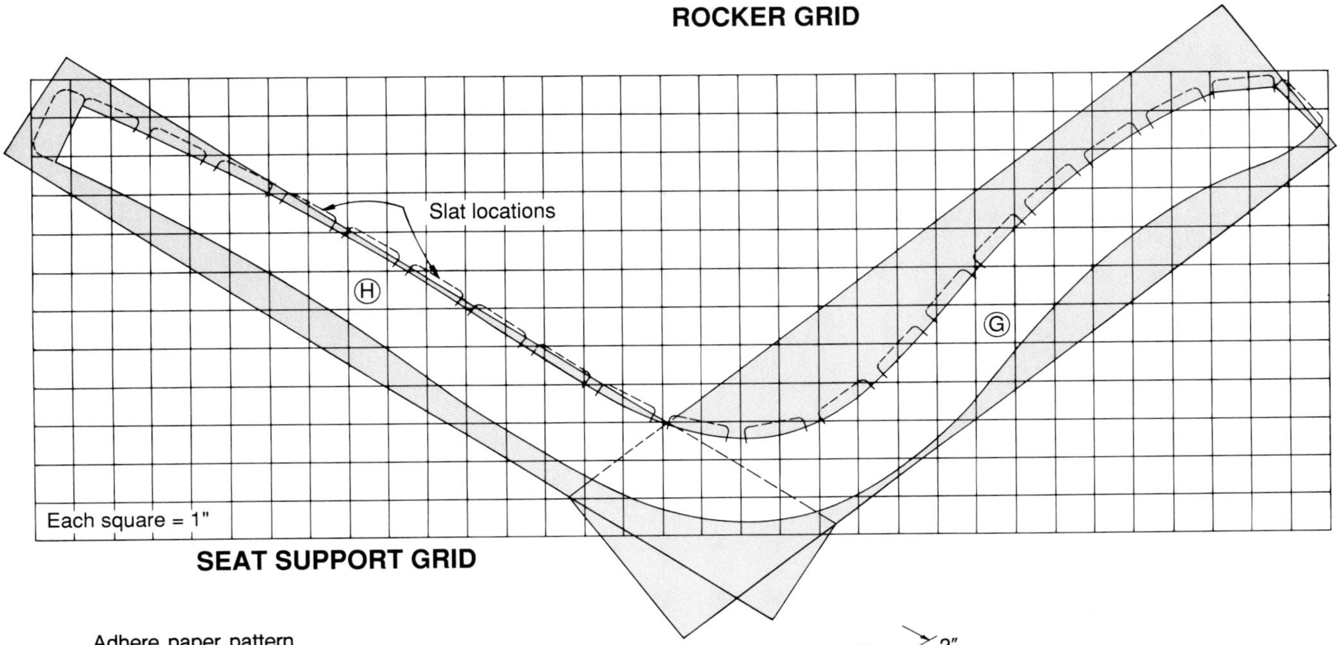
Slat locations
H
G
Each square = 1"

SEAT SUPPORT GRID

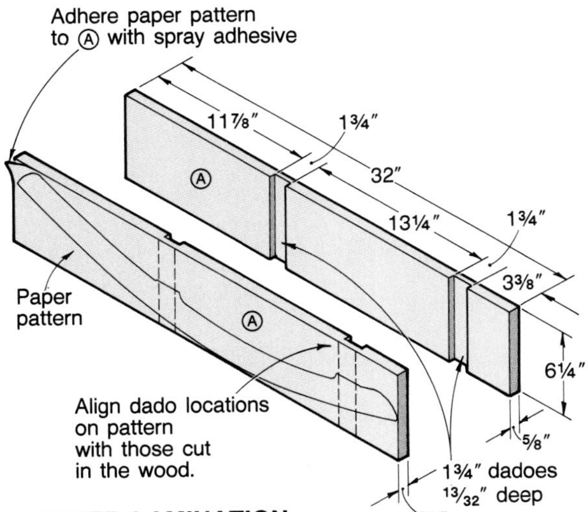
Adhere paper pattern to A with spray adhesive
11⅞″
1¾″
32″
13¼″
1¾″
3⅜″
6¼″
5⁄8″
A
A
Paper pattern
Align dado locations on pattern with those cut in the wood.
1¾″ dadoes 13⁄32″ deep
5⁄8″

ROCKER LAMINATION

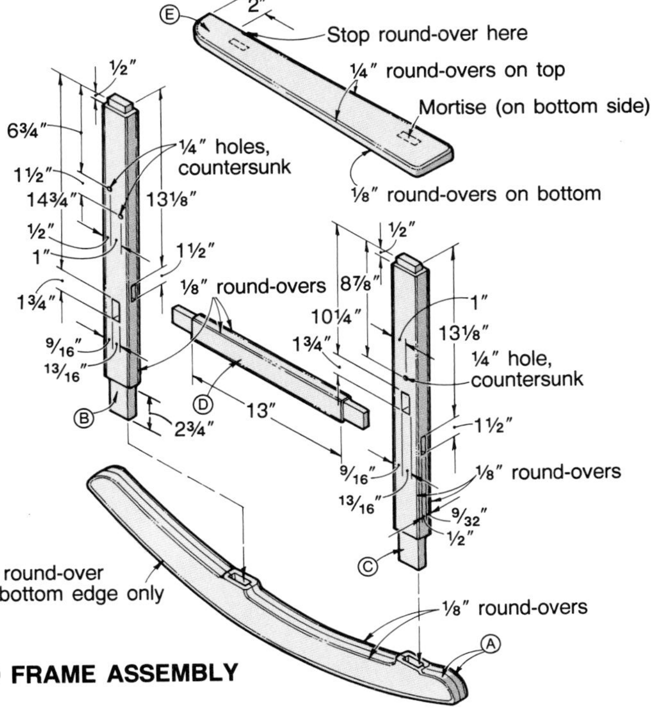
E
2″
Stop round-over here
¼″ round-overs on top
Mortise (on bottom side)
⅛″ round-overs on bottom
½″
6¾″
¼″ holes, countersunk
1½″
14¾″
13⅛″
½″
1″
1½″
1¾″
⅛″ round-overs
9⁄16″
13⁄16″
B
2¾″
D
13″
½″
8⅞″
10¼″
1″
13⅛″
1¾″
¼″ hole, countersunk
1½″
9⁄16″
13⁄16″
⅛″ round-overs
9⁄32″
½″
C
¼″ round-over on bottom edge only
⅛″ round-overs
A

END FRAME ASSEMBLY

Lazy-Days Porch Rocker

continued

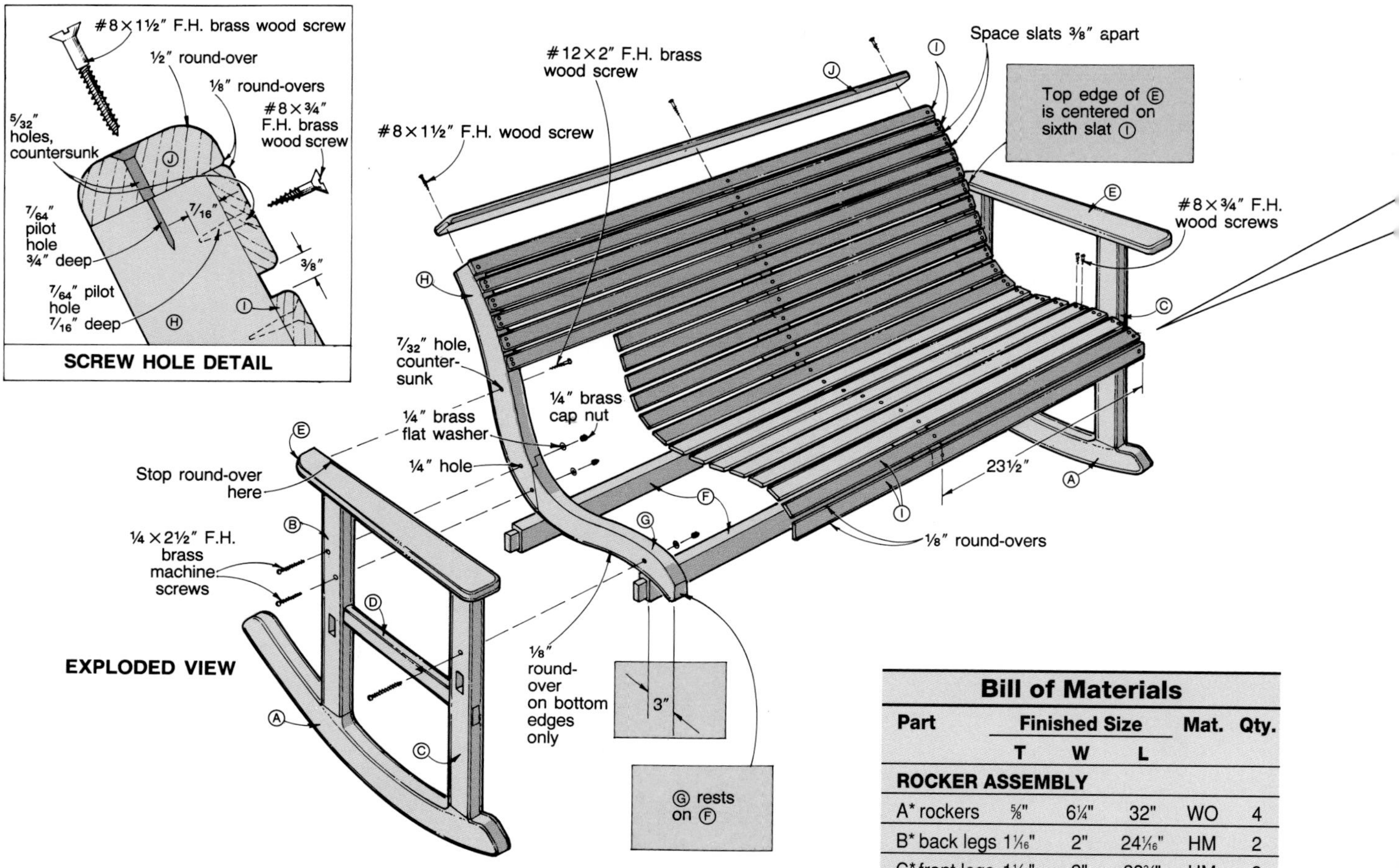

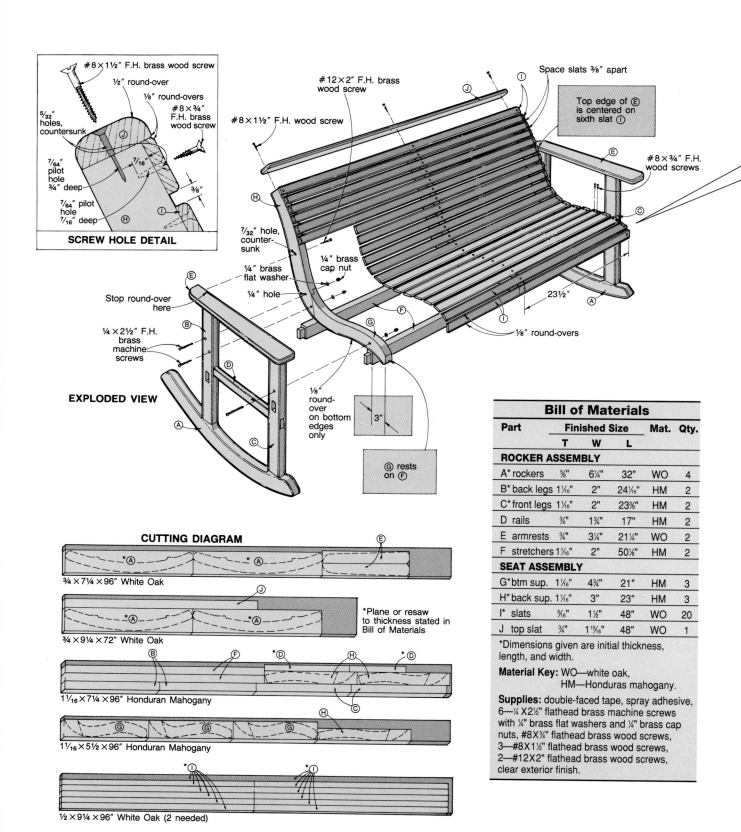

#8×1½″ F.H. brass wood screw
½″ round-over
⅛″ round-overs
#8×¾″ F.H. brass wood screw
5/32″ holes, countersunk
7/64″ pilot hole ¾″ deep
7/16″
⅜″
7/64″ pilot hole 7/16″ deep
SCREW HOLE DETAIL
#12×2″ F.H. brass wood screw
#8×1½″ F.H. wood screw
Space slats ⅜″ apart
Top edge of Ⓔ is centered on sixth slat Ⓘ
#8×¾″ F.H. wood screws
7/32″ hole, counter-sunk
¼″ brass cap nut
¼″ brass flat washer
¼″ hole
Stop round-over here
¼×2½″ F.H. brass machine screws
23½″
⅛″ round-overs
EXPLODED VIEW
⅛″ round-over on bottom edges only
3″
Ⓖ rests on Ⓕ

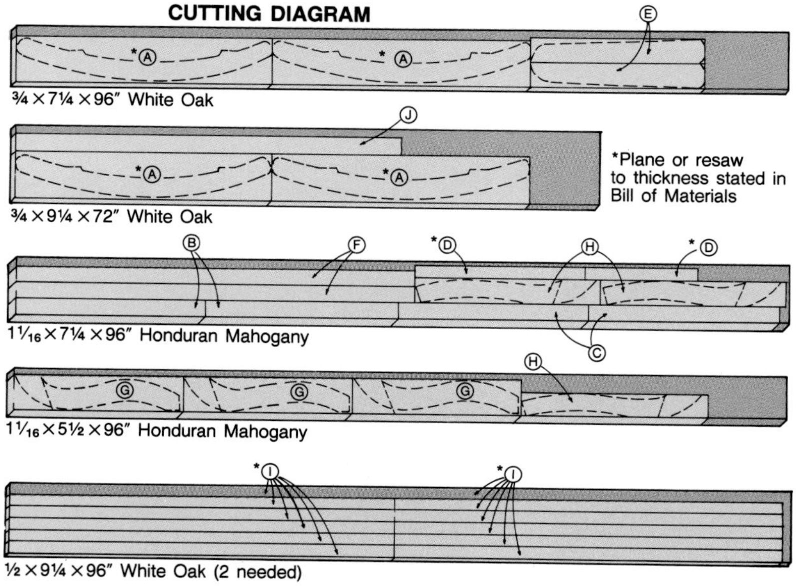

CUTTING DIAGRAM
¾×7¼×96″ White Oak
¾×9¼×72″ White Oak
*Plane or resaw to thickness stated in Bill of Materials
1 1/16×7¼×96″ Honduran Mahogany
1 1/16×5½×96″ Honduran Mahogany
½×9¼×96″ White Oak (2 needed)

Bill of Materials

Part	Finished Size T	W	L	Mat.	Qty.
ROCKER ASSEMBLY					
A* rockers	⅝"	6¼"	32"	WO	4
B* back legs	1 1/16"	2"	24 1/16"	HM	2
C* front legs	1 1/16"	2"	23⅜"	HM	2
D rails	¾"	1¾"	17"	HM	2
E armrests	¾"	3¼"	21¼"	WO	2
F stretchers	1 1/16"	2"	50⅛"	HM	2
SEAT ASSEMBLY					
G* btm sup.	1 1/16"	4¾"	21"	HM	3
H* back sup.	1 1/16"	3"	23"	HM	3
I* slats	5/16"	1½"	48"	WO	20
J top slat	¾"	1 15/16"	48"	WO	1

*Dimensions given are initial thickness, length, and width.

Material Key: WO—white oak, HM—Honduras mahogany.

Supplies: double-faced tape, spray adhesive, 6—¼ X2½" flathead brass machine screws with ¼" brass flat washers and ¼" brass cap nuts, #8X¾" flathead brass wood screws, 3—#8X1½" flathead brass wood screws, 2—#12X2" flathead brass wood screws, clear exterior finish.

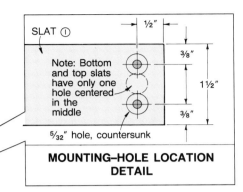

SLAT ①

Note: Bottom and top slats have only one hole centered in the middle

½"
⅜"
1½"
⅜"

5/32" hole, countersunk

MOUNTING–HOLE LOCATION DETAIL

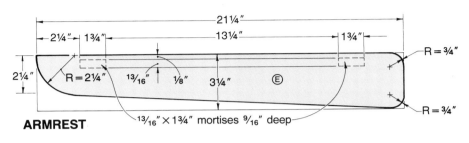

21¼"
2¼" 1¾" 13¼" 1¾"
R = ¾"
2¼" R = 2¼" 13/16" ⅛" 3¼" Ⓔ
R = ¾"
ARMREST
13/16" × 1¾" mortises 9/16" deep

FORMING THE TENONS

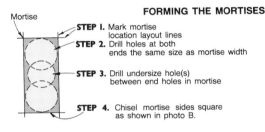

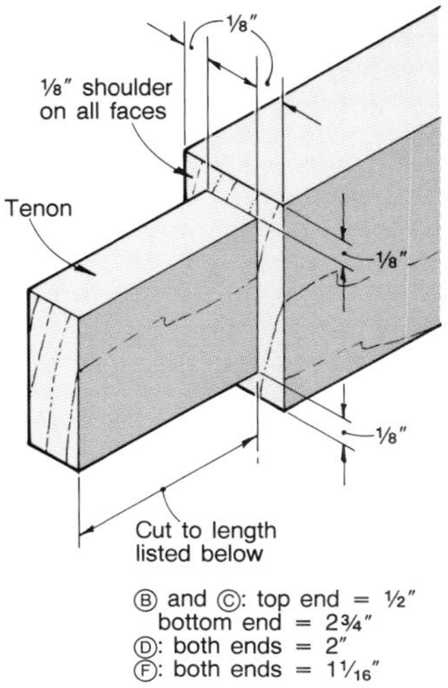

⅛"
⅛" shoulder on all faces
Tenon
⅛"
⅛"
Cut to length listed below

Ⓑ and Ⓒ: top end = ½"
bottom end = 2¾"
Ⓓ: both ends = 2"
Ⓕ: both ends = 1 1/16"

Mortise

FORMING THE MORTISES

STEP 1. Mark mortise location layout lines
STEP 2. Drill holes at both ends the same size as mortise width
STEP 3. Drill undersize hole(s) between end holes in mortise
STEP 4. Chisel mortise sides square as shown in photo B.

at *right*, use a square to mark the mortise, tenon, and hole locations on each leg. Next, mark the tenon locations on each end of the rails.

3 Following the four-step procedure on the drawing at *far right*, form the mortises. Then, cut tenons on the legs and rails.

4 For securing the seat assembly to the end frames later, drill and countersink a pair of ¼" holes in each back leg (B) and one in each front leg (C).

5 Cut two armrest blanks (E) to 3¼x21¼" from ¾"-thick white oak. Using the Armrest drawing for reference, transfer the pattern to one of the pieces. Next, using the method described earlier, tape the armrests together, cut to shape, sand the edges smooth, separate the armrests, and remove the tape.

6 Mark the location for a pair of 9/16"-deep mortises on the bottom of each armrest (E).

7 Rout ⅛" and ¼" round-overs on parts A, B, C, D, and E where shown on the End Frame Assembly and Exploded View drawings.

8 Glue and clamp each end frame assembly, checking for square.

NOW, ADD THE STRETCHERS, AND JOIN THE END ASSEMBLIES

1 Cut the stretchers (F) to size. Mark and cut 1 1/16"-long tenons on the ends of each stretcher.

2 Glue the pair of stretchers between the end frames as shown in Photo A. (To ensure that the assembly would stay square, we clamped square corner braces in place and left them there until the glue dried.)

3 Position an armrest on the top of each end assembly, and verify that the marked mortises match the tenon locations on the top of the legs. Re-mark if necessary.

4 Drill overlapping holes 9/16" deep where marked. Then, as shown in Photo B on *page 16*, chisel the mortise sides square, and finish forming the mortise.

5 Glue and clamp an armrest to the top of each end-frame assembly. Immediately wipe off glue squeezed

A

We used 90° corner braces to hold the rocker frame pieces square while the glue dried.

out of the mortise and tenon joints. Later remove the clamps and sand the rocker assembly smooth.

AND NOW FOR THE SLAT-SUPPORT ASSEMBLIES

1 Rip and crosscut three pieces of 1 1/16" mahogany stock to 4¾x21" for the bottom-slat supports (G) and three pieces to 3x23" for back-slat supports (H).

continued

Lazy-Days Porch Rocker

continued

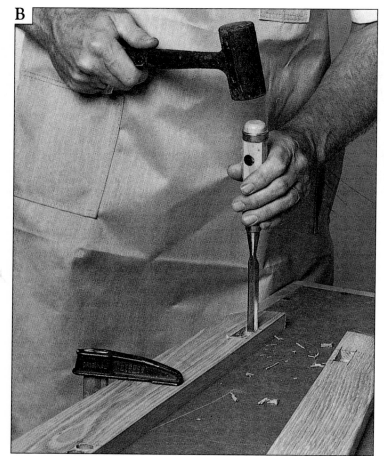

B

Use a mallet and chisel to finish shaping the mortises.

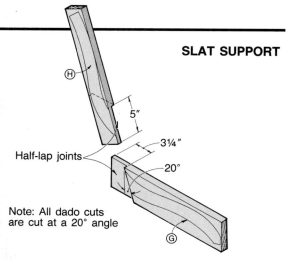

SLAT SUPPORT

Half-lap joints

5"

3¼"

20°

Note: All dado cuts
are cut at a 20° angle

H

G

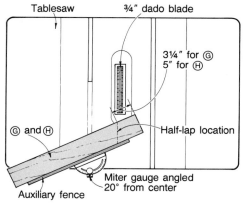

Tablesaw

¾" dado blade

3¼" for G
5" for H

G and H

Half-lap location

Miter gauge angled
20° from center

Auxiliary fence

CUTTING THE HALF LAPS

2 Using the Slat Support drawing *top right* for reference, mark the location of the half-lap joint on one end of each slat support (G, H).

3 Mount a ¾"-wide dado blade to your tablesaw. Elevate the blade to cut exactly half the thickness of your stock. (We used scrap the same thickness as the supports, and made test cuts to verify blade height.) Angle the miter gauge 20° from center. Cut a half-lap on one end of each of the six slat supports where shown on the drawing *above right*.

4 Dry-clamp the three supports (one G and one H per support) to check the fit. Glue and clamp each of the three supports.

5 Following the method described to form the rockers and armrests, tape the supports together, transfer the pattern outlines, cut the supports to shape, and sand the edges. Then, using a try square, transfer the slat (I) locations to the top front edge of each slat support assembly (G, H). Pry the pieces apart, remove the double-faced tape, and finish-sand the supports, being careful not to sand away the slat location lines.

6 Rout ⅛" round-overs along the bottom and back edges of each slat support where shown on the Exploded View drawing.

IT'S TIME TO FASTEN THE SLATS TO THE SLAT SUPPORTS

1 From ⁵⁄₁₆"-thick oak (we planed thicker stock to size), cut 20 seat slats (I) to 1½x48". From ¾" stock, cut the top slat (J) to size.

2 Rout a ⅛" round-over along the top edges and ends of each ⁵⁄₁₆" slat (I) and a ½" round-over along the top edges and ends of the top slat (J). Next, rout a ⅛" round-over along the bottom front edge of the top slat.

3 Drill the countersunk screw holes in each slat where dimensioned on the Exploded View drawing and accompanying Mounting Hole Location detail. (We clamped a fence and a stop-block to our drill-press table to position the holes from slat to slat.)

4 As shown in the drawing *opposite*, place the three slat supports on your benchtop. Clamp a large hand-screw clamp to each to hold the pieces upright.

5 Screw the top slat (J) to the three slat supports. Then, fasten one of the ⁵⁄₁₆" slats (I) to the opposite end

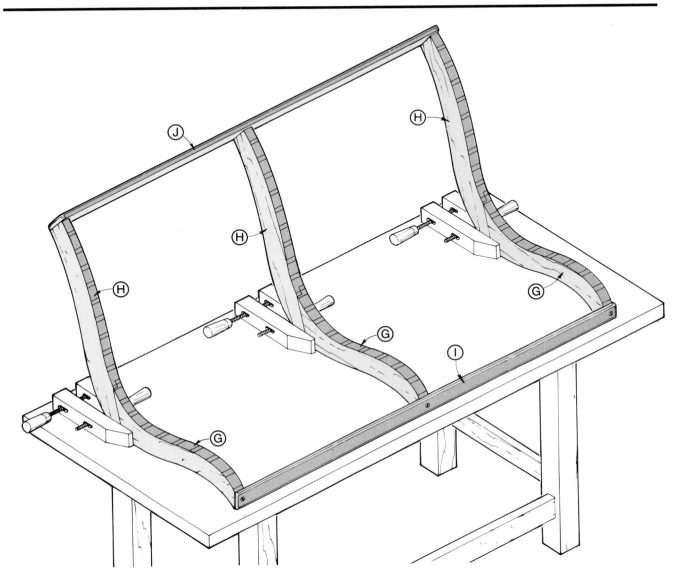

of the assembly where shown in the drawing on the seat support pattern on *page 13*.

6 Following the layout marks on the slat supports, fasten the remaining seat slats (I).

FINISHING UP

1 With a helper, position the seat assembly on the rocker assembly where dimensioned in the tinted boxes on the Exploded View

drawing. Once correctly positioned, clamp the seat in place.

2 Using the previously drilled ¼" holes in the front and rear legs as guides, drill ¼" holes through the slat supports. Using ¼" machine screws, fasten the two assemblies.

3 Working from the back inside, drill a ⁷⁄₃₂" shank hole through the back seat support (H) and a ⁹⁄₆₄" pilot hole 1" deep into the inside edge of the armrests. Drive

a #12x2" flathead brass wood screw through the support and into the armrest.

4 Remove the screws, and separate the seat assembly from the rocker assembly. (We found it easier to sand the assemblies when separated.) Finish-sand both assemblies and apply the finish. (We applied three coats of spar varnish.) Later, fasten the two assemblies back together.

Leafy Lodging Birdhouse

A birdhouse in the original style

Decorative birdhouses usually look like places people would hang around. So, here's one that almost any bird will recognize as home: a tree. Woodworkers will see something even more in this one: a fun pre-springtime project.

Note: *You'll need ½"-thick redwood or cedar for the birdhouse. (We planed a 34"-long redwood 1x12 to ½" thick, and then cut it to 16" and 18" lengths for our stock.)*

Enlarge the pattern *opposite* 150 percent. Trace the *red* outline and the *black* lines onto the ½x11¼x16" stock.

Bandsaw or scrollsaw Part A around the *red* outline. Bore the 1⅛" entrance hole where shown. Woodburn the *black* lines, and then sand the piece on both sides.

Cut the sides (B), back (C), bottom (D), and roof (E) to the sizes shown on the Cutting Diagram. Tilt your tablesaw blade to 15°, and bevel-rip a ⅞" strip 18" long. Bevel one end of Part B and one edge of Part D, as indicated. Cut cleats F and G to length.

Glue house Parts B, C, and D together. Glue the long cleat (G) to the bottom front edge of the house, beveled side down.

Drill and countersink where indicated, and drive in #6x1" flathead brass wood screws. Drill ventilation holes on both sides. Fasten a ¾" galvanized pipe floor flange to the bottom of the house with four machine screws. Drill the drainage holes where shown.

Position the house assembly on the backside of front piece (A). Center it side to side with the floor 3" below the bottom of the entrance hole. Drill a ⅛" hole through the center of each cleat into, but not through, the front piece. Glue the house assembly in place, and secure it with a screw through each cleat.

Attach the roof (E) with a 6" length of brass continuous hinge. Install a 1" brass hook and eye to latch the roof closed.

Paint the foliage with acrylics. (We used Ceramcoat jubilee green for the leaves and thalo green for the shaded areas.) Apply a clear finish overall, a weatherproof one if you'll be hanging your birdhouse outside.

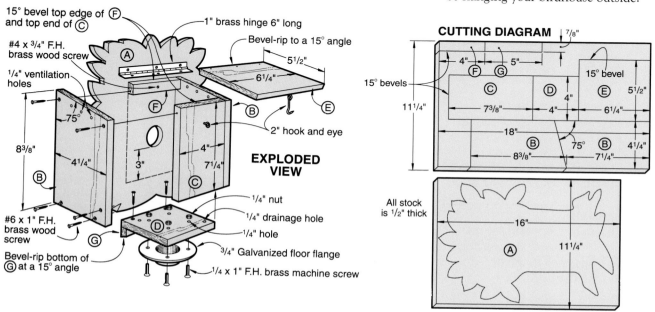

EXPLODED VIEW

CUTTING DIAGRAM

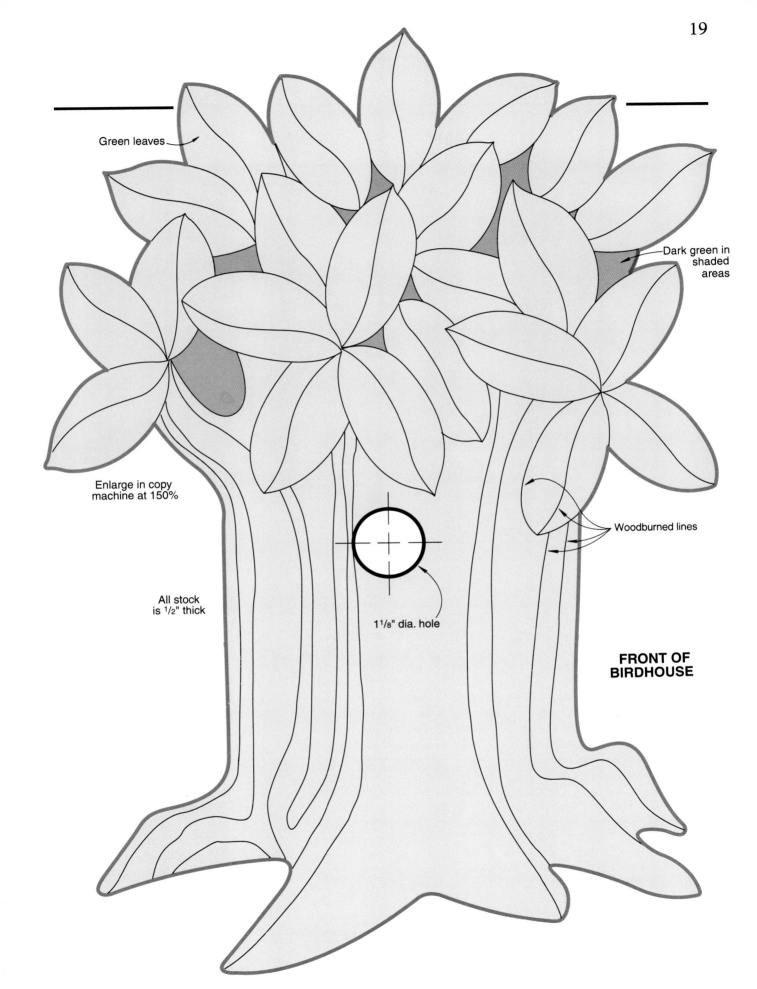

Green leaves

Dark green in shaded areas

Enlarge in copy machine at 150%

Woodburned lines

All stock is 1/2" thick

1 1/8" dia. hole

FRONT OF BIRDHOUSE

Seeds-and-Such Snack Shop

For birds on the move

When Pat Schlarbaum, songbird specialist with Iowa's Department of Natural Resources, stopped by WOOD® magazine with this feeder, we saw some new concepts that needed explaining. We have run bird feeders before, but none quite like this. It didn't take long, however, for Pat to quickly put our concerns to rest with his thorough knowledge of birds and their feeding habits. Now, we believe this may be our best-ever feeder.

ALL FEEDERS ARE NOT CREATED (OR CONSTRUCTED) EQUAL

This bird feeder design appeals to a variety of birds and their feeding habits. In designing it, I wanted to provide a healthy, durable structure that both people and birds could enjoy for a lifetime.

When songbirds feed from a seed supply that's damp and sometimes infested with Aspergillosis (a fungal disease), it can kill them. For this reason, I've designed a feeder that specifically keeps seed dry and minimizes the threat of this disease.

The proportions of the feeder include an overhang that aids in keeping the feeding area dry. The recessed trough controls seed waste. An attached screen underneath allows for aeration. I designed this cedar feeder to be large enough to let birds of different species, particularly territorial ones like the nuthatch, feed at the same time without bothering one another.

To hold seed between their toes while eating, songbirds such as chickadees and tufted titmice require a crevice in tree bark to hold their seed while they peck it open. However, birds that typically feed on the ground, like cardinals and juncoes, use the platform when feeding. To accommodate both types of birds, I use tree branches for perches on my feeders. I've found that oil (black) sunflower seeds are preferred by the most desirable species. They're widely available at home centers, hardware stores, and garden shops. *Note: For the construction of this feeder, we purchased 1x10" cedar boards at a local home center. Then, we selected areas between the splits and knots for the pieces. Our stock came ⅞" thick and planed on one side. We planed the rough opposite side for a ¾" finished thickness.*

START WITH THE BASE

1 Cut the feeder base (A) to size. Lay out and mark the centerpoints for the ½" drain holes where dimensioned on the Parts View drawing. Drill the holes.

2 Cut the two perch strips (B) to size. Lay out, then drill and

continued

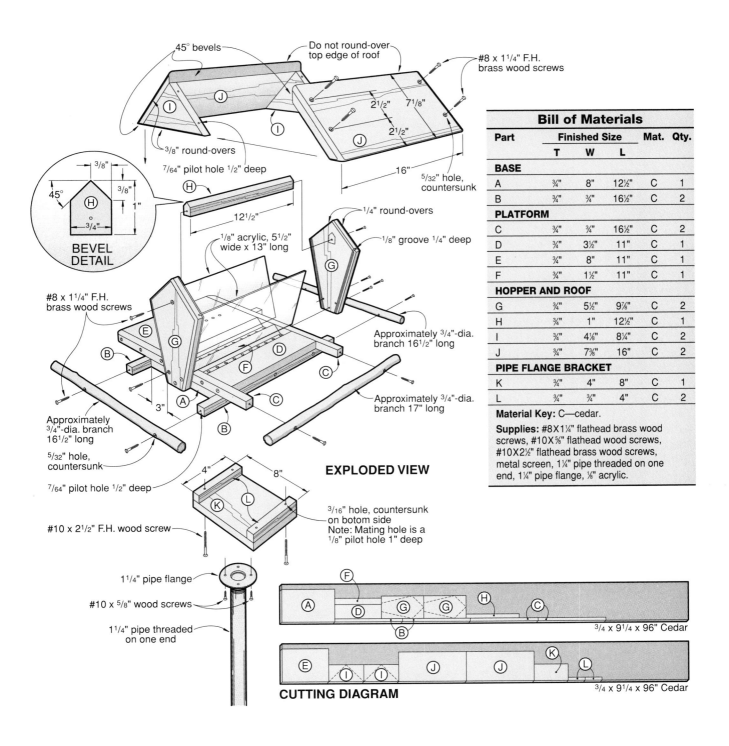

45° bevels

Do not round-over top edge of roof

#8 x 1¼" F.H. brass wood screws

J

I

I

J

2½" 7⅛"

2½"

3/8" round-overs

7/64" pilot hole ½" deep

16"

5/32" hole, countersunk

BEVEL DETAIL

3/8"

3/8"

45°

H

1"

3/4"

H

12½"

1/8" acrylic, 5½" wide x 13" long

1/4" round-overs

1/8" groove ¼" deep

G

G

#8 x 1¼" F.H. brass wood screws

E

B

G

A

D

F

C

C

3"

B

Approximately ¾"-dia. branch 16½" long

5/32" hole, countersunk

7/64" pilot hole ½" deep

Approximately ¾"-dia. branch 16½" long

Approximately ¾"-dia. branch 17" long

#10 x 2½" F.H. wood screw

4"   8"

K   L

3/16" hole, countersunk on botom side
Note: Mating hole is a 1/8" pilot hole 1" deep

EXPLODED VIEW

1¼" pipe flange

#10 x 5/8" wood screws

1¼" pipe threaded on one end

Bill of Materials

Part	Finished Size			Mat.	Qty.
	T	**W**	**L**		
BASE					
A	¾"	8"	12½"	C	1
B	¾"	¾"	16½"	C	2
PLATFORM					
C	¾"	¾"	16½"	C	2
D	¾"	3½"	11"	C	1
E	¾"	8"	11"	C	1
F	¾"	1½"	11"	C	1
HOPPER AND ROOF					
G	¾"	5½"	9⅞"	C	2
H	¾"	1"	12½"	C	1
I	¾"	4⅛"	8¼"	C	2
J	¾"	7⅜"	16"	C	2
PIPE FLANGE BRACKET					
K	¾"	4"	8"	C	1
L	¾"	¾"	4"	C	2

Material Key: C—cedar.

Supplies: #8X1¼" flathead brass wood screws, #10X⅝" flathead wood screws, #10X2½" flathead brass wood screws, metal screen, 1¼" pipe threaded on one end, 1¼" pipe flange, ⅛" acrylic.

F

A   D   G   G   H   C

B

3/4 x 9¼ x 96" Cedar

E

I   I   J   J   K   L

CUTTING DIAGRAM

3/4 x 9¼ x 96" Cedar

Seeds-and-Such Snack Shop

continued

countersink three mounting holes in each strip where located on the Base Assembly drawing *opposite*. **Note:** *So it can stand up to the elements, construct your feeder using Titebond II water-resistant glue, slow-set epoxy, or resorcinol.*

3 Glue and screw the perch strips (B) to the base (A).

4 Cut a piece of metal screen wire to 4¼x12". Use masking tape or duct tape to hold the screen in position where shown on the Base Assembly drawing. Then, secure the screen with #18x½" nails. Remove the tape.

ADD THE FEEDING PLATFORM

1 Cut the platform ends (C) to size. Then, cut the platform pieces (D, E, F) to size, bevel-ripping the edges where shown on the Base Assembly drawing. For safety, we started with a 5"-wide piece of stock, and bevel-ripped Part F from one edge.

2 Dry-clamp the pieces together in the configuration shown on the drawing. Mark the centerpoints, and drill and countersink mounting holes through the C parts and into the ends of D, E, and F where shown.

3 Glue and screw the platform (C, D, E, F) together. Mark the radii, and cut or sand the two rounded corners of the platform to shape where shown on the Base Assembly drawing.

4 Drill mounting holes, and then glue and screw the platform to the base where shown on the Exploded View and Base drawings.

NEXT, LET'S ADD THE HOPPER AND ROOF ASSEMBLIES

1 Using the dimensions on the Parts View drawing, lay out the hopper

ends (G), drill the countersunk mounting holes, and cut these pieces to shape.

2 Cut or rout a ⅛" groove ¼" deep ⅜" in from the edges where shown on the Parts View.

3 Cut the cross member (H) to size, bevel-ripping the top edges. (See the Bevel detail on the Exploded View drawing.)

4 Cut the roof pieces (I, J) to size. (See the Parts View and Exploded View drawing for reference.)

5 Drill the mounting holes, and then glue and screw the hopper ends (G) to the base and platform assembly. Secure the cross member (H) between the end pieces.

6 Assemble the roof (I, J).

7 Cut the pipe flange bracket pieces (K, L). Drill the holes, and glue and screw them to the bottom of the base, being careful not to cover the drainage holes.

8 Have two pieces of ⅛" clear acrylic cut to fit the hopper

grooves. Secure a pipe flange to the bottom of bracket (K, L).

NATURAL PERCHES ARE FOR THE BIRDS

1 Cut or prune straight branches about ¾" in diameter to the lengths shown on the Exploded View drawing. Seal the ends of the branches to prevent cracking.

2 Drill the mounting holes through the branches and secure them to the perch strips (B) and platform ends (C) where shown on the Exploded View drawing. Mount the branches so they come in contact where they cross.

3 Mount the feeder to 1¼" pipe that has the top end threaded to mate with the flange. If possible, position your feeder near bushes or evergreens for shelter and in an area protected from strong winds. Lift the roof assembly off the feeder, fill with bird seed, and watch the birds come home to feed.

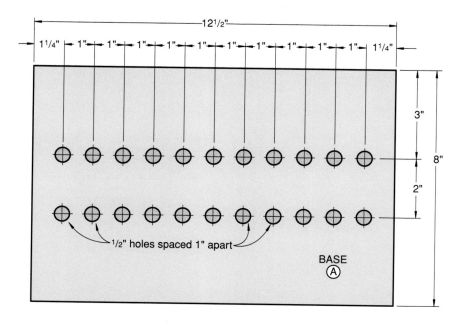

½" holes spaced 1" apart

BASE
A

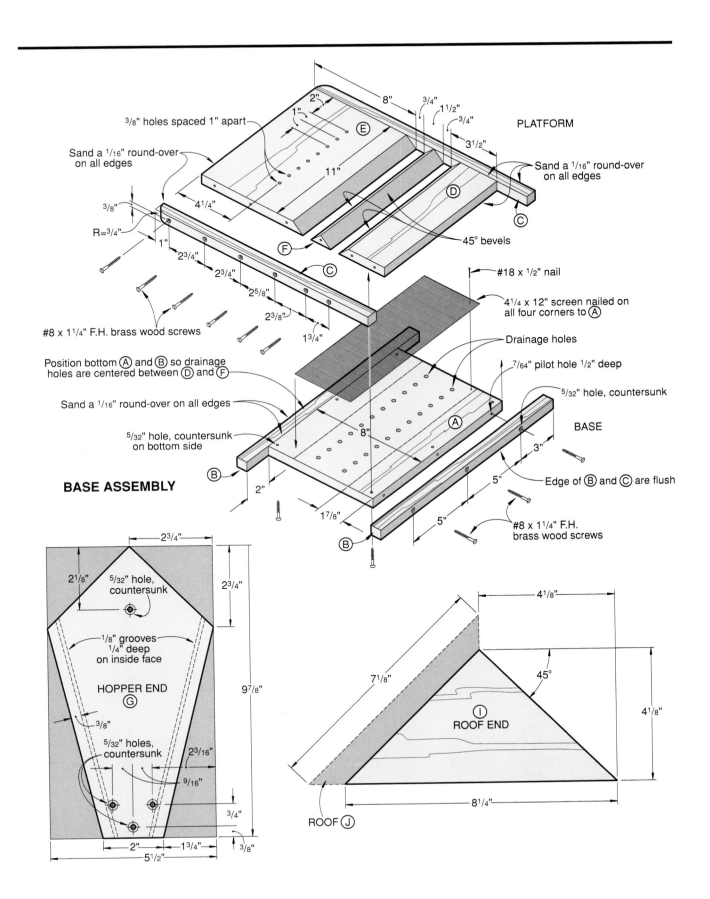

3/8" holes spaced 1" apart

Sand a 1/16" round-over on all edges

2"
1"
8"
3/4"
1 1/2"
3/4"
3 1/2"

PLATFORM

Sand a 1/16" round-over on all edges

11"

E

D

C

3/8"
R=3/4"
4 1/4"
1"
2 3/4"
2 3/4"
2 5/8"
2 3/8"
1 3/4"

F

C

45° bevels

#18 x 1/2" nail

4 1/4 x 12" screen nailed on all four corners to A

#8 x 1 1/4" F.H. brass wood screws

Position bottom A and B so drainage holes are centered between D and F

Sand a 1/16" round-over on all edges

5/32" hole, countersunk on bottom side

Drainage holes

7/64" pilot hole 1/2" deep

5/32" hole, countersunk

8"

A

BASE

BASE ASSEMBLY

B

2"

1 7/8"

3"

5"

5"

Edge of B and C are flush

#8 x 1 1/4" F.H. brass wood screws

B

2 3/4"

2 1/8"

5/32" hole, countersunk

2 3/4"

1/8" grooves 1/4" deep on inside face

HOPPER END
G

9 7/8"

3/8"

5/32" holes, countersunk

2 3/16"

9/16"

3/4"

2"
1 3/4"
3/8"
5 1/2"

4 1/8"

45°

I
ROOF END

7 1/8"

4 1/8"

8 1/4"

ROOF J

Craftsman-Style Wall Lantern

Turn-of-the-century looks fresh today

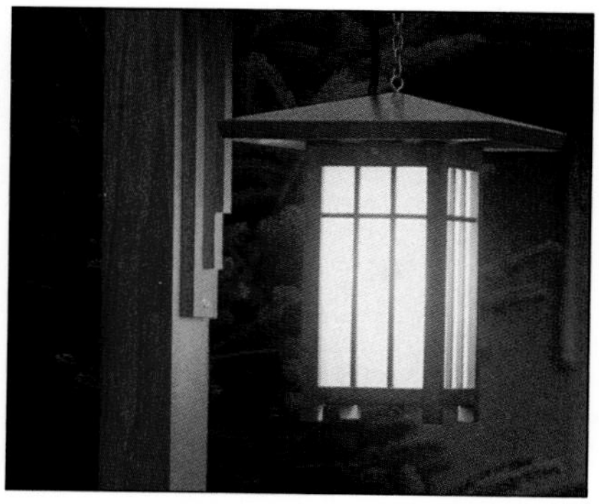

Want to replace your dated exterior lights with something more stylish? Now, with this pleasing outdoor light, you can. We accented our design with stained glass, a decorative grille, and a large overhanging roof. To install, consider post-mounting your light as shown here, or attach it to your house adjacent to an exterior door. Build several and use them to brighten up your deck or patio.

Start with the Lantern Frames

Note: *To enable your light(s) to stand up to the elements, adhere the pieces using Titebond II water-resistant glue or slow-set epoxy.*

1 From ¾" Honduras (genuine) mahogany (not Philippine mahogany, which is not a true mahogany, and is not as durable), cut the frame stiles (A), bottom rails (B), and top rails (C) to the sizes listed in the Bill of Materials.

2 Glue and clamp each of the four frames together in the configuration shown on Step 1 of the Frame Assembly drawing.

3 To strengthen the weak butt joints, use a doweling jig and drill a ⅜" hole 1½" deep at each joint where shown on Step 1 of the Frame Assembly drawing and as shown in Photo A.

4 Cut sixteen ⅜" dowels to 1¾" long. Glue a dowel in each hole. Later, trim the protruding dowels flush with the outside edges of each frame. Sand both surfaces of each frame.

5 Fit your table-mounted router with a rabbeting bit, and rout a ¼" rabbet ⅜" deep along the back inside edge of each frame. Chisel the round-routed corners square.

6 Tilt your tablesaw blade to 45°, and bevel-rip both edges of each frame as shown in Step 2 of the Frame Assembly drawing.

A

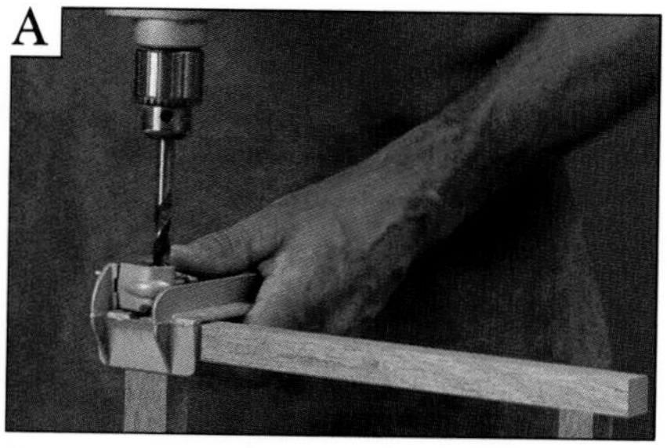

Using a doweling jig for alignment, drill a ⅜" dowel hole at each butt joint.

7 To glue the frames together, lay the frames bevel side down on your workbench. Apply masking tape along the three mating edges where shown in Step 3 of the drawing. Carefully flip the assembly over, and apply glue to the mating beveled edges.

8 Stand the assembly upright, and apply tape along the remaining corner. As shown in Photo B, use a pair of band clamps to clamp the four frames together. Not only does the masking tape help hold the pieces in place while you apply the band clamps, it also prevents glue from squeezing out onto the outside of the frames.

9 For attaching to the roof assembly later, drill and countersink a mounting hole in two opposite top rails where shown on the Exploded View drawing.

Now, Let's Add the Decorative Grilles

1 Resaw or plane thicker stock to ¼" thick, and then rip three ¼x¼x40"

continued

B

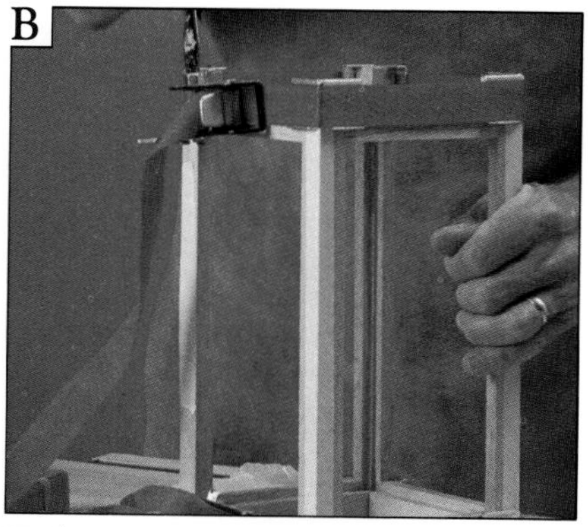

Tighten a pair of band clamps to secure the four frames until the glue dries.

Bill of Materials

Part	Finished Size T	W	L	Mat.	Qty.
FRAMES					
A stiles	¾"	¾"	12"	M	8
B bottom rails	¾"	¾"	4⅝"	M	4
C top rails	¾"	1"	4⅝"	M	4
GRILLES					
D uprights	¼"	¼"	9½"	M	8
E crossbars	¼"	¼"	4⅝"	M	4
ROOF					
F supports	¾"	1 7/16"	15"	M	2
G roof	¾"	6¼"	12"	M	4
H block	¾"	1½"	4⅝"	M	1
HANGER					
I upright	¾"	2¼"	17⅜"	M	1
J support	¾"	1"	14⅜"	M	1
K crossbars	¾"	1"	11"	M	2
L block	¾"	¾"	2"	M	1
POST (optional)					
M sides	¾"	3½"	10'	M	2
N sides	¾"	2"	10'	M	2
O cap	¾"	3½"	3½"	M	1

Material Key: M—Honduras mahogany.

Supplies: ¼" dowel stock, ⅜" dowel stock, two galvanized shingle nails with the heads cut off, #10 brass screw eyes, #8X1¼" flathead brass wood screws, #8X1½" flathead brass wood screws, #10X1½" flathead brass wood screws, #10X2½" flathead brass wood screws, #10 brass finish (countersunk) washer, #8X¾" panhead screws, ½X4"-diameter ceiling pan, Romex connector, silicone sealant, four stained-glass panels, keyless porcelain socket, #16/2 neoprene insulated wire, #3 straight-link brass-plated machine chain 3" long, exterior finish.

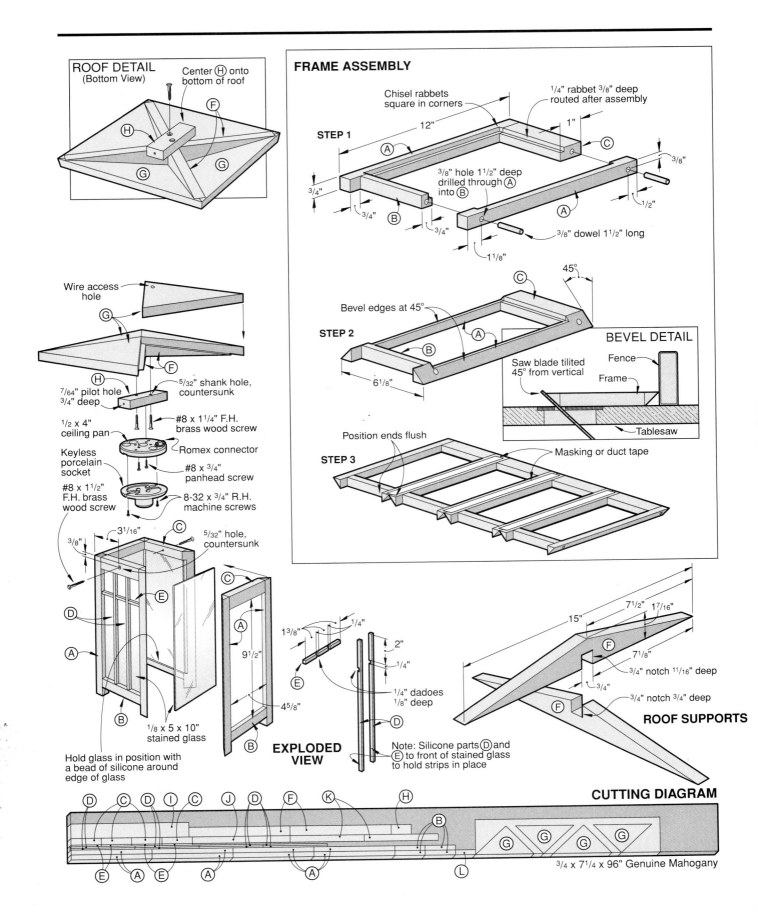

ROOF DETAIL
(Bottom View)

Center (H) onto bottom of roof

FRAME ASSEMBLY

Chisel rabbets square in corners

1/4" rabbet 3/8" deep routed after assembly

STEP 1

12"

1"

3/4"

3/8"

3/8" hole 1 1/2" deep drilled through (A) into (B)

3/4"

3/4"

3/8" dowel 1 1/2" long

1/2"

1 1/8"

45°

STEP 2

Bevel edges at 45°

6 1/8"

BEVEL DETAIL

Saw blade tilted 45° from vertical

Fence

Frame

Tablesaw

STEP 3

Position ends flush

Masking or duct tape

Wire access hole

7/64" pilot hole 3/4" deep

5/32" shank hole, countersunk

#8 x 1 1/4" F.H. brass wood screw

1/2 x 4" ceiling pan

Keyless porcelain socket

Romex connector

#8 x 3/4" panhead screw

#8 x 1 1/2" F.H. brass wood screw

8-32 x 3/4" R.H. machine screws

3 1/16"

3/8"

5/32" hole, countersunk

9 1/2"

1 3/8"

1/4"

2"

1/4"

1/4" dadoes 1/8" deep

4 5/8"

1/8 x 5 x 10" stained glass

EXPLODED VIEW

Note: Silicone parts (D) and (E) to front of stained glass to hold strips in place

Hold glass in position with a bead of silicone around edge of glass

15"

7 1/2"

1 7/16"

7 1/8"

3/4" notch 11/16" deep

3/4"

3/4" notch 3/4" deep

ROOF SUPPORTS

CUTTING DIAGRAM

D C D I C J D F K H

E A E A A B L

G G G G

3/4 x 7 1/4 x 96" Genuine Mahogany

Craftsman-Style Wall Lantern

continued

pieces for grille parts. Crosscut eight upright grille parts (D) and four crossbars (E) from the 40"-long strips.

2 Fit your tablesaw with a ¼" dado blade, and cut dadoes in the grille parts where dimensioned on the Exploded View drawing. (We screwed a wooden auxiliary fence to our miter gauge. Then, we clamped a stopblock to the auxiliary fence to ensure consistency in the positioning of the dadoes from piece to piece.)

3 Glue the four grille assemblies together, checking for square.

TOP YOUR LANTERN WITH A STYLISH ROOF

1 Using the dimensions on the Roof Supports drawing on *page 25* for reference, cut the roof-support blanks (F) to 1⁷⁄₁₆x15". Mark the location of the tapers and mating-notches. Cut the dadoes, and then bandsaw the tapers. Glue the two parts together.

2 Using the dimensions on the Parts View drawing, lay out the roof-piece (G) outline onto a piece of hardboard or ¼" plywood. Cut the template to shape. Use the template to mark four roof-piece outlines on the mahogany stock as laid out on the Cutting Diagram.

3 Tilt your bandsaw table 10°, and cut the four roof pieces where shown. Test-fit the pieces on top of the roof supports (F). Tilt the table on your disc sander, and sand the mating edges if necessary for a tight fit.

4 Using masking tape as we did earlier with the lantern frames, glue and tape the roof pieces together. Later, glue the roof assembly (four Gs) to the roof supports (two Fs).

5 Cut the roof block (H) to size. Drill a pair of mounting holes, and screw it to the bottom side of the roof assembly where shown on the Roof detail accompanying the Exploded View drawing.

MAKE A HANDSOME HANGER FOR YOUR LANTERN

1 Rip and crosscut the hanger parts (I, J, K, L) to the sizes listed in the Bill of Materials.

2 Lay out and mark the notches where shown on the Parts View drawing. Cut the notches. Mark the ¼" hole centerpoints on the support (J), crossbars (K) and block (L) and drill the holes.

3 Glue and screw the support (J) to the upright (I). Mark the location and drill the ⅜" wire access hole through J and I.

4 Snip the heads off of two galvanized shingle nails. Tap them into the inside face of one crossarm where shown on the Section View drawing. The nails will hold the electrical cord in place later.

5 Glue the two crossarms to the upright/support assembly and block (L), checking the assembly for square and squeezing the headless galvanized nails between the two pieces.

6 Using the previously drilled holes in the crossarms as guides, drill ¼" holes through the support, upright, and block. Cut four pieces of ¼" dowel stock to 2½" long. Glue the dowels in the holes just drilled and where shown on the Hanger Assembly drawing. Later, trim the ends of the dowels flush with the outside edges of the crossarms.

FINISH THE PARTS, AND ADD THE ELECTRICALS AND GLASS

1 Stain the project if desired and add the finish.

2 Have four pieces of stained glass cut to fit the rabbeted openings (we bought a glass called Kokomo 11 ML at a local stained-glass store). Fit the glass panels into the openings, and secure them to the frames with clear silicone sealant.

3 Drill the pilot holes, and thread a #10 brass screw eye into the roof

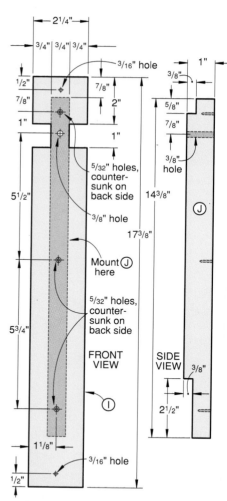

PARTS VIEW

and hanger block where shown on the Section View drawing. Cut the brass-plated chain to length, and connect the chain to the screw eyes.

4 Drill a wire-access hole through the roof where shown on the

Section View drawing. Fasten a
½x4"-diameter ceiling pan to
the roof block (H). Connect a
#16/2 insulated wire to the keyless
porcelain socket, and run the opposite end of the wire through the hole
in the ceiling pan, roof, and bracket.
Connect the porcelain socket to the
ceiling pan. Secure the wire by tight-
ening the screws in the Romex
connector at the ceiling pan.

5 Connect the insulated wire
from the light fixture to the wire
from your house. Screw the hanger
assembly to the wall. Fill the gap
around the wire in the roof with
silicone sealant. Screw a 60-watt
bulb into the socket and give your
new light a try.

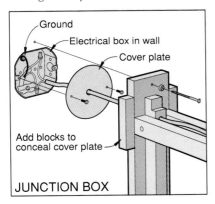

GROUND
Electrical box in wall
Cover plate
Add blocks to conceal cover plate

JUNCTION BOX

JUNCTION BOX

If you intend to mount your light
directly to your house and over a
switch-operated junction box, drill
a hole in the center of the cover
plate, run wire through it, make
the connections, and screw the
plate to the junction box where
shown on the Junction Box drawing. Screw the light to the wall,
and then cut and add a pair of
blocks for each side of the upright
to hide the cover plate.

See the Post Mount drawing for
details on hanging the lantern from a
post. Check local codes for depth to
bury the wire and post bottom. To
make the post, we bought 10' boards,
and buried the bottom end of the
post 30" in the ground.

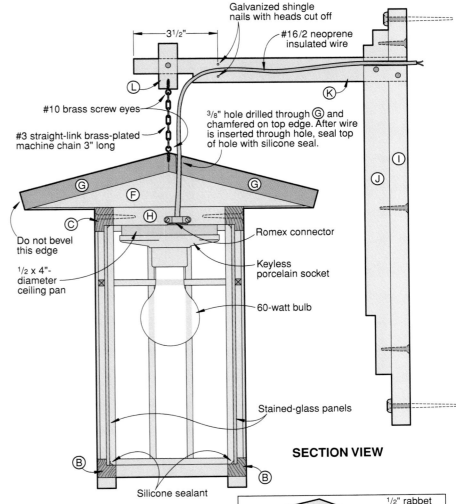

Galvanized shingle nails with heads cut off
#16/2 neoprene insulated wire
3½"
#10 brass screw eyes
#3 straight-link brass-plated machine chain 3" long
⅜" hole drilled through G and chamfered on top edge. After wire is inserted through hole, seal top of hole with silicone seal.
Do not bevel this edge
½ x 4"-diameter ceiling pan
Romex connector
Keyless porcelain socket
60-watt bulb
Stained-glass panels
Silicone sealant

SECTION VIEW

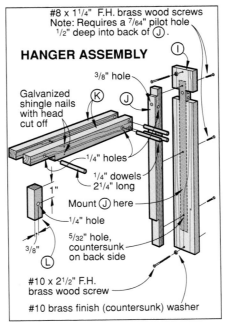

#8 x 1¼" F.H. brass wood screws
Note: Requires a 7/64" pilot hole ½" deep into back of J.

HANGER ASSEMBLY

⅜" hole
Galvanized shingle nails with head cut off
¼" holes
¼" dowels 2¼" long
Mount J here
1"
¼" hole
5/32" hole, countersunk on back side
3/8"
#10 x 2½" F.H. brass wood screw
#10 brass finish (countersunk) washer

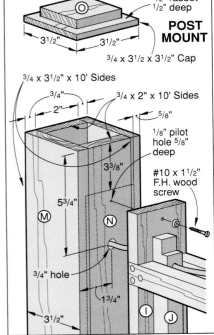

POST MOUNT
½" rabbet ½" deep
3½" 3½"
¾ x 3½ x 3½" Cap
¾ x 3½" x 10' Sides
¾"
2"
¾ x 2" x 10' Sides
5/8"
⅛" pilot hole 5/8" deep
#10 x 1½" F.H. wood screw
3⅜"
5¾"
¾" hole
1¾"
3½"

Plant Hanger from Paradise

With a cockatoo that caws attention to it

Your tropical plant will look right at home hanging from this colorful wall bracket. Build several of these easy scrollsawed hangers, and turn almost any room into a green and growing paradise.

1 Cut three pieces of Baltic birch plywood ⅛ x10x10". Temporarily laminate two of them, good sides out, with double-faced tape.

2 Enlarge the pattern, *opposite*, with a photocopying machine set to 141 percent. With spray adhesive, affix the pattern to the laminated stock.

3 Drill ⅛" blade start holes where indicated. Starting with the small triangular area on the left side,

insert the scrollsaw blade through each hole to cut along the *red* pattern lines. (We used a No. 7 scrollsaw blade, .045x.017" with 11.5 teeth per inch.)

4 After you complete the interior cuts, separate the two pieces. Leave the pattern attached. Sandwich the remaining piece of stock between the two cutouts, with the patterned piece on top. Glue the three together, aligning the edges, and clamp. When dry, cut the outside shape, following the *purple* pattern line.

5 Cut a ¾x1½x12" top arm and a ¾x1½ x11" back for the hanger. Starting from one end, rout a ⅜x⅜" groove 9⅜" long centered on one side of each. Miter-cut the grooved end,

making the grooved side the short face. On the other end, mark and saw a 1½" radius.

6 Drill a ¼" hole where shown on the top arm. Drill a ½" counter-bore ¼" deep on the ungrooved side. Dry-assemble the parts to test their fit. Finish-sand all parts.

7 Paint with acrylic artist's colors, following the color scheme shown or your own. When painting the foliage, go a little way onto the tongue that fits into the grooved top arm and back; this prevents bare wood from showing along the edges. For the bird, we painted the front view on both sides.

8 Glue the parts together and clamp. Finish the top arm and back with clear polyurethane.

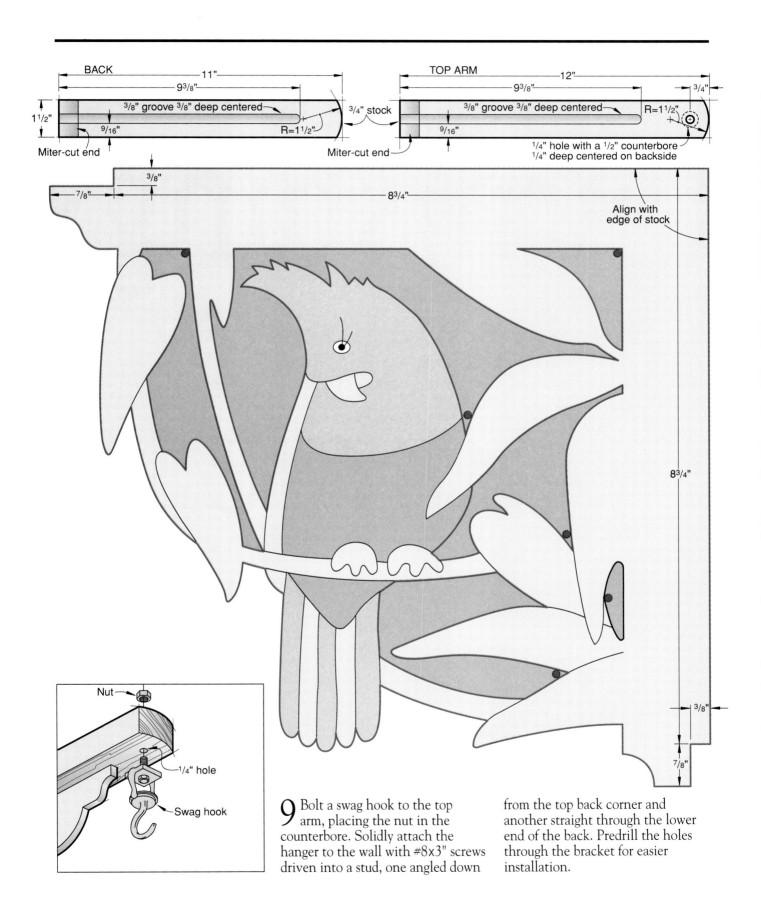

BACK

11"

9³⁄₈"

³⁄₈" groove ³⁄₈" deep centered

³⁄₄" stock

1¹⁄₂"

9⁄₁₆"

R=1¹⁄₂"

Miter-cut end

TOP ARM

12"

9³⁄₈"

³⁄₄"

³⁄₈" groove ³⁄₈" deep centered

9⁄₁₆"

R=1¹⁄₂"

Miter-cut end

¹⁄₄" hole with a ¹⁄₂" counterbore
¹⁄₄" deep centered on backside

³⁄₈"

7⁄₈"

8³⁄₄"

Align with
edge of stock

8³⁄₄"

³⁄₈"

7⁄₈"

Nut

¹⁄₄" hole

Swag hook

9 Bolt a swag hook to the top arm, placing the nut in the counterbore. Solidly attach the hanger to the wall with #8x3" screws driven into a stud, one angled down from the top back corner and another straight through the lower end of the back. Predrill the holes through the bracket for easier installation.

Fine Furnishings for the Home

Craftsmanship comes to the fore in this series of projects that showcases quality furnishings and other accessories for your home. As sturdy as they are beautiful, here are pieces that will be admired and used for generations.

Elegant Oak Dining Table

Dine in turn-of-the-century style

Style, sturdiness, and expandability make this the perfect dining table for either a traditional or contemporary home. We modeled our solid-oak design after popular turn-of-the-century Mission furniture. Our table includes slides and leaves so it can comfortably seat up to eight. Also, there's no need to shop around for matching chairs—you'll find the plan for the slat-back version shown on *page 38*.

FOR A WOBBLE-FREE TABLE, START WITH THE NOTCHED FEET

1 From ¾"-thick stock, rip and crosscut six pieces to 3⅝" wide by 34" long for the feet (A). As dimensioned on the Foot Lamination drawing on *page 32*, the length shown (34") is 1" longer than the finished length to allow for trimming the ends in Step 5.

2 Mark and cut a pair of 2x2⅝" notches in two of the six pieces where shown on the Foot

Lamination drawing. (We band-sawed the notches to shape.)

3 Spread an even coat of glue on the mating surfaces of the three pieces making one foot. With the edges and ends flush and a *notched piece in the middle*, glue and clamp the pieces face-to-face to form one foot (A). Remove any glue from the notches before it hardens. Repeat the process to laminate the second foot.

continued

Elegant Oak Dining Table

continued

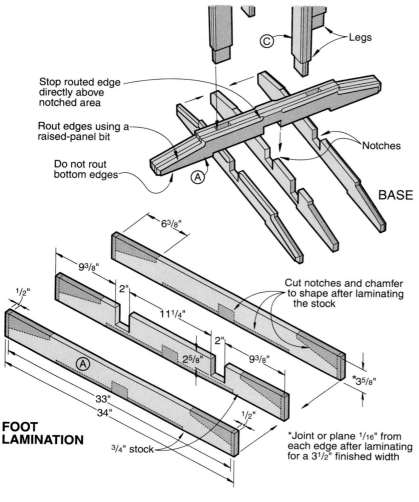

Legs

Stop routed edge directly above notched area

Rout edges using a raised-panel bit

Do not rout bottom edges

Notches

BASE

6³/₈"

9³/₈"

2"

11¹/₄"

Cut notches and chamfer to shape after laminating the stock

1/2"

2"

2⁵/₈"

9³/₈"

*3⁵/₈"

33"

34"

1/2"

FOOT LAMINATION

³/₄" stock

*Joint or plane ¹/₁₆" from each edge after laminating for a 3¹/₂" finished width

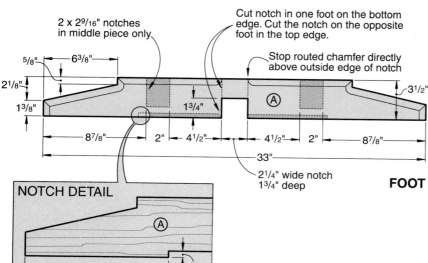

2 x 2⁹/₁₆" notches in middle piece only

Cut notch in one foot on the bottom edge. Cut the notch on the opposite foot in the top edge.

Stop routed chamfer directly above outside edge of notch

5/8"   6³/₈"

2¹/₈"

1³/₈"

1³/₄"

3¹/₂"

8⁷/₈"   2"   4¹/₂"   4¹/₂"   2"   8⁷/₈"

33"

2¹/₄" wide notch 1³/₄" deep

FOOT

NOTCH DETAIL

8⁵/₈"   1/4"

4. Scrape the glue from the bottom edge of each foot, and then joint or plane that edge flat, removing no more than ¹/₁₆" of stock. Now, joint or plane the opposite edge for a 3¹/₂" finished width.

5. Cut the feet to length (33"), trimming an equal amount from both ends to keep the notches equally spaced from the center.

6. Using the dimensions on the Foot drawing for reference, mark and cut the notched recess across the bottom, the chamfered top ends, and the mating 1¾x2¼" notches on each foot. *Note that the notch in one foot is cut in the bottom edge while the notch in the other foot is cut in the top surface.* Sand the cut edges smooth to remove saw marks.

7. Fit your table-mounted router with a raised-panel bit (we used a Bosch 85583M). Rout along the edges of each foot where shown on the Foot and Base drawings.

ADD THE CROSS MEMBERS AND UPRIGHTS TO FINISH THE BASE

1. Using the dimensions on the Cross Member drawing, cut 10 pieces for the two cross members (B). As noted on the drawing, *the length of the middle piece must be the same as the distance between the notches in the top of the feet.*

2. With the edges and ends flush, dry-clamp each cross member. Check the alignment of the mortises in the cross members against the notches in the feet. Trim the cross member parts if necessary for alignment. Laminate the pieces to form the two cross members.

3. Cut the mating ¹⁷/₃₂x2¼" notches centered from end to end in the cross members. When mating the cross members together at the notches, the top and bottom surfaces of the cross members must be flush.

4 Miter-cut a ¾" chamfer across the ends of each cross member.

5 For mounting the tabletop to the cross members later, drill and countersink a pair of ¼" mounting holes in each cross member, 1¼" from the ends where shown on the Cross Member drawing and accompanying Screw detail. Spread glue in the notches, and clamp the cross members together.

6 Cut the four uprights (C) to size (we laminated two ¾" pieces for each 1½"-thick upright). Using the Tenon detail accompanying the Cross Member drawing, cut a tenon on both ends of each upright.

7 Rout a ¼" chamfer along each edge of each upright.

ASSEMBLE THE BASE, AND ADD THE SLATS

1 Dry-fit the base pieces (A, B, C) to check the fit. Trim if necessary, and then sand smooth.

2 Glue and clamp the base (A, B, C) together, checking for square. Remove any excess glue now with a damp cloth, or wait until it forms a tough skin and remove it with a chisel.

3 Cut the slats (D) to size.

4 To form the slat trim (E), cut a piece of stock to ⅜x½x48". Cut or rout a ⅛" chamfer along one edge of the 48"-long strip. See the Exploded View drawing and accompanying details for reference.

5 Cut the spacers (F, G, H) to size. (For safety, we made the double miter-cuts on the ends of a long piece of stock for Parts H, miter-cutting the parts on a hand miter box. Then, we crosscut the H's to length from the ends of the long stock.)

6 Dry-fit the slat assembly (D, E, F, G, H) between the feet and cross members to check the fit. Then, glue and clamp the pieces in place where shown on the Slat and Spacer detail accompanying the Exploded View drawing on *page 34*.

continued

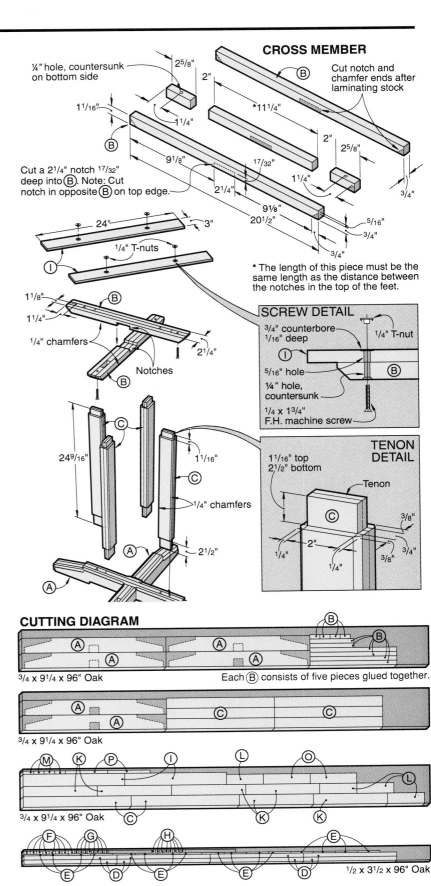

Elegant Oak Dining Table

continued

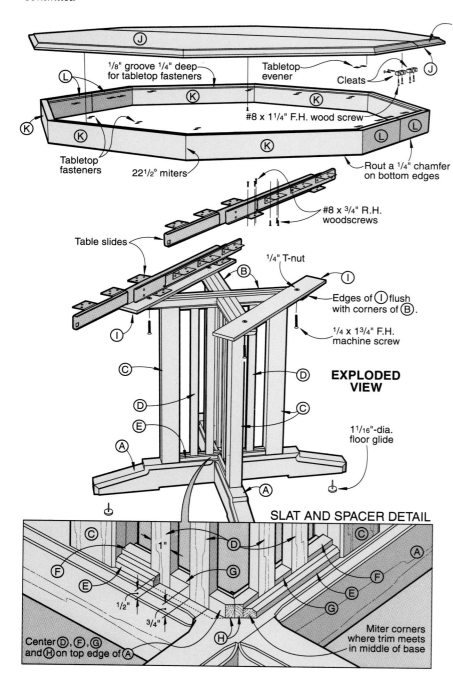

Rout table edge with a raised-panel bit

1/8" groove 1/4" deep for tabletop fasteners

Tabletop evener

Cleats

#8 x 1 1/4" F.H. wood screw

Tabletop fasteners

22 1/2° miters

Rout a 1/4" chamfer on bottom edges

#8 x 3/4" R.H. woodscrews

Table slides

1/4" T-nut

Edges of Ⓘ flush with corners of Ⓑ.

1/4 x 1 3/4" F.H. machine screw

EXPLODED VIEW

1 1/16"-dia. floor glide

Center Ⓓ, Ⓕ, Ⓖ and Ⓗ on top edge of Ⓐ.

SLAT AND SPACER DETAIL

1"

1/2"

3/4"

Miter corners where trim meets in middle of base

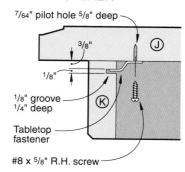

TABLETOP FASTENER

7/64" pilot hole 5/8" deep

3/8"

1/8"

1/8" groove 1/4" deep

Tabletop fastener

#8 x 5/8" R.H. screw

Bill of Materials					
Part	**Finished Size**			**Mat.**	**Qty.**
	T	**W**	**L**		
BASE					
A* feet	2 1/4"	3 1/2"	33"	LO	2
B* cross members	1 1/16"	2 1/4"	20 1/2"	LO	2
C uprights	1 1/2"	2 1/2"	24 3/16"	LO	4
D slats	1/2"	1"	21"	O	8
E* trim	3/8"	1/2"	5 1/8"	O	16
F* spacers	1/2"	3/4"	1 1/2"	O	8
G* spacers	1/2"	3/4"	1"	O	8
H* spacers	1/2"	3/4"	7/8"	O	8
I supports	3/4"	3"	24"	O	2
TABLETOP (2 HALVES)					
J* tabletop halves	1 1/16"	22 3/16"	44 3/8"	EO	2
K rails	3/4"	2 1/2"	17 1/2"	O	6
L rails	3/4"	2 1/2"	8 3/4"	O	4
M cleats	3/4"	3/4"	2 1/2"	O	4
ONE LEAF					
N* leaf	1 1/16"	11"	44 3/8"	EO	1
O rails	3/4"	2 1/2"	11"	O	2
P cleat	3/4"	3/4"	10"	O	2

*Initially cut parts marked with an * oversized. Then, trim each to finished size according to the how-to instructions.

Material Key: LO—laminated oak, O—oak, EO—edge-joined oak.

Supplies: 4—1/4 X 1 3/4" flathead machine screws, #8 X 3/4" roundhead wood screws, #8 X 1 1/4" flathead wood screws, #8 X 1 1/2" flathead wood screws, #8 X 5/8" roundhead screws, waxed paper, stain, finish.

Cutting Diagram

Ⓙ Ⓙ Ⓙ Ⓙ

1 1/16 x 9 1/4 x 96" Oak (three 9 1/4"-wide boards required for Ⓙ)

Ⓝ Ⓝ Ⓝ

1 1/16 x 5 1/2 x 96" Oak

Note: Cut splines from 1/4" plywood

7 Next, cut the table-slide supports (I) to size. Position and clamp them on the top of the cross members where shown on the Exploded View drawing. Using the previously drilled ¼" mounting holes in the cross members (B) as guides, mark the centerpoints and drill the ⁵⁄₁₆" mounting holes and T-nut depressions in each support. See the Screw detail accompanying the Cross Member drawing for reference.

NOW, EDGE-JOIN NARROWER STOCK FOR THE TABLETOP

1 To form the two halves (J) for the tabletop, cut 1¹⁄₁₆"-thick stock to the sizes listed on the Tabletop Assembly drawing. Only one half is shown, so be sure to cut two pieces for every one shown.

2 Lay out the pieces for the best grain match. Mark the edges that will receive the splines. See the Tabletop Assembly for location.

3 Fit your router with a ¼" slotting cutter. Rout ¼" slots centered along the marked edges of the tabletop pieces, stopping 1¼" from the ends. See the Spline detail accompanying the Tabletop Assembly drawing for reference.

4 From ¼" stock (we used plywood), cut ¹⁵⁄₁₆"-wide splines to the lengths listed on the Tabletop Assembly drawing. (Before cutting, make sure the ¼" plywood fits snugly in the ¼" slots. We've found some ¼" plywood is undersized, making for a sloppy fit.) Now, cut or sand the ends of each spline to the shape shown on the full-sized Spline End pattern.

5 Glue, spline, and clamp one tabletop half together, checking that the top remains flat. Repeat for the other tabletop half. Remove excess glue.

6 Mark the layout lines, and cut the tabletop halves to shape. See the Tabletop Assembly and Tabletop Half drawings for dimensions.

continued

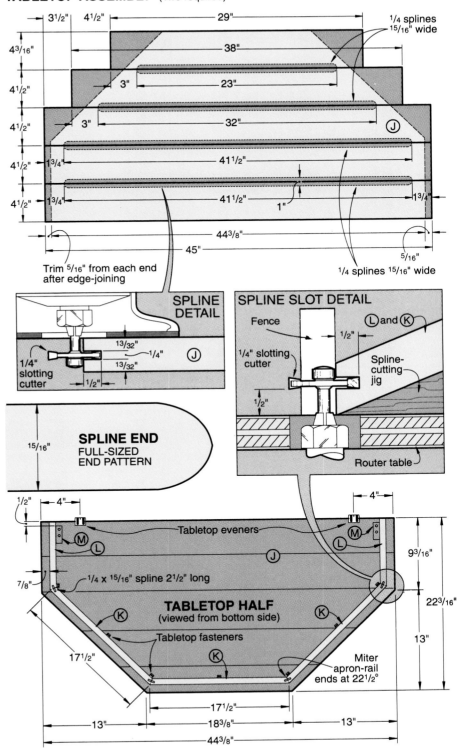

TABLETOP ASSEMBLY (Two required)

SPLINE DETAIL

SPLINE SLOT DETAIL

SPLINE END
FULL-SIZED END PATTERN

TABLETOP HALF
(viewed from bottom side)

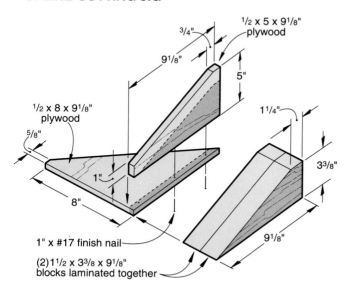

Elegant Oak Dining Table

continued

SPLINE-CUTTING JIG

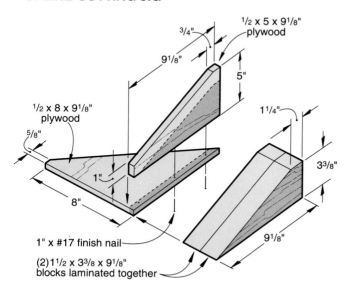

3/4"

1/2 x 5 x 9⅛"
plywood

9⅛"

5"

1/2 x 8 x 9⅛"
plywood

5/8"

1"

8"

1" x #17 finish nail

(2)1½ x 3⅜ x 9⅛"
blocks laminated together

1¼"

3⅜"

9⅛"

Using the spline-cutting jig for support, rout slots across the ends of the apron rails.

NEXT, ADD THE APRON RAILS AND HARDWARE

1 Cut the apron rails (K, L) to the sizes listed in the Bill of Materials. Miter the ends at the angle shown on the Tabletop Half drawing.

2 Cut a ⅛" groove ¼" deep along the top inside edge of each apron rail where shown on the Tabletop Fastener detail accompanying the Exploded View drawing.

3 Rout a ¼" chamfer along the bottom edges of each apron rail.

4 Build the Spline-Cutting Jig shown *above*.

5 Raise the bottom edge of the slotting cutter ½" above the top surface of the router table. As shown in the photo *above right*, rout a slot across both ends of each long apron rail (K) and across the mitered end of each short apron rail (L).

6 Lay a blanket on top of your workbench. Then, position the tabletop halves upside down and edge to edge with the ends aligned. Attach the tabletop eveners where

shown on the Tabletop Half drawing. The eveners align with each other on each half.

7 Position the apron rails (K, L) on the tabletop halves, positioning the square-cut ends of the short apron rails (L) with the inside edge of the tabletop half. To keep glue off the tabletop bottom, slide waxed paper between the apron rails and tabletop. Glue and spline the apron rails together. Use masking tape to hold the mitered-splined joints tight and the pieces in place until the glue has dried. (We used large handscrew clamps to temporarily clamp the pieces to the tabletop bottom until the glue dried.) Later, remove the clamps, waxed paper, and masking tape.

8 Carefully position the apron assembly on the tabletop bottom. Slide one end of each tabletop fastener into the ⅛" groove in the apron rails, and screw the opposite end of the fastener to the tabletop bottom.

9 With the ends flush and the slides parallel to each other, attach the

slides to the base supports where shown on the Exploded View drawing.

10 With the tabletop still upside down, position the base (also upside down) on the bottom side of the tabletop. Position the slides so that they are perpendicular to the joint line of the tabletop halves. Drill mounting holes, and fasten the slides to the tabletop.

BUILD A LEAF (OR TWO, OR THREE)

1 Edge-join stock for each 11"-wide leaf (N), cutting the pieces 1" extra in length. Crosscut the ends square, trimming the leaves to the same length as the tabletop. (To ensure the correct length, we positioned our leaves next to the tabletop halves to mark the cutoff lines.)

2 Turn the table right side up, and position the leaves on the slides between the tabletop halves (J). Attach the tabletop eveners to the leaves, mating them to the eveners already attached to the tabletop halves. Keep the leaves in place for routing in the next step.

3 Using the same raised-panel bit used earlier to rout the feet, rout the top edges of the tabletop and the ends of the leaf.

4 Cut the leaf apron rails (O) to size, and chamfer the bottom outside edge of each.

5 Cut the apron-rail cleats (P) to size. Drill mounting holes through them to the sizes stated on the Leaf drawing. Fasten the cleats to the apron rails, and then attach the apron rail/cleats to the bottom of the leaf, making sure the leaf apron rails align with the tabletop apron rails.

FINISHING UP

1 With the leaves in place, sand the top of the tabletop assembly flush and smooth.

2 Remove the slides from the tabletop and base. (To maintain alignment between the tabletop and leaves, we didn't remove the eveners.) Finish-sand the base, tabletop, and leaves.

3 Stain the pieces (we used WOOD-KOTE gelled Danish walnut stain). Apply the finish. (We applied Minwax fast-drying clear-gloss polyurethane, followed by a final coat of Minwax fast-drying clear semi-gloss polyurethane.) To help prevent warping later due to moisture absorption from the atmosphere, add as many coats of finish to the bottom of the tabletop and leaf as you do to the top.

4 Reattach the slides to the supports and tabletop halves as shown in the photo *above right*.

5 Nail the floor glides to the bottom of the feet.

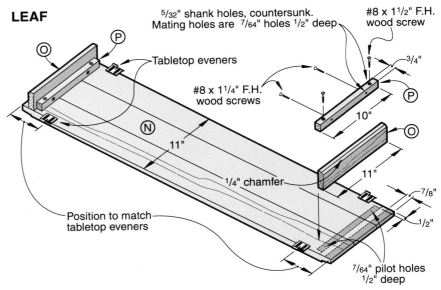

Attach the metal slides to the slide supports (I) and then secure them to the bottom of the tabletop halves.

BUYING GUIDE

• **Mission table hardware.** One pair of ball-bearing steel slides, 2" high by 40" long; one pack (10 pair) of tabletop eveners; two packs of tabletop fasteners (10/pack) one pack of ¼"-20 T-nuts (10/pack); 4—1¹⁄₁₆"-diameter floor glides. Kit No. 85812. For current prices, contact The Woodworkers' Store, 21801 Industrial Blvd., Rogers, MN 55374-9514, or call 612/428-3200 or 800/279-4441 to order.

Elegant Oak Dining Chairs

A comfortable seat for fine dining

Complement the distinguished-looking table featured on *page 31* with a set of these elegant matching chairs. Mortise-and-tenon joinery makes for rock-solid construction, and our padded-seat design guarantees an oh-so-comfortable dining experience.

Note: *The instructions, Bill of Materials, and Cutting Diagram are for one chair. Adjust for the number of chairs you plan to build. To lay out the rear legs, you can enlarge the Rear Leg grid on page 40.*

START WITH THE FRONT LEGS

1 Use 1½"-thick stock for the front legs (A) if you have it. If not, rip and crosscut four pieces of ¾"-thick stock to 1⅞" wide by 18" long. To allow for trimming later, these dimensions are slightly larger in length and width than those on the Front Legs drawing.

2 Spread an even coat of glue on the mating surfaces. With the edges and ends flush, glue and clamp two pieces face-to-face to form each leg. Repeat the process to laminate the second front leg.

3 Scrape the glue from one edge of each leg, and then joint or plane that edge flat, removing no more than 1/16" of stock. Now, rip the opposite edge for a 1¾" width. Crosscut both ends of each leg for a finished length of 17½".

4 Mark the locations for the mortises and dowel holes where shown on the Front Legs drawing. Be sure to lay out the legs in pairs that contain a left and a right leg.

5 Cut the mortises and drill the dowel holes in each leg. (To form the mortises, we drilled overlapping holes to remove most of the waste stock, and then chiseled the mortises square. You also can leave the ends of the mortises round, and use a rasp to round the ends of the mating tenons.)

6 Mark a pair of taper lines on two surfaces (the same surfaces as the mortises) of each leg where shown on the Front Legs drawing and accompanying Taper detail. Bandsaw the tapers where marked (you could also make the cuts using a taper jig). Sand the tapered surfaces smooth to remove the saw marks.

LAY OUT, CUT, AND MACHINE THE REAR LEGS

1 From 1 1/16"-thick stock, cut two pieces 4" wide by 35" long for the rear legs (B). Then, cut a piece of thin plywood or hardboard to the same size for use as a template in the next step.

2 Cut a piece of paper to 4x35", and mark 1" grid lines on it. Transfer the rear-leg outline, dowel-hole centerline, tenon, and mortise locations from the Rear Leg Side View drawing on *page 40*. Refer to the Tenon detail for dimensions when laying out the tenon. (To lay out the curved front and back outlines, we cut a ¼"-thick strip of wood to 1" wide by 37" long. Using a helper to position the flexible strip of wood, we positioned one edge of the strip against the marked points on the gridded paper.

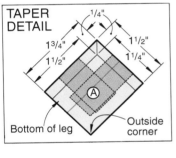

TAPER DETAIL

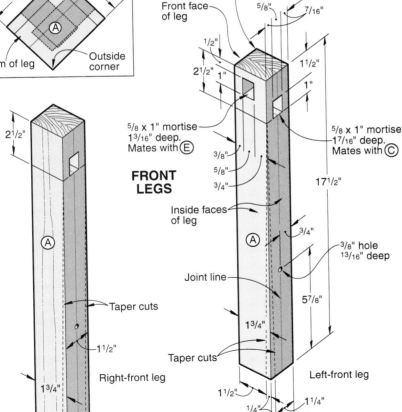

FRONT LEGS

continued

Elegant Oak Dining Chairs

continued

Holding the wood strip firmly in place, we marked the curves for the front and back edges of the leg.) Keep flat the 2"-wide area where the top rail (C) joins the rear leg.

3 Using spray adhesive, adhere the paper pattern to the 4x35" template stock. Cut the template to shape.

4 Using double-faced tape, adhere the two leg blanks together face-to-face, with the edges and ends flush. Next, apply spring clamps to position and hold the template on the leg blanks where shown in the photo *below* and dimensioned on the Rear Leg Side View drawing.

5 As shown in the photo, use a square to transfer the mortise location and dowel-hole center-lines to the rear leg blanks. Next, transfer the leg outline. Separate the template from the leg blanks. Drill the dowel holes (we did this on our drill press, using a brad-point bit). Next, chisel the mortises to shape.

6 Bandsaw the rear legs to shape, and bandsaw the tenons to shape. (We used a ¼" blade.) Sand the edges of the legs smooth. Using a wood wedge, pry the legs apart.

THE UPPER RAILS COME NEXT

1 From 1¹⁄₁₆"-thick stock, cut the upper side rails (C) to the size listed in the Bill of Materials.

2 Using the dimensions on the Tenon details accompanying the Side Frame Assembly drawing on *page 42*, carefully lay out a tenon on each end of the upper side rails (C).

3 Cut the tenons. (We cut them out of scrap stock first to verify the settings. We did this on a tablesaw using a miter gauge fitted with an auxiliary fence and stop-block. The stopblock helped ensure even-lengthed tenons.) Check the fit of the tenons in their mating mortises and trim if necessary. For reference when gluing the same joints later during assembly, make matching marks on both mating pieces at each joint.

continued

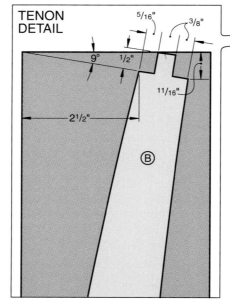

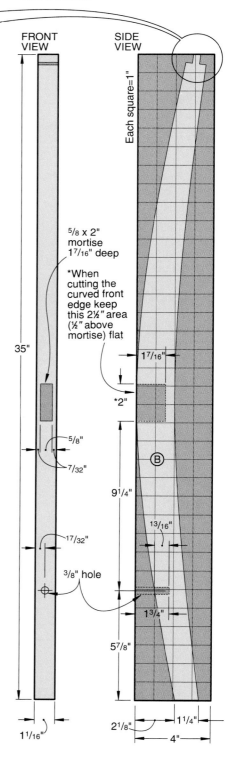

Transfer the mortise location, dowel-hole centerline, and leg outline to the rear leg blanks from the template.

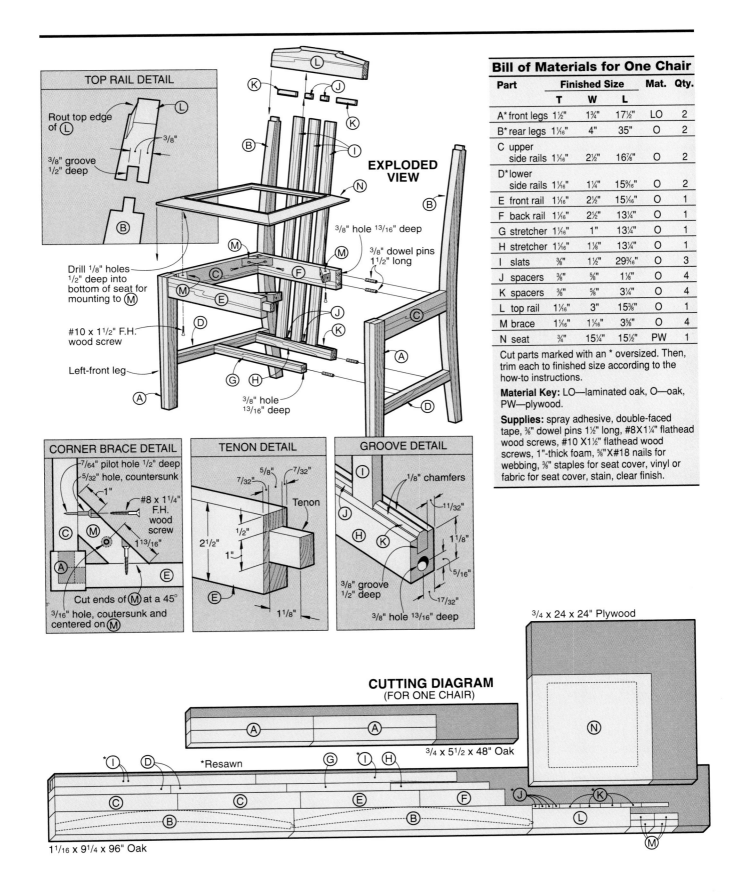

TOP RAIL DETAIL

Rout top edge of Ⓛ

3/8"

3/8" groove 1/2" deep

Drill 1/8" holes 1/2" deep into bottom of seat for mounting to Ⓜ

#10 x 1 1/2" F.H. wood screw

Left-front leg

EXPLODED VIEW

3/8" hole 13/16" deep

3/8" dowel pins 1 1/2" long

3/8" hole 13/16" deep

Bill of Materials for One Chair

Part	Finished Size			Mat.	Qty.
	T	**W**	**L**		
A* front legs	1 1/2"	1 3/4"	17 1/2"	LO	2
B* rear legs	1 1/16"	4"	35"	O	2
C upper side rails	1 1/16"	2 1/2"	16 7/8"	O	2
D* lower side rails	1 1/16"	1 1/4"	15 5/16"	O	2
E front rail	1 1/16"	2 1/2"	15 1/16"	O	1
F back rail	1 1/16"	2 1/2"	13 1/4"	O	1
G stretcher	1 1/16"	1"	13 1/4"	O	1
H stretcher	1 1/16"	1 1/8"	13 1/4"	O	1
I slats	3/8"	1 1/2"	29 3/16"	O	3
J spacers	3/8"	5/8"	1 1/8"	O	4
K spacers	3/8"	5/8"	3 1/4"	O	4
L top rail	1 1/16"	3"	15 5/8"	O	1
M brace	1 1/16"	1 1/16"	3 5/8"	O	4
N seat	3/4"	15 1/4"	15 1/2"	PW	1

Cut parts marked with an * oversized. Then, trim each to finished size according to the how-to instructions.

Material Key: LO—laminated oak, O—oak, PW—plywood.

Supplies: spray adhesive, double-faced tape, 3/8" dowel pins 1 1/2" long, #8X1 1/4" flathead wood screws, #10 X1 1/2" flathead wood screws, 1"-thick foam, 5/8"X#18 nails for webbing, 3/8" staples for seat cover, vinyl or fabric for seat cover, stain, clear finish.

CORNER BRACE DETAIL

7/64" pilot hole 1/2" deep

5/32" hole, countersunk

1"

#8 x 1 1/4" F.H. wood screw

1 13/16"

Cut ends of Ⓜ at a 45°

3/16" hole, countersunk and centered on Ⓜ

TENON DETAIL

5/8"

7/32"

7/32"

Tenon

1/2"

2 1/2"

1"

1 1/8"

GROOVE DETAIL

1/8" chamfers

11/32"

1 1/8"

5/16"

17/32"

3/8" groove 1/2" deep

3/8" hole 13/16" deep

CUTTING DIAGRAM
(FOR ONE CHAIR)

3/4 x 24 x 24" Plywood

Ⓝ

Ⓐ   Ⓐ

3/4 x 5 1/2 x 48" Oak

*Ⓘ   Ⓓ   *Resawn   Ⓖ   *Ⓘ   Ⓗ   *Ⓙ   Ⓚ

Ⓒ   Ⓒ   Ⓔ   Ⓕ   Ⓛ

Ⓑ   Ⓑ   Ⓜ

1 1/16 x 9 1/4 x 96" Oak

Elegant Oak Dining Chairs

continued

4 Mark the pair of dowel-hole centerpoints on the *inside* face, rear end of each upper rail (C) where dimensioned on the Tenon detail at *far right*.

NOW, CUT THE LOWER RAILS

1 From 1¹⁄₁₆"-thick stock, cut the lower side rails (D) to size plus 1" in length.

2 Using the dimension on the Side Frame drawing and angles shown on the Section View drawing, miter-cut the ends of the lower side rails. Next, mark the centerpoints and drill dowel holes in the inside face of each rail where dimensioned on the Section View drawing.

3 To drill the hole in each end of the rails, mark their centerpoints. Extend a reference line *parallel* to the top and bottom edges of the rail. Secure the rail in a bench vise. Chuck a ³⁄₈" brad-point bit into your portable drill. Align the bit with the marked lines, and drill the holes to ¹³⁄₁₆" deep.

4 Mark the centerpoints, and drill the dowel holes for Parts G and H where located on the Section View drawing.

5 Dry-clamp the side frame rails (C, D) between the legs (minus the dowels) to check the fit, and trim if necessary.

SHAPE THE RAILS AND STRETCHERS

1 Cut the front rail (E) to size. Using the Tenon Detail accompanying the Exploded View drawing on *page 41* for dimensions, machine a tenon on both ends.

2 Cut the back rail (F) to size.

3 To transfer the dowel-hole centerpoints to the ends of the back rail (F), position ³⁄₈" dowel

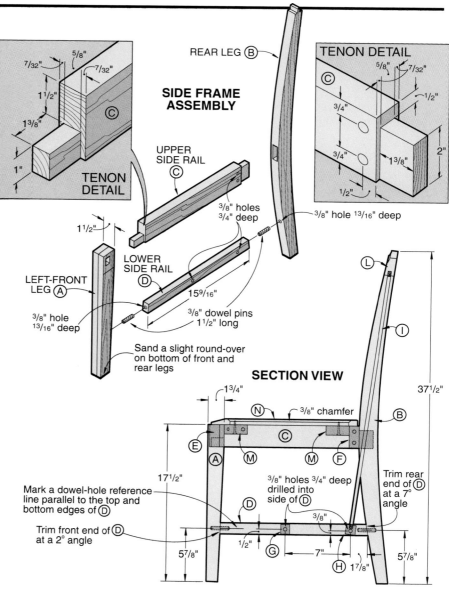

SIDE FRAME ASSEMBLY

TENON DETAIL

SECTION VIEW

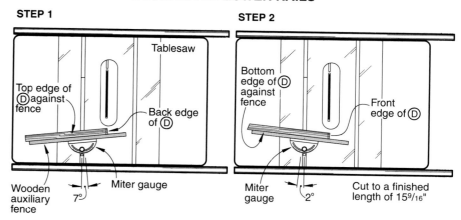

CUTTING THE LOWER RAILS

STEP 1

STEP 2

Cut to a finished length of 15⁹⁄₁₆"

centers (you'll need four) in the previously drilled dowel holes in the back inside surface of the upper rails (C). Clamp the front and back rails (E, F) between the side frame assemblies.

4 With the assembly dry-clamped, cut the front stretcher (G) and rear stretcher (H) to fit snugly between the lower rails (D).

5 Drill a dowel hole centered in each end of the front stretcher (G). Mark the dowel-hole center-points on the ends of the rear stretcher (H) where dimensioned on the Groove detail accompanying the Exploded View drawing. Drill the holes.

SLIP IN THE SLATTED BACKREST

1 Cut and sand the backrest slats (I) to size. They're easier to sand now than when glued in place.

2 Cut a piece of stock to ⅜"x⅝"x20" for spacers (J, K). Cut or rout a pair of ⅛" chamfers along one edge of the 20" strip where shown on the Groove detail accompanying the Exploded View drawing. Then, crosscut the middle spacers (J) to length from the long strip.

3 Using the Part View drawing for reference, cut the backrest top rail (L) to shape.

4 Fit your table-mounted router with a raised-panel bit with a ½" cutter (we used a Bosch 85583M). Rout along the top front edges of the backrest top rail (L). Do not rout the ends, bottom, or back of the rail.

5 Cut a ⅜" groove ½" deep along the bottom edge of the backrest top rail (L) and along the top edge of the rear stretcher (H). The top rail groove is cut ⅜" from the *back* face. The groove in the rear stretcher is centered.

6 Stain the slats and back surface of the back rail (F). It's easier to do this now than with the chair assembled. (We used WOODKOTE Danish walnut stain.)

7 Glue, dowel, and clamp the stretchers (E, F, G, H) between the side frames. To angle the rear stretcher (K), stick one end of a slat in the groove in the rear stretcher, and align the top end of the slat with the rear leg tenons. (To give us a bit more working time, we used white glue.)

8 Working from the center out, glue and clamp the slats, spacers, and top rail (L) in place. Doing this now will automatically angle the rear stretcher (H). (We used masking tape to hold the spacers in place until the glue dried.)

9 Miter-cut the braces (M) to length. Drill the holes, and then glue and screw them to the chair frame. See the Corner Brace detail accompanying the Exploded View drawing for reference.

10 Finish-sand and stain the chair and apply the finish. (We applied two coats of Minwax fast-drying clear-gloss polyurethane, followed by a coat of Minwax fast-drying clear semi-gloss poly-urethane.)

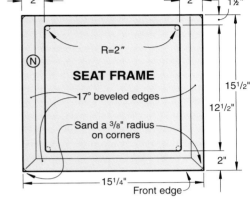

ADD THE OH-SO-COMFORTABLE PADDED SEAT

1 From ¾" fir plywood, cut the seat frame (N) to shape. The outside edges of the seat should be ⅛" in from the outside edges of the top rails (C, E, F).

2 Using the Seat Frame drawing *above*, lay out and cut the border for the opening with a jigsaw. (We drilled ⅜" blade start holes first.) Sand the cut edges.

3 Tilt your tablesaw blade 17° from vertical, and rip the front and side top edges of the seat frame where shown on the Bevel-Ripping the Seat Frame drawing on *page 44*.

4 Rout a ⅜" chamfer along the inside top edge of the seat-frame opening. Sand a ⅜" radius on the sharp front corners of the seat frame to round them off. Sand a slight round-over on all edges.

5 Starting at the center and working out, nail one end of the center piece of webbing to the seat frame, pull the opposite end tight, nail it in place, and cut off the excess. Nail the other four strips running front to back in place. See the Buying Guide for our chair web-bing source. Starting at the front and working back, weave and nail the remaining webbing in place where shown on the Forming the Seat drawing and accompanying detail.

continued

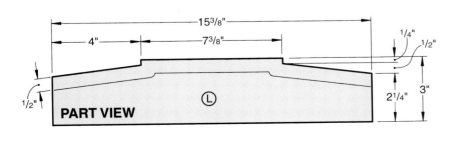

Elegant Oak Dining Chairs

continued

6 To help hold the 1"-thick seat foam in place when applying it in the next step, cover all four edges of the plywood seat frame with double-faced (carpet) tape. (We purchased our foam at an upholstery supply store.) Left untaped, the foam tends to pull away from the edges.

7 Lay the seat frame on a piece of 1" foam. Use a utility knife with a sharp blade to trim the edges of the foam flush with the edges of the seat frame.

8 Cut a piece of vinyl (or fabric) to 24" square, and lay it good side down on your workbench. Position the seat frame, foam side down, centered over the vinyl.

9 Staple the back edge of the vinyl to the bottom side of the seat frame. Pull the front edge of the vinyl tight over the frame to remove any ripples, and staple the vinyl in place. See the Staple detail accompanying the Forming the Seat drawing. Fold the corners until they're smooth, pull tight, and staple the sides of the vinyl to the frame. Trim the vinyl on the bottom side of the seat frame where shown on the detail.

10 Position and center the seat on the chair frame. Use the previously drilled holes in the braces as guides to drill pilot holes in the bottom side of the seat frame. Drive screws through the four braces into the seat frame to fasten it securely to the chair.

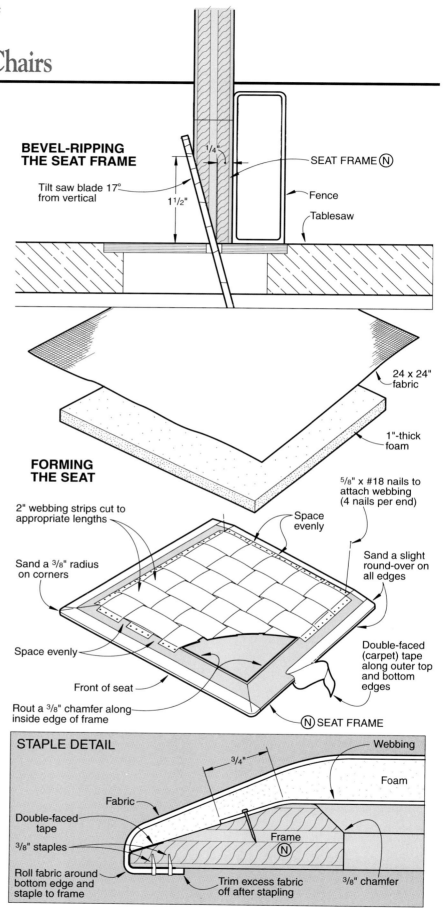

BEVEL-RIPPING THE SEAT FRAME

Tilt saw blade 17° from vertical

1/4"

1 1/2"

SEAT FRAME N

Fence

Tablesaw

24 x 24" fabric

1"-thick foam

FORMING THE SEAT

2" webbing strips cut to appropriate lengths

Sand a 3/8" radius on corners

Space evenly

Front of seat

Space evenly

Rout a 3/8" chamfer along inside edge of frame

5/8" x #18 nails to attach webbing (4 nails per end)

Sand a slight round-over on all edges

Double-faced (carpet) tape along outer top and bottom edges

N SEAT FRAME

STAPLE DETAIL

Webbing

Fabric

Foam

Double-faced tape

3/8" staples

3/4"

Frame N

Roll fabric around bottom edge and staple to frame

Trim excess fabric off after stapling

3/8" chamfer

Worth-Every-Minute Wall Clock

Build this timeless statement in leaded glass

With our leaded-glass technique article on *page 49,* why not practice what we've preached by building this beautiful wall-mounted pendulum clock? You'll be surprised how easy the whole project goes together (we've kept the clock and glass-panel construction simple on purpose). See the Buying Guide at the end of the article for our source of supplies.

Note: *See the following techniques article for information on assembling the glass-panel insert used in the door of this clock.*

Let's start with the solid oak clock case

1 From ¾" oak stock, cut the clock case sides (A) and upper and lower members (B) to the sizes listed in the Bill of Materials.

2 Cut or rout a ¾" rabbet ¼" deep across both ends of each side piece (A). Cut a ¼" rabbet ½" deep along the back inside edges of the sides (A). See the Exploded View drawing for reference.

3 Sand the inside surfaces of Parts A and B. Glue and clamp the pieces. Check for square and that the *front* edges are flush.

4 Cut the top and bottom pieces (C) to size.

5 Tilt your tablesaw blade 45° from vertical, position your fence, and cut a chamfer along the front and side edges of the top and bottom. Use a pushblock for stability and to minimize grain tear-out. Sand the chamfers to remove the machining marks.

6 Center the top and bottom pieces (C) side-to-side on the top and bottom of the clock case. Then, with the back edges flush with the sides (A), glue and clamp them in place.

continued

Worth-Every-Minute Wall Clock
continued

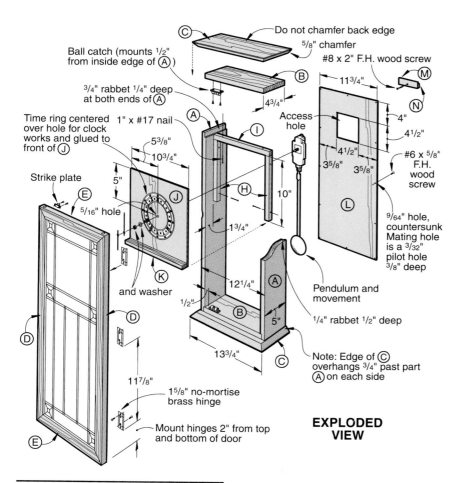

Ball catch (mounts ½" from inside edge of (A))

Do not chamfer back edge

⅝" chamfer

#8 x 2" F.H. wood screw

¾" rabbet ¼" deep at both ends of (A)

Access hole

Time ring centered over hole for clock works and glued to front of (J)

Strike plate

5/16" hole

and washer

1" x #17 nail

5⅜"

10¾"

5"

1¾"

12¼"

½"

13¾"

11⅞"

1⅝" no-mortise brass hinge

Mount hinges 2" from top and bottom of door

11¾"

4¾"

10"

3⅝"   3⅝"

4½"

4"

4½"

5"

#6 x ⅝" F.H. wood screw

9/64" hole, countersunk Mating hole is a 3/32" pilot hole ⅜" deep

Pendulum and movement

¼" rabbet ½" deep

Note: Edge of (C) overhangs ¾" past part (A) on each side

EXPLODED VIEW

Bill of Materials

Part	Finished Size			Mat.	Qty.
	T	W	L		
CASE					
A sides	¾"	5"	28"	O	2
B U & L members	¾"	4¾"	11¼"	O	2
C top & bottom	¾"	6½"	13¾"	O	2
DOOR					
D* stiles	¾"	1¼"	27¾"	O	2
E* rails	¾"	1¼"	12¼"	O	2
F stops	3/16"	¼"	25¾"	O	2
G stops	3/16"	¼"	10¼"	O	2
CLOCK FACE ASSEMBLY					
H supports	¾"	¾"	10"	O	2
I support	¾"	¾"	10¾"	O	1
J face	¼"	10¾"	10¾"	OP	1
K ledge	¾"	1¼"	10¾"	O	1
L back	¼"	11¾"	28"	OP	1
HANGING BLOCK					
M front	⅜"	2"	4"	O	1
N back	⅜"	1"	4"	O	1

*Initially cut parts oversized. Then, trim to finished size according to the how-to instructions.

Material Key: O—oak, OP—oak plywood.
Supplies: ¾"X#17 brads, 1" X#17 nails, ¼" dowel stock, #8X2" flathead wood screws, #6X⅝" flathead wood screws, stain, finish.

NOW, LET'S CONSTRUCT THE DOOR FRAME

1 Cut the door stiles (D) and rails (E) to size plus 2" in length.

2 Cut or rout a ¼" rabbet 3/16" deep along the back edge of each piece. See the Door drawing and accompanying Glass Stop detail for reference.

3 Miter-cut the stiles and rails to length. Glue and clamp the pieces together, checking the door frame for square and that it lies flat.

4 Using a doweling jig for alignment, drill a ¼" hole in each corner of the door frame where shown on the Door drawing.

5 Cut four pieces of ¼" dowel stock to 1⅝" long. Sand a chamfer on one end of each dowel. Apply glue and insert the dowels—chamfered end first—into the dowel holes just drilled. Later, trim the protruding

ends of the dowels flush with the edges of the door frame.

6 Assemble the glass insert for the door using the method described in the techniques article and the Leaded-Glass Pattern shown *opposite*.

7 Cut the glass stops (F, G) to size, miter-cutting the ends.

NEXT, MACHINE THE REMAINING PIECES

1 Cut the clock-face supports (H, I) to size. Drill pilot holes, then glue and brad them to the inside of the clock case where shown on the Exploded View drawing. Immediately remove excess glue.

2 From ¼" oak plywood, cut the clock face (J) to size. Check the fit in the opening. Then, mark the shaft hole centerpoint where dimensioned on the Exploded View

drawing, and drill the shaft hole through the face. Check the fit of the clock shaft through the hole. Some movements might require a different-sized hole.

3 Cut the clock-face ledge strip (K) to size, and glue and clamp it to the front of the clock face.

4 Glue and clamp the clock-face assembly (J, K) to the supports (H, I).

Wrap sandpaper around a 1" dowel and sand the finger recess to shape.

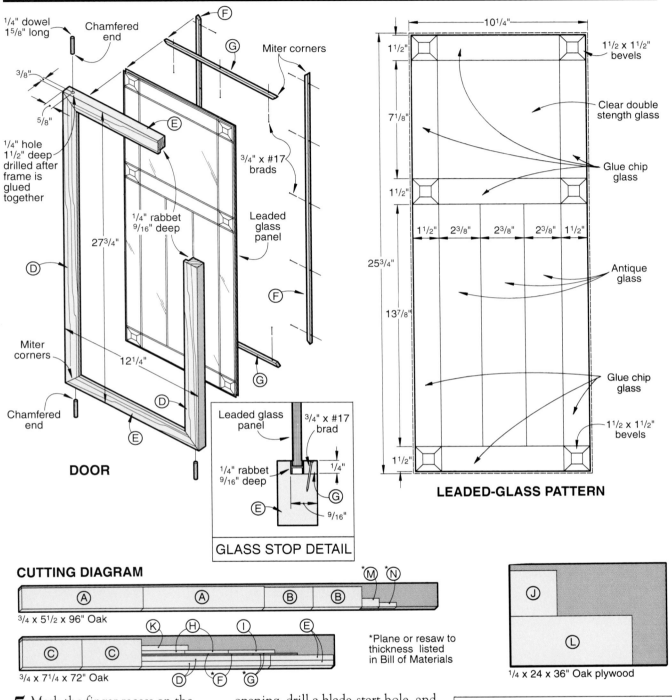

DOOR

1/4" dowel 1⁵/₈" long

Chamfered end

3/8"

5/8"

1/4" hole 1¹/₂" deep drilled after frame is glued together

27³/₄"

1/4" rabbet ⁹/₁₆" deep

Miter corners

D

12¹/₄"

Chamfered end

E

D

Miter corners

F

G

3/4" x #17 brads

Leaded glass panel

F

G

GLASS STOP DETAIL

Leaded glass panel

3/4" x #17 brad

1/4" rabbet ⁹/₁₆" deep

1/4"

E

G

⁹/₁₆"

LEADED-GLASS PATTERN

10¹/₄"

1¹/₂"

7¹/₈"

1¹/₂"

25³/₄"

1¹/₂" 2³/₈" 2³/₈" 2³/₈" 1¹/₂"

13⁷/₈"

1¹/₂"

1¹/₂ x 1¹/₂" bevels

Clear double stength glass

Glue chip glass

Antique glass

Glue chip glass

1¹/₂ x 1¹/₂" bevels

CUTTING DIAGRAM

A   A   B   B   *M *N

3/4 x 5¹/₂ x 96" Oak

K H I E
C   C
D *F *G

3/4 x 7¹/₄ x 72" Oak

*Plane or resaw to thickness listed in Bill of Materials

J
L

1/4 x 24 x 36" Oak plywood

5 Mark the finger recess on the front outside edge of the left-hand side piece (A) where shown on the Finger Recess drawing. Wrap sandpaper around a 1"-diameter dowel, and sand the recess to shape as shown in the photo *opposite.*

6 Measure the rabbeted opening, and cut the clock-case back (L) to size. Lay out the 4½"-square access

opening, drill a blade-start hole, and cut the opening to size.

7 Cut the clock-hanger block parts (M, N) to size. Drill mounting holes and glue and screw the parts. To help keep the completed clock plumb and prevent the hanger block from rubbing against the wall, adhere
continued

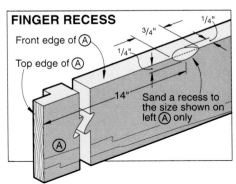

FINGER RECESS

1/4" 3/4" 1/4"

Front edge of A

Top edge of A

14"

Sand a recess to the size shown on left A only

A

Worth-Every-Minute Wall Clock

continued

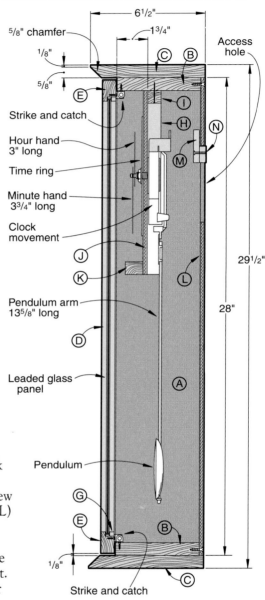

HANGER BLOCK

3/8"   4"   5/32" hole, countersunk on back side

1 x 4" 100-grit sandpaper strip glued to face of Ⓝ

1"   1/2"   2"   2"   Ⓜ   Ⓝ

SECTION VIEW

6 1/2"   1 3/4"   5/8" chamfer   Access hole   1/8"   5/8"   Ⓔ   Ⓒ   Ⓑ   Ⓘ   Ⓗ   Ⓝ   Ⓜ

Strike and catch

Hour hand 3" long

Time ring

Minute hand 3 3/4" long

Clock movement

Ⓙ   Ⓚ   Ⓛ   Ⓐ   Ⓓ   29 1/2"   28"

Pendulum arm 13 5/8" long

Leaded glass panel

Pendulum   Ⓖ   Ⓔ   Ⓑ   1/8"   Ⓒ

Strike and catch

a piece of sandpaper to the exposed face of Part N where shown on the Hanger Block drawing.

ADD THE FINISH, GLASS PANEL, HARDWARE, AND MOVEMENT

1 Finish-sand the clock case, door, stops, and back panel. Stain as desired, and apply a clear finish.

2 Install the glass panel in the door. To do this, snip the head off a #17x3/4" brad, chuck the brad into your portable drill, and use the brad as a bit to drill angled pilot holes through the glass stops and into the door frame. See the Glass Stop detail accompanying the Door drawing for reference.

3 Center and brad (or epoxy) the timing ring to the front of the clock face (J).

4 Attach the no-mortise hinges to the front edge of the right-hand door stile (D) where dimensioned on the Exploded View drawing. Then, fasten the hinges to the door stile. When positioning the door for attaching the hinges to the clock case, leave an 1/8" gap between the clock case and top and bottom of the door.

5 Attach the ball catches to the clock case and mating positions on the back of the door.

6 Stick the clock shaft through the hole in the clock face (J), and fasten the movement (minus the pendulum) to the clock face with the external-threaded nut and washer. Trim the metal hands (we used a scissors) to the lengths stated on the Section View drawing. Add the hands to the protruding clock shaft. Add the battery.

7 Drill mounting holes, and screw the oak plywood back panel (L) into the rabbet in the rear of the clock case.

8 Fasten the hanger block to the wall, and slip the clock onto it. See the Section View drawing for reference.

9 Cut the wood pendulum arm to 13 5/8" long. Hang the pendulum and set the time.

BUYING GUIDE

• **Clock movement and hardware.** Mini-quartz movement with wood pendulum and brass disc, etched time ring, straight hands, antique brass no-mortise hinges, and two polished-brass ball catches. Stock No. 4910. For current prices, contact Turncraft Clocks, Inc., P.O. Box 100, Mound, MN 55364-0100, or call 800/544-1711 to order.

• **Glass and leading.** 6—1 1/2x1 1/2" beveled-glass squares, 1—10x15" clear semi-antique glass, 1—18x24" single chip glass, 1—8x10" clear double-strength glass, 3—6' pieces 1/4" RH lead came. Kit No. 8030WM. For current prices, contact Delphi Stained Glass, 2116 E. Michigan Ave., Lansing, MI 48912, or call 800/248-2048 to order.

Leaded-Glass Panels

A clear winner!

I f you've admired the striking beauty of leaded panels made of clear, stained, or beveled glass, you may be surprised at how easily you can make one. With our instructions and a modest investment in tools and supplies,

you can create simple, but elegant, panels such as the one shown in the inset *above*. And, you'll find endless woodworking applications for such panels—as with the pendulum-clock project on *page 45*.

A HANDFUL OF ITEMS TO HELP YOU GET STARTED

For an investment of less than $150, you can buy the essential tools and supplies for making leaded-glass panels. Here's a listing and the approximate prices of the items shown on *pages 50–51*.

continued

Leaded-Glass Panels

continued

1. Whiting powder ($2 for 1 pound)

2. Glazing cement ($6 for 1 pound)

3. Round-H lead came, ¼" wide ($2.30 for a 6' length)

4. Came-stretching vise ($4)

5. Glass ($4–$10 per square foot for most types)

6. Horseshoe nails (75¢ per dozen)

7. Glass cutter ($4–$30; the least expensive models work fine, and the higher-priced versions have carbide wheels for longer life)

8. Cork-backed straightedge ($4)

9. Three-bladed pattern shears ($10)

10. Running pliers ($10)

11. Breaker/grozer pliers with ⅜"-wide jaws ($10)

12. Flush-cutting lead nippers ($7–$22)

13. Flux ($3 for 4 ounces)

14. Flux brush (35¢)

15. 80- to 100-watt soldering iron with 700° temperature control and ⅜"-wide tip ($40–$70)

16. 50/50 solder ($6 for a 1-pound spool)

If you live near a large city, you'll find these tools and supplies at a stained-glass store. Or, you can order them from the source in the Buying Guide on *page 55.*

LET'S START BY MAKING OUR PATTERN

To keep things simple, we'll show you how to make a panel with glass pieces having straight edges only. As your skills improve, you may want to try free-form design using curved pieces of glass.

First, determine the exact width and height of your panel. Lay out these dimensions on a piece of paper (shown by the dashed line in the drawing *opposite, top right*), and mark solid lines ⅛" inside the dashed lines on all sides.

Note: *We suggest you use H-channel lead came for the inside and border of your panel. This way, you can trim some of the lead from the border of the panel to help it fit into its frame. U-channel lead came does not afford you this option.*

Now, select the beveled pieces for your design. You can choose these pre-cut pieces in many sizes and shapes such as squares, rectangles, diamonds, and triangles. The catalog listed in the Buying Guide on *page 55* carries a full line of beveled glass.

Draw centerlines for locating the beveled glass as shown *opposite*. Place and align the bevels on the paper, being careful to leave a ¹⁄₁₆" gap where they meet each other. With a sharp pencil trace around the bevels.

Now, lay out the rest of your pattern as shown *opposite, far right*. We refer to this pattern as the *glazing copy* because you'll use it to reassemble your glass pieces later.

Choose your glass for the rest of the pattern. We selected glue-chip glass, a heavily textured clear glass, for the border pieces of the finished panel on *page 49.* You also can substitute a colored glass for these border pieces as we did in the how-to photos throughout this article. For the interior pieces we chose antique glass with subtle distortions.

Now, with carbon paper make a *cutting copy* by tracing the solid lines of your glazing copy onto a piece of heavy paper. With the carbon paper still in place, number each pattern piece. Separate the two patterns, and cut the cutting copy into separate pieces with a three-bladed shears. As shown *opposite left*, the shears remove ³⁄₆₄" of your pattern to make room for the lead came. Cut carefully and in straight lines. Since your bevel pieces come precut, you must be sure to cut on the *outside* of the lines touching or surrounding the bevels (that's why we placed the bevels ¹⁄₁₆" apart).

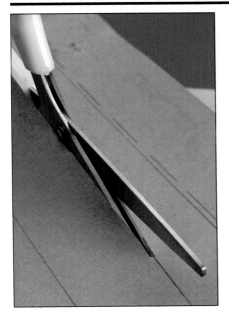

Three-bladed pattern shears remove 3/64" of your pattern to allow room for the lead came.

READY TO CUT SOME GLASS? IT'S A SNAP!

Although cutting glass may seem at first to be a hazardous activity, we found it safe and easy to do once we learned a few basic methods. To get started, attach a cutting-pattern piece to a piece of glass with rubber cement.

If you're working with a textured glass, attach the pattern to the smooth side of the glass. Done this way, the textured side of the glass will face away from you when you look at the front of the completed panel (the

HOW TO LAY OUT YOUR PATTERN

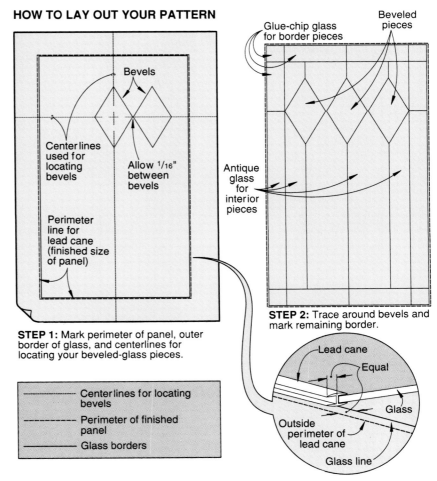

STEP 1: Mark perimeter of panel, outer border of glass, and centerlines for locating your beveled-glass pieces.

— — — — Centerlines for locating bevels

– – – – Perimeter of finished panel

——— Glass borders

STEP 2: Trace around bevels and mark remaining border.

side with the bevels facing you). However, if you want the textured side of the glass to face you, just reverse the pattern before attaching it to the smooth side of the glass.

Safety Note: *Always wear eye protection whenever you cut, groze (chip away), or grind glass.*

continued

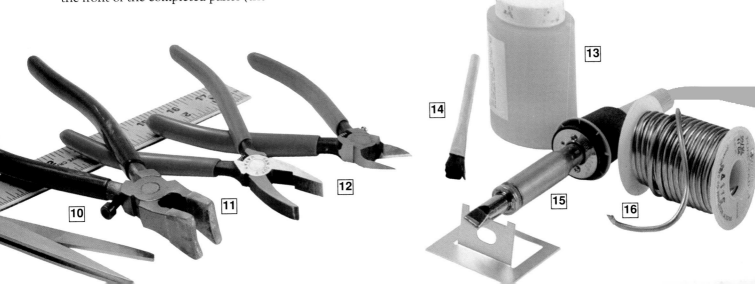

Leaded-Glass Panels

continued

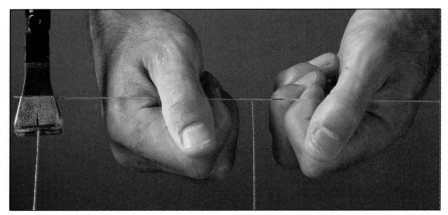

You can use a running pliers *(left)* or your hands to break glass along straight scoring lines. The pliers come in especially handy when cutting narrow pieces.

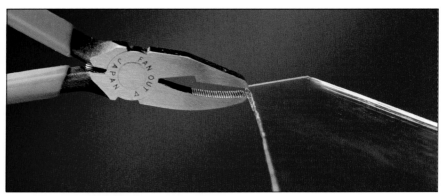

A breaker/grozer pliers helps you trim glass to fit within your pattern lines. Remember to keep the curved jaw down, and take small, controlled bites.

Hold the lead came firmly in a pair of pliers and stretch it 1" for every 1' of length. This quick procedure straightens the came and makes it stiff.

CUTTING GLASS: A TYPICAL SUCCESSION OF CUTS

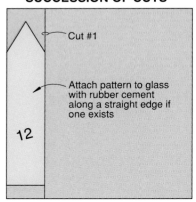

Cut #1

Attach pattern to glass with rubber cement along a straight edge if one exists

12

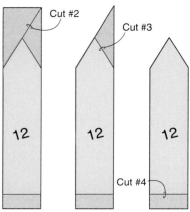

Cut #2

Cut #3

12   12   12

Cut #4

To make a cut, score along one side of the pattern with your glass cutter. Be careful to keep your score line right alongside the edge of the pattern or just inside it. Use a straightedge to keep your long cuts straight. Now, grasp the glass on either side of the scoring line as shown *top left*.

To break the glass, twist both wrists so your palms face upward. This may be hard to do when cutting narrow pieces, so at these times use a running pliers as shown on the *left* side of the *top* photo. These pliers have curved jaws that create the same pressure that your hands would otherwise. The drawing *above* shows a typical succession of cuts.

After cutting each piece, check to see if any portion of the glass extends past the pattern. If so, you'll need to carefully gnaw away at these protrusions with a breaker/grozer pliers as shown *opposite, center.* When using this handy tool, remember to keep the curved jaw down.

IT'S TIME TO ASSEMBLE THE GLASS AND LEAD

To determine how much lead came you'll need, add up the length of all the solid pattern lines and add 15 percent. The came comes in limp, 6'-long strands. Before using the came, you need to straighten and stiffen it by stretching it as shown *opposite bottom.* To do this, lock one end of the strand in a came-stretching vise clamped to one end of your bench. Now, hold the other end solidly in a pair of hand pliers, and pull the came, stretching it about 6". Be careful not to bend the taut came. Then, cut it into two equal lengths for convenient handling.

Note: *For health reasons, do not eat or drink while handling lead came. And, be sure to wash your hands after every work session.*

Set the came strips aside, and staple your glazing copy to a flat piece of ¾" plywood that's at least 2" larger than the paper pattern on all sides. Position the plywood and pattern on a bench so the longest side of the panel faces you. Screw two ⅜"-thick, 1"-wide wooden cleats with straight edges along the dashed lines on the bottom and left side of the pattern. (If you're left-handed, screw the cleats to the bottom and right side of the pattern.)

With your flush-cutting lead nippers, cut two lengths of lead that fit along the inside corner of the two cleats. (Because solder will cover this joint later, you don't need to miter the ends.) Cut these so they extend slightly past your outside pattern lines. To make a clean cut, hold the came and nippers as shown *above right.*

Starting in this corner, tuck your first piece of glass into the channels in the lead came. Tap this piece (and all others) to make sure it goes completely into the channel. Then, check that the piece does not go beyond your pattern lines. If so, trim away some glass with your breaker/grozer pliers, or by lightly touching the edge to a belt sander

Position your lead came and nippers this way for clean cuts.

with 120-grit abrasive. Assemble your panel by working out from the bottom left corner toward the top right corner.

Note: *Plan the joints of your inside lead pieces so your panel has as many long pieces as possible and a minimum number of joints. The drawing on page 54 shows how we worked out the joint placement in our sample panel.*

SOME TIPS FOR CUTTING AND POSITIONING THE LEAD CAME

For smooth-looking soldered joints later, you should cut your lead pieces so they butt up against each other without a gap. (Never
continued

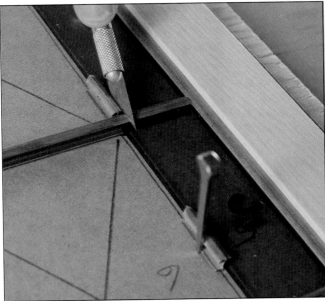

Use lead scraps to accurately guide your cutoff marks. This scrap substitutes for a full-length piece of came that you cut later.

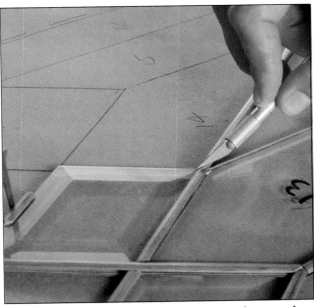

Align your lead cutoff mark with the bevels at the top and bottom of the diamonds.

Leaded-Glass Panels

continued

leave a gap greater than ⅟₁₆"; if you do, you'll have to fill it with a small piece of lead before soldering.) And, be sure to position the came in straight lines throughout the panel. To ensure your success, follow these tips:

• Hold your glass and came in place with horseshoe nails as you work. Use scraps of came as cushions between the nails and glass. Also use scraps to help you mark the position of your cuts with a slim knife as shown on *page 53, bottom left.*

• Since solder covers joints completely, you usually don't have to miter lead came at corners. But, diamond-shaped bevels do require mitered cuts. In our sample we cut the miters on the right and left corners of the beveled pieces by eyeballing the necessary angle and nipping the lead until it fit. At the top and bottom of the bevels, we marked the cut by following the line formed by the intersecting bevels as shown on *page 53, bottom right.*

• When cutting miters of 45° or more, you may find that the "heart" of the lead came interferes with your

TYPICAL LEAD CANE JOINTS

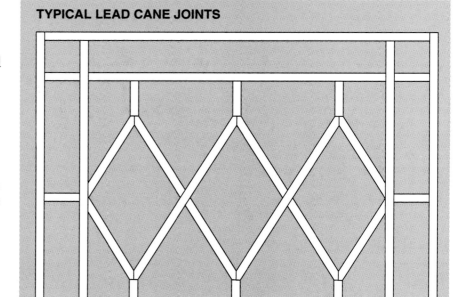

nippers. In these cases, remove a short length of the heart as shown *below left.* To do this, cut along both sides of the heart, then bend the heart back and forth until it breaks off.

• To butt a piece of came up against the mitered joint at the bottom of a diamond-shaped bevel, make cutoff marks on the mitered pieces as shown *below right.*

• Don't jam your glass and lead tightly together. A slight amount of play helps you adjust the pieces for

proper alignment during soldering. However, don't leave so much space between the glass and came that you have visible gaps in the panel.

ADD SOLDER FOR SOLID JOINTS

With your glass and lead came in place, tack two more cleats around the perimeter of your pattern as shown *opposite, top center.* Make certain that the panel does not extend past your dashed line. If it

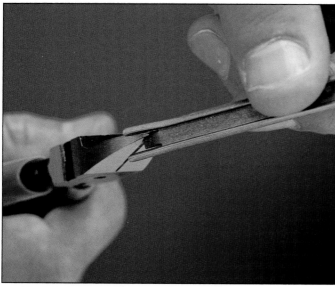

With your flush-cutting lead nippers, remove the heart of the lead came prior to cutting miters of 45° or more.

Mark and cut mitered lead pieces so they form clean, gap-free joints with butting pieces of came.

does, check the fit of your glass pieces against your pattern, and readjust as needed. Also, double-check to make sure that all of the lead pieces align in straight rows. *Note: You'll find that with time and practice your soldering technique will improve greatly, so it pays to practice on scrap came.*

Brush some flux on all of the joints on the top side of the panel. The flux helps the solder adhere and flow into the joint.

When your soldering iron becomes hot enough to melt the solder, hold the solder between the joint and the soldering iron as shown on *page 49*. The iron will quickly melt the solder. Hold the soldering iron on the joint for two or three seconds, until the solder flows evenly across the joint. You may need to move the iron in a small circular motion to smooth the solder, but be careful not to spread the solder more than ¼" past the joint. Then, lift the iron straight up and off the joint.

Use no more solder than necessary for a smooth joint. (See the photos *far right* for examples of well done and poorly executed soldered joints). Try to keep the joint as flat as possible. To fill small gaps, turn the tip of your soldering iron vertical before lifting it off the gap.

When you finish soldering, wipe away all excess flux. Temporarily remove two cleats and flip the panel over. Flux and solder the joints on the other side. Check both sides to make sure you didn't miss any joints.

THE FINAL STEPS: GLAZING AND CLEANING

To prevent the glass from rattling within the lead channels, and to weatherproof the panel, you need to work glazing cement into the space between the lead came and the glass.

Add two more cleats to make your project square and secure prior to soldering. (Remove the horseshoe nails before positioning the cleats.)

Scrub the whiting into your panel to clean and polish it.

To do this, apply a glob of cement to the panel and work it under the lead, using a scrub brush as shown *top right*.

After glazing both sides, sprinkle some whiting (powdered chalk) onto one side and work it around with a clean scrub brush as shown *above*. The whiting will pick up the excess glazing cement and leave the glass looking smooth and polished. Repeat this procedure on the other side of the panel. Lay the panel on a flat surface and let the cement cure for about 24 hours.

With a toothpick or other pointed object, remove the excess cement from along the edges of the lead came. Finally, lightly sprinkle some whiting on the panel and scrub it

Work the glazing cement under the came with a scrub brush.

Strive for flat, smooth, small, and unobtrusive solder joints such as the example at *right*. Shown at *left* is a poorly soldered joint. Oops!

again with a clean brush. You're done! (For information on how to install leaded glass panels in a wood frame, see the instructions in the Pendulum Clock project on *page 45*.)

BUYING GUIDE
• For a complete catalog of leaded-glass supplies, including tools, glass, books, videos, kits, and designs, contact Delphi Stained Glass, 2116 E. Michigan Ave., Lansing, Ml 48912, or call 800/248-2048.

Woven-Wood Hamper

Good-looking storage

Here's a storage hamper that's so good looking, you won't want to hide it in a closet. Designer Keith Raivo uses a thin-strip weave to make a practical accessory work as a decorative accent.

Note: See the Buying Guide at the end of the article for our source of 1" copper nails.

MARK AND CUT THE BASE AND THE FORM PIECES

1 From ¾" AC exterior plywood, cut two pieces to 14½x21" for the base and form blanks (A).

2 With the edges and ends flush, adhere the two pieces of plywood with double-faced tape or a few beads of hot-melt adhesive. Using the dimensions on the Parts View drawing, mark the base outline on the top piece. Bandsaw the two pieces to shape, and sand their edges flush. Pry the pieces apart, and remove the double-faced tape or hot-melt adhesive.

3 On the piece you'll use for the base, lightly mark the upright positions with a pencil where shown on the Parts View drawing. On the other piece, which you'll use as the form, mark and cut the hand-hold opening.

NOW, CUT AND ADD THE UPRIGHTS TO THE BASE

Note: When ripping the ⅟₁₆" and ⅛"-thick strips, we recommend cutting several extra; it's easy to break them when weaving Also, you can cut the

C

Glue, spline, and clamp the lid together in two steps to help ensure a flat lid.

Sanded round-over on top edges

Sand a slight chamfer

3/32" holes

1/8" holes to form corners

(P)

HINGE
(FULL-SIZED PATTERN)

3 Paying close attention to the direction of grain indicated on the Lid Assembly drawing, cut 1/8"-thick splines (M) to the sizes shown on the drawing.

4 As shown in Photo C, glue, spline, and clamp the two lid side pieces (L) to the back piece (K). You want the ends of the splines flush with the *outside* edges of the lid. Check that the ends of the back piece are flush with the edges of the side pieces and that the surfaces are flush and level.

5 Sand a slight round-over along the inside edge of the lid parts where shown on the Exploded View drawing.

6 Cut the lid weavers (N, O) to size. Sand a taper on both ends of each. Soak the pieces, and weave them in place where shown on the Lid Assembly drawing.

7 With the lid weavers in place, glue, spline, and clamp the lid front (J) to the previously formed lid assembly (K, L).

8 To form the hinge joint, cut the lid back (K) into two pieces where shown on the Lid Assembly drawing. Tape the two pieces back together edge to edge.

9 Turn the hamper upside down, and carefully center it on the lid assembly. Set the point of a compass 3/8" from the lead, and mark a line 3/8" from the outside edge of the hamper onto the lid bottom.

10 Bandsaw the taped-together lid to shape, and sand the cut edges smooth. Rout a 3/8" round-over along the top outside edge of the lid (see the Hinge detail accompanying the Exploded View drawing for reference.) Sand a slight round-over along the bottom outside edge. Remove the tape.

NOW, SHAPE THE HINGES, AND ATTACH THE LID

1 Using the full-sized hinge pattern on the Parts View drawing, lay out two hinges (P) including the openings and nail-hole centerpoints onto 1/2" walnut.

2 Using a scrollsaw or coping saw, cut the hinges to shape. Drill a blade-start hole, and cut the openings to shape. Drill three pilot holes in each hinge.

3 Sand a 1/8" round-over on the top outside edge of each hinge. Sand a slight chamfer on the front and back edges of each opening. (For reference, see the Hinge detail accompanying the Exploded View drawing.)

4 Mark the hinge-hole locations on the lid back (K) 5/16" from the cut edge where shown on the Lid Assembly drawing. Cut the hinge holes in the lid back to shape.

5 Cut the lid support (Q) to the size listed in the Bill of Materials. Place the lid support on the top of the hamper, and trace the hamper interior shape onto the piece. Bandsaw the piece to shape.

6 Clamp the lid support (Q) to the inside back edge of the hamper with the top edges flush. Clamp the lid back (K) to the support so the lid back protrudes 3/8" beyond the

continued

Woven-Wood Hamper

continued

outside edge of the hamper. Trace the hinge-hole locations from the lid back onto the lid support. Remove the pieces, and form the hinge holes in the support where marked.

7 With the hinge holes aligned, glue and clamp the support and lid back to the hamper.

8 To pin the leather hinge strip to the support later, drill a 3/32" hole through the front edge of the support (Q) and into the hinge hole.

9 From 1/8"-thick leather, cut two strips 1/2" wide by 5" long for the hinge straps. Push one end of the strap though the hole in the hinge. Stick both ends through the hole in the lid back (K). Repeat with the other hinge. (We bought our leather at Tandy—you also could get it at a shoe-repair store.) Drive a 1" copper nail through the previously drilled holes in the lid support to fasten the hinge strap to the support.

10 Align the lid on the hamper, and glue and nail the hinges to the lid.

11 Using the Support Strap drawing for reference, drill pilot holes, and attach a pair of 8" leather straps to the hamper and lid.

FINALLY, ADD THE FINISH

1 Sand the hamper smooth. (We used a flap sander and just lightly

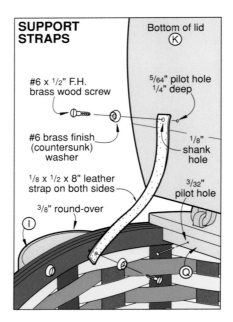

sanded the hamper, but not the lid, to smooth any grain raised from the soaking of the pieces.)

2 Cover the exposed leather with masking tape. Apply the finish of your choice. (We sprayed on several coats of polyurethane.) If you apply the finish with a brush, do it lightly to prevent runs on the uprights and weavers. Remove the masking tape from the leather.

BUYING GUIDE

• **Copper nails.** 2mmx1" nails with rose-type head, 100 nails per kit. For current prices, contact Faering Design, Inc., P.O. Box 805, Shelburne, VT 05482. No phone orders please.

The Safe-and-Simple Thin-Strip Ripper

For edging and weaving with ease

Ripping thin strips between the tablesaw blade and fence can be risky business. But, if you need these strips for edging plywood shelves, adding inlay strips, or for use with our hamper on *page 56,* we've come across a jig that makes the process super simple. It allows you to cut strip after strip, achieving uniform thickness without the worry of kickback.

CUT THE PARTS AND ASSEMBLE THE JIG

1 From ¾" plywood, cut the base (A) to 7" wide by 10" long.

2 Referring to the Top View drawing of the base for location, mark the four centerpoints for the ⁵⁄₁₆" holes. Drill the holes where marked. Now use a straightedge to mark lines from hole to hole to lay out the pair or ⁵⁄₁₆"-wide slots 3½" long on the plywood base.

3 Using a scrollsaw or jigsaw, cut along the marked lines to form the ⁵⁄₁₆"-wide slots. Sand or file the cut edges of each slot.

4 Mark diagonals on the base to locate the center, and drill a hole for the handle to the size stated on the Exploded View drawing. Sand the base smooth, sanding a slight chamfer along one edge to allow for sawdust buildup.

5 Fasten a 2"-diameter knob (we used a cabinet knob) to the base, making sure the head of the mounting screw doesn't protrude below the bottom surface.

6 Cut the miter-gauge slot guide (B) to the width and depth of your miter-gauge slot, and cross-cut it to 10" long. The guide should fit snugly in the slot; a loose fit can result in uneven thin strips later. Our guide measured ⅜" thick by ¾" wide. For the guide to slide easily in the slot, you may need to lightly sand one edge. Mark the centerpoints for the two ¼" holes. Drill and countersink the holes.

7 Check that the screw heads don't protrude. Then, epoxy a ¼x1½" flathead machine screw in each countersunk hole. Wipe off excess epoxy.

8 Fasten the guide to the base with ¼" washers and wing nuts.

continued

The Safe-and-Simple Thin-Strip Ripper

continued

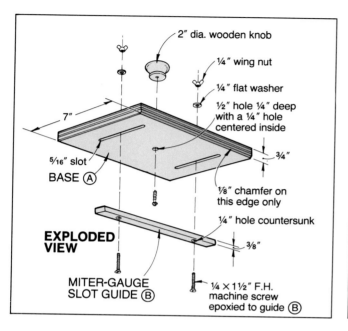

2" dia. wooden knob

¼" wing nut

¼" flat washer

½" hole ¼" deep with a ¼" hole centered inside

7"

¾"

⁵⁄₁₆" slot

BASE (A)

⅛" chamfer on this edge only

¼" hole countersunk

EXPLODED VIEW

⅜"

MITER-GAUGE SLOT GUIDE (B)

¼ × 1½" F.H. machine screw epoxied to guide (B)

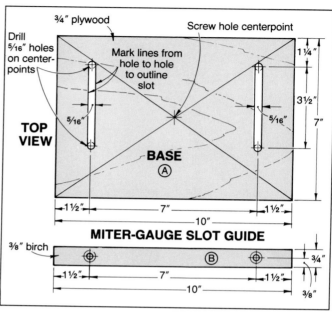

¾" plywood

Screw hole centerpoint

Drill ⁵⁄₁₆" holes on center-points

Mark lines from hole to hole to outline slot

1¼"

3½"

TOP VIEW

⁵⁄₁₆"

⁵⁄₁₆"

7"

BASE (A)

1½"   7"   1½"

10"

MITER-GAUGE SLOT GUIDE

⅜" birch

(B)

¾"

1½"   7"   1½"

10"

⅜"

HOW TO USE THE JIG TO RIP SOME THIN STRIPS

Loosen the wing nuts, and position the inside chamfered edge of the base parallel to the saw blade, leaving a gap between the blade and the base equal to the width of the strips desired. Tighten the wing nuts. See Step 1 of the drawing *below* for reference. Place the stock to be ripped next to the jig. Then, move the rip fence against the stock where shown in Step 2 of the drawing. Remove the jig, start the saw, and cut a thin strip as shown in Step 3 of the drawing. Use a pushstick to keep your fingers safely away from the blade. Position the jig in the miter-gauge slot. Repeat Steps 2 and 3 of the drawing to cut the next thin strip. Keep repeating the process until you feel uncomfortable with the distance between the blade and the fence (we stop at about ¾").

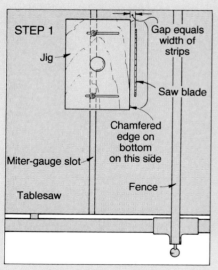

STEP 1

Jig

Gap equals width of strips

Saw blade

Chamfered edge on bottom on this side

Miter-gauge slot

Tablesaw

Fence

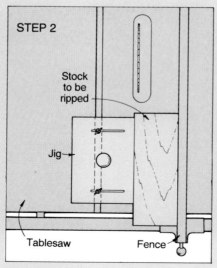

STEP 2

Stock to be ripped

Jig

Tablesaw

Fence

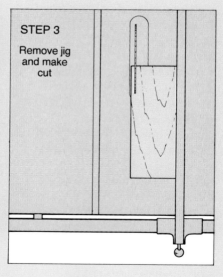

STEP 3

Remove jig and make cut

Bow-Front Table

A beautiful blend of contrasting hardwoods

Does a wall in your home suffer from a sheer lack of visual interest? If so, then let this beautiful bow-front table help you create an area worthy of high praise. As shown *above,* the table serves as the staging area for numerous complementary decorations. And, from a woodworker's point of view, you'll like learning how to bend wood and taper table legs.

START BY BUILDING THE FORM

1 Cut a piece of ¾" plywood to 14x39" for the form base. Using

the dimensions on the Lamination Form drawing, mark the screw-hole centerpoints on the bottom side of the base for attaching the 2x4 supports in the next step. Note that the two outside supports get two screws each. Working from the bottom side, drill and countersink a ⁵/₃₂" shank hole at each marked centerpoint.

2 Crosscut seven pieces of 2x4 to 4" long for the form supports. Mark diagonals on one end of five of the supports to find center. Then, mark a dividing line across the width on one end of each of the two remaining

supports. Mark the hole centerpoints on these two remaining supports.

3 Drill a ⁵/₆₄" pilot hole 1" deep into each 2x4 support at each marked centerpoint. Using 3" drywall screws (no glue), secure the 2x4 supports to the top face of the base where shown on the Lamination Form drawing on *page 66.* (To allow the five middle supports to pivot and conform to the natural bend of the bowed rail [A], we used only one screw in each.)

4 For aligning the front pieces when laminating the front later, mark a reference line on the center 2 x4 support where shown on the Lamination Form drawing.

HERE'S HOW TO LAMINATE THE BOWED FRONT RAIL

1 From one end of a 4x8 sheet of ⅛" oak plywood, crosscut six pieces 48" wide by 4" long (remember to measure length *with* the grain). See the Cutting Diagram for reference.

2 Cover the form and 2x4 supports with waxed paper.

3 Use spring clamps to dry-clamp the plywood strips together with the ends and edges flush. Mark an alignment line across the top edge, centered from end to end, on the plywood pieces. Remove the clamps.

4 Using a 3"-wide paint roller, apply white woodworkers glue to the mating surfaces of each layer. Now, using handscrew clamps or C-clamps and 4"-tall blocks of wood, glue the oak plywood strips together and against the supports as shown in Photo A on *page 67 top left.* Keep the bottom edges of the plywood flush with each other and firmly against the plywood base. Position the marked alignment lines on the top edges of the strips so that they align with each other and with the reference mark on the middle support.

5 Before the glue dries, scrape off as much of it as possible from the *continued*

Bow-Front Table

continued

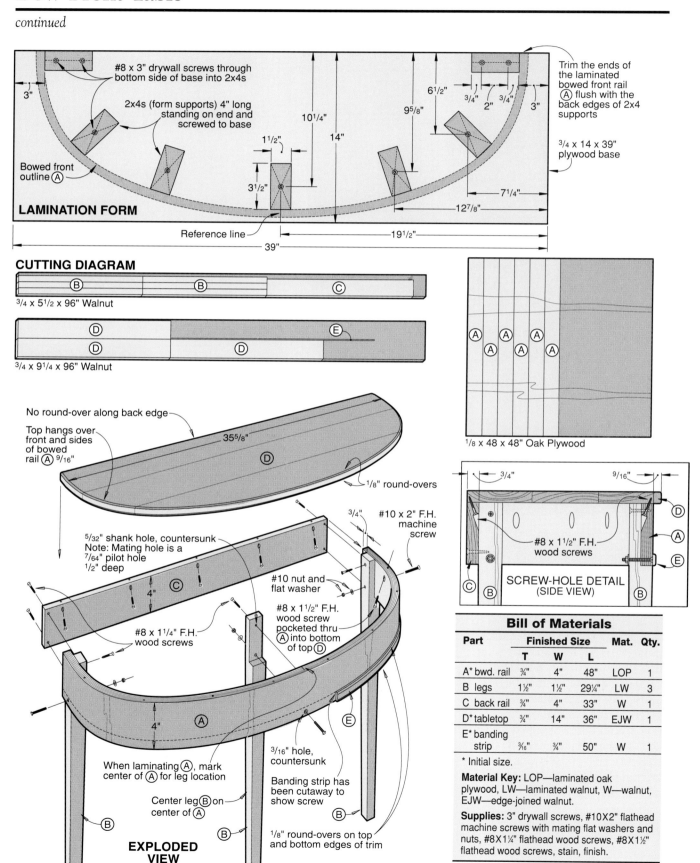

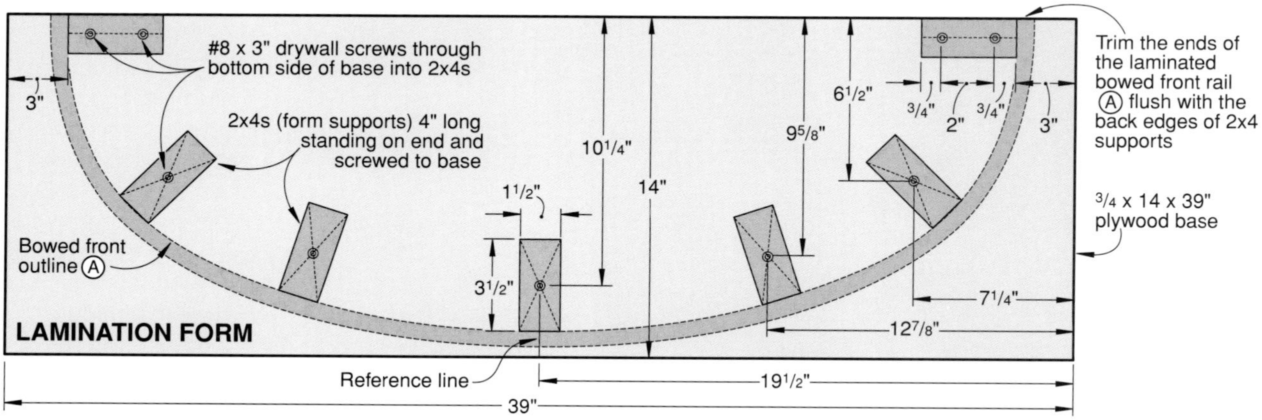
#8 x 3" drywall screws through bottom side of base into 2x4s
3"
2x4s (form supports) 4" long standing on end and screwed to base
10¹/4"
14"
9⁵/8"
6¹/2"
3/4"
2"
3/4"
3"
Trim the ends of the laminated bowed front rail Ⓐ flush with the back edges of 2x4 supports
3/4 x 14 x 39" plywood base
1¹/2"
3¹/2"
Bowed front outline Ⓐ
7¹/4"
12⁷/8"
LAMINATION FORM
Reference line
19¹/2"
39"

CUTTING DIAGRAM

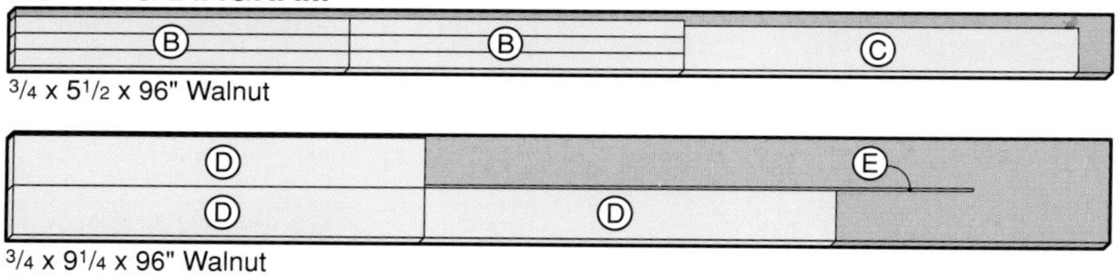
Ⓑ
Ⓑ
Ⓒ
3/4 x 5¹/2 x 96" Walnut
Ⓓ
Ⓔ
Ⓓ
Ⓓ
3/4 x 9¹/4 x 96" Walnut

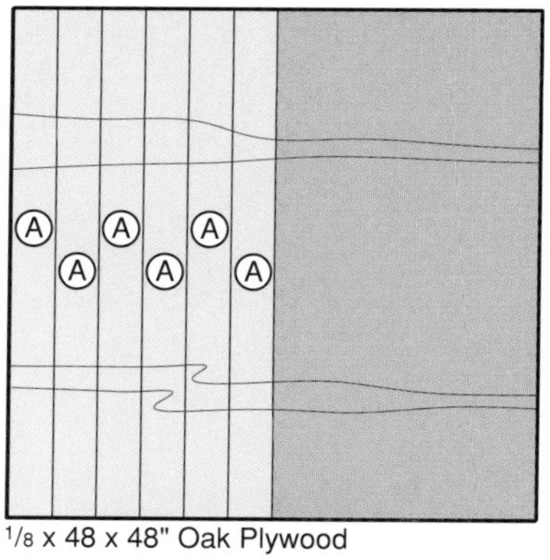
Ⓐ Ⓐ Ⓐ Ⓐ Ⓐ Ⓐ
1/8 x 48 x 48" Oak Plywood

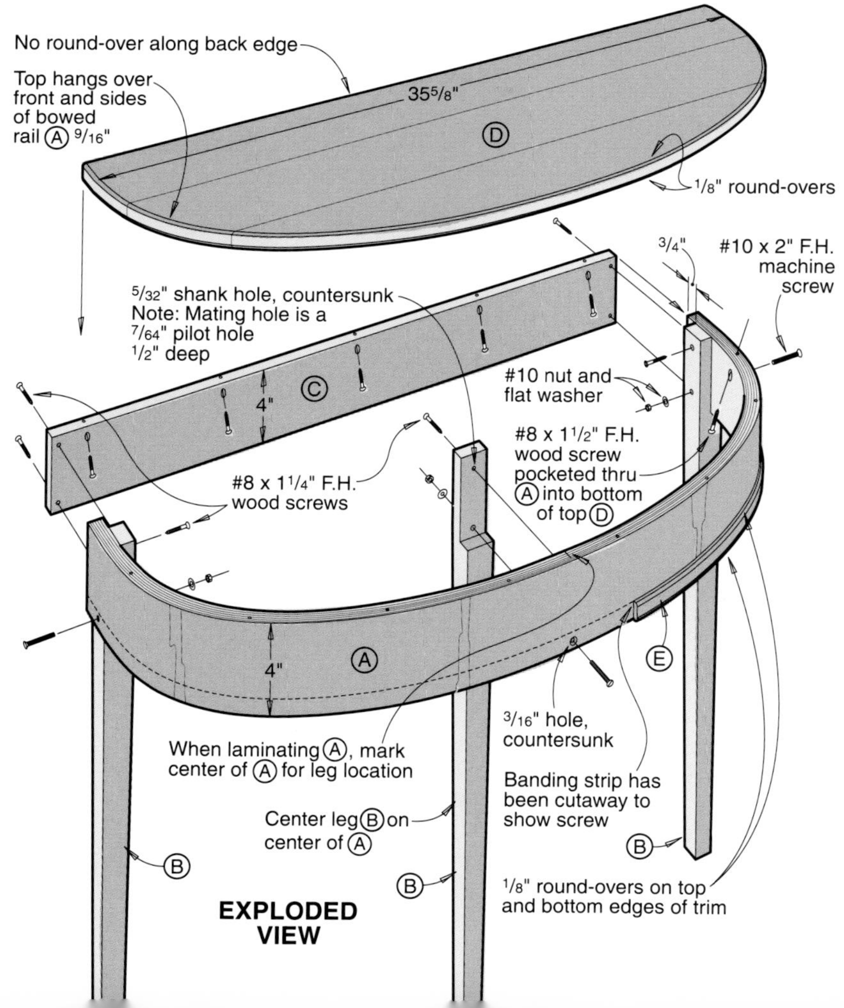
No round-over along back edge
Top hangs over front and sides of bowed rail Ⓐ 9/16"
35⁵/8"
Ⓓ
1/8" round-overs
3/4"
#10 x 2" F.H. machine screw
5/32" shank hole, countersunk
Note: Mating hole is a 7/64" pilot hole 1/2" deep
4"
Ⓒ
#10 nut and flat washer
#8 x 1¹/2" F.H. wood screw pocketed thru Ⓐ into bottom of top Ⓓ
#8 x 1¹/4" F.H. wood screws
4"
Ⓐ
Ⓔ
3/16" hole, countersunk
Banding strip has been cutaway to show screw
When laminating Ⓐ, mark center of Ⓐ for leg location
Center leg Ⓑ on center of Ⓐ
Ⓑ
Ⓑ
Ⓑ
1/8" round-overs on top and bottom edges of trim
EXPLODED VIEW

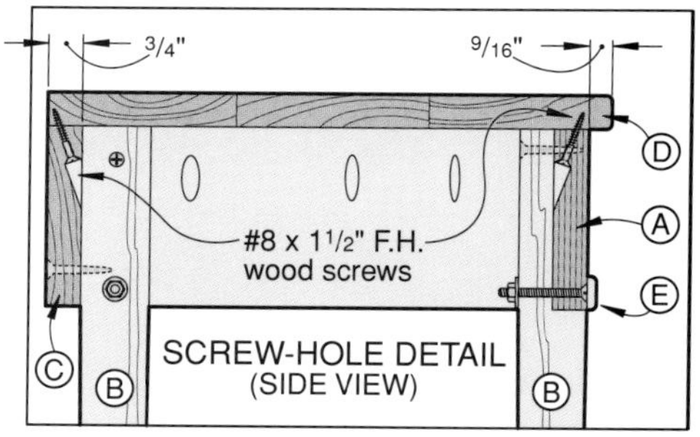
3/4"
9/16"
Ⓓ
#8 x 1¹/2" F.H. wood screws
Ⓐ
Ⓔ
Ⓒ
Ⓑ
SCREW-HOLE DETAIL (SIDE VIEW)
Ⓑ

Bill of Materials

Part	Finished Size			Mat.	Qty.
	T	W	L		
A* bwd. rail	¾"	4"	48"	LOP	1
B legs	1½"	1½"	29¼"	LW	3
C back rail	¾"	4"	33"	W	1
D* tabletop	¾"	14"	36"	EJW	1
E* banding strip	3/16"	¾"	50"	W	1

* Initial size.

Material Key: LOP—laminated oak plywood, LW—laminated walnut, W—walnut, EJW—edge-joined walnut.

Supplies: 3" drywall screws, #10X2" flathead machine screws with mating flat washers and nuts, #8X1¼" flathead wood screws, #8X1½" flathead wood screws, stain, finish.

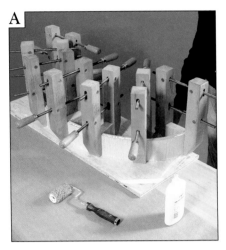

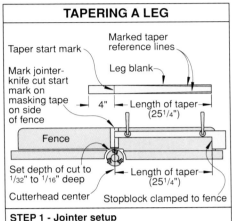

TAPERING A LEG

Taper start mark

Marked taper reference lines

Mark jointer-knife cut start mark on masking tape on side of fence

Leg blank

4" ⊢— Length of taper (25¼")

Fence

Set depth of cut to 1/32" to 1/16" deep

Cutterhead center

⊢— Length of taper (25¼")

Stopblock clamped to fence

STEP 1 - Jointer setup

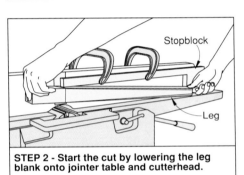

Stopblock

Leg

STEP 2 - Start the cut by lowering the leg blank onto jointer table and cutterhead.

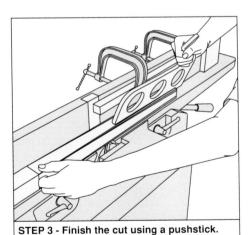

STEP 3 - Finish the cut using a pushstick.

STEP 4 - Repeat steps 2 and 3 until your cut reaches the taper reference line.

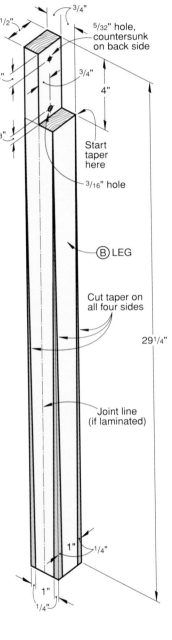

1½" 3/4"

5/32" hole, countersunk on back side

3/4" 3/4"

4"

3/8"

Start taper here

3/16" hole

Ⓑ LEG

Cut taper on all four sides

29¼"

Joint line (if laminated)

1" 1/4"

1" 1/4"

top edge of the lamination. Wipe off any squeeze-out that dribbles down the front face of the outermost layer. Allow the lamination to dry overnight.

6 Using a handsaw, trim the ends of the lamination flush with the back edges of the form supports. See the Lamination Form drawing for reference.

7 Remove the clamps, and scrape off any remaining glue from the top and bottom edges of the bowed lamination (A). Next, sand both edges smooth. Set the bowed lamination aside for now.

NOW, LET'S MAKE THE LEGS

1 To form the legs (B), laminate two ¾x1½x29¼" pieces together face-to-face, use furniture squares, or crosscut three pieces of 1½x1½" stock to 29¼" long.

2 Lay out and cut a ¾x4" notch on the top inside face of each leg where shown on the Leg drawing.

3 Mark taper-cut reference lines on all four surfaces of each leg. Then, make a mark 4" down from the notched end of each leg.

4 To cut the tapers on each leg, follow the procedure described on the Tapering A Leg drawing.

5 Cut the back rail (C) to size.

6 Using the hole sizes stated on the Exploded View drawing, drill mounting holes and screw the two back legs to the back rail (C). Use a

framing square to check that the legs are square to the rail.

7 Verify that the alignment marks made when laminating the bowed front still indicate the front center of the bowed front; adjust if necessary. Glue and clamp the center leg, centered on the front rail. Check for square.

8 Drill the mounting holes, and secure the back rail (C) to the front rail/leg assembly.

TOPPING THE TABLE

1 Edge-join enough ¾"-thick stock to form a blank for the tabletop (D) that measures 14" wide by 36" long.

continued

Bow-Front Table

continued

POCKET SCREW-HOLE LOCATIONS

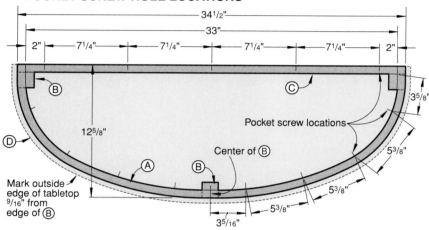

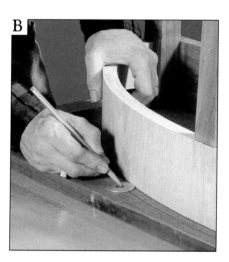

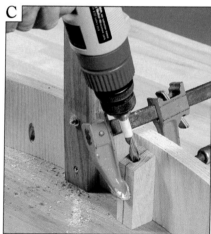

2 To copy the front-rail profile and create a ⁹⁄₁₆" overhang on the blank, start by setting the blank good side down on your workbench. As shown in Photo B, position a ³⁄₈" fender washer next to the rail, place the lead of your pencil inside the hole, and trace the overhang outline onto the bottom side of the tabletop blank. (You could also use a compass to mark the ⁹⁄₁₆" overhang.)

3 Bandsaw the tabletop to shape. Sand the bandsawed edge to a smooth, continuous arc.

4 Rout ⅛" round-overs along the top and bottom edges of the rounded front (do not rout along the straight back edge). Sand the base and tabletop smooth.

5 To attach the tabletop to the base (front and back rails), start by building the pocket screw-hole jig shown on *page 69*.

6 To strengthen the glue joint joining the legs to the front rail, drill the mounting holes and screw and bolt the three legs to the laminated bowed-front rail (A). See the Exploded View drawing and accompanying Screw-Hole detail for reference.

7 Clamp the tabletop to the base, centered from side to side and with the back edges flush. Next, mark the location reference lines where located on the Pocket Screw-Hole Locations drawing. As shown in Photo C, align the guide with the marks, clamp the guide to the front rail, and drill the angled mounting holes. Drive screws through these holes to secure the tabletop to the base.

SECURE THE LEGS, AND ADD THE WALNUT BANDING TRIM

1 To form the banding strip (E), rout ⅛" round-overs along one edge of a piece of ¾"-thick walnut 50" long. Then, rip a ³⁄₁₆"-thick strip from the routed edge.

2 Glue the ³⁄₁₆"-wide walnut banding strip to the bowed front rail where shown on the Exploded View drawing and accompanying

Screw-Hole detail. (We used sliding-head type clamps to hold the strip in place until the glue dried.) Later, trim the ends of the strip flush with the back surface of the back rail.

3 Finish-sand the table and apply the finish. (We used a walnut stain on the oak front rail and left the walnut pieces natural. Then, we brushed on two coats of gloss polyurethane, followed by one coat of satin polyurethane.)

Pocket-Hole Drill Guide

For your portable drill

Equipped with this handy shop aid, you can drill quick, accurate pocket holes for fastening face frames to cabinets, aprons to tabletops, and other similar tasks requiring angled mounting holes. To build the drill guide shown at *left*, just follow the instructions on the drawings *below*. Then, try it on our bow-front table on *page 65*.

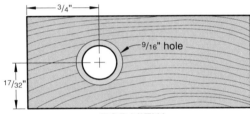

TOP VIEW

3/4"

9/16" hole

17/32"

STEP ONE

From $1^{1}/_{16}$" stock, cut a block to $2^{3}/_{8}$ x $3^{1}/_{2}$". Adhere the full-sized pattern to it. Locate and bore a $^{9}/_{16}$" hole, using a spade bit in the drill press. Bandsaw the guide to shape.

STEP TWO

Clamp a 3" length of $^{1}/_{4}$" iron pipe ($^{9}/_{16}$" O.D.) into a machinist's vice. Using a $^{3}/_{8}$" twist drill, slowly ream out the inside of the pipe to $^{3}/_{8}$". Epoxy the pipe into the $^{9}/_{16}$" hole, flush with the top of the block. After epoxy sets up, hacksaw the pipe off at an angle to match the block. Use a stationary sander to sand the pipe flush. Break sharp edges of steel with a file and emery cloth.

FULL-SIZED PATTERNS

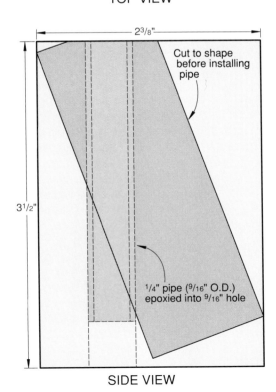

2 3/8"

Cut to shape before installing pipe

3 1/2"

1/4" pipe (9/16" O.D.) epoxied into 9/16" hole

SIDE VIEW

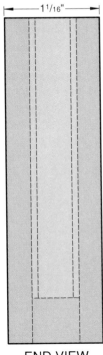

1 1/16"

END VIEW

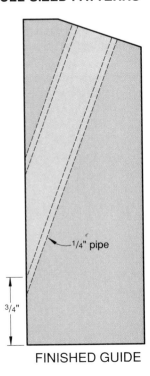

1/4" pipe

3/4"

FINISHED GUIDE

Down-to-Business Oak Desk

Practicality made beautiful with raised panels

It would cost you about $1,500 to buy a raised-panel, solid-oak desk like the one shown here. But if you're willing to invest some time and effort, you can build this enduring, traditional furniture piece for about $350. And look what you get for your money— frame-and-panel construction, a smooth, attractive top, and a trio of drawers, one of which is large enough for hanging files. We've wrapped the oak-and-frame panels around the desk, allowing you to position it against a wall or to sit in the middle of a room as shown *above*. Best of all, you can proudly say you made it yourself.

START WITH END AND MIDDLE FRAME AND PANEL ASSEMBLIES

Note: To machine the panels (H), see the technique article on page 76 on how to make raised panels. To make the jig used to form the panels, see page 82.

1 To construct the two end frames and middle frame, cut the stiles (A, B), top rails (C), and bottom rails (D) to the sizes listed in the Bill of Materials. (We used red oak.) Note that you'll use two of the five stiles (B) for the large front frame.

2 Cut the front frame top rail (E), bottom rail (F), and mullions (G) to size.

3 Edge-join narrower stock to make up the raised-panel blanks (H). Following the tablesaw and router method and illustration from the techniques article on *page 76*, machine the panels.

4 Cut ¼" grooves ⅜" deep along the appropriate edges of A, B, C, D, E, F, and G. Also make grooves along the ends of Parts C, D, E, F, and G where shown on the Frame Construction, End View, and Front View drawings. (To cut the grooves in the right place, we laid out the frames in the configuration shown on the End View and Front View drawings. Next, we marked the edges and ends needing the grooves, and did the cutting to these marked edges.)

5 Using ¼" stock (we selected plywood), cut the splines to the sizes dimensioned on the Frame Construction, End View, and Front View drawings.

6 Finish-sand and stain the raised panels. Staining the panels now prevents the exposure of an unstained line later if the panels happen to shrink slightly.

7 Glue and clamp the front frame together as shown in the photo *opposite right*. Check that the front frame clamps square and flat.

8 Before gluing and clamping the end and middle frames together study the Assembling the Frames drawing on *page 74*. Notice that the panels in the left-hand and middle frames face one direction; the right-hand frame, the opposite direction. Once the pieces are in the correct configuration, glue and clamp the end frames and middle frame, letting them sit that way overnight.

9 Mark and cut the notch for the top rail (K) in the middle frame where shown on the Assembling the Frames drawing. Finish-sand both sides of each frame, being careful not to sand the previously stained panels.

ASSEMBLE THE DRAWER UNIT

1 Cut a couple of corner braces like that shown *opposite*.

2 Cut the rails (I, J, K) to size. The long rail (K) should measure 1½" less than the overall length of the front frame. For proper fitting drawers and slides later, be careful to cut the short rails to the exact length listed in the Bill of Materials.

3 Glue and clamp the rails (I, J, K) in place where shown on the drawing titled Assembling the Frames and the Exploded View drawing. Use the corner braces cut in Step 1 to help hold the assembly square. Drill countersunk mounting holes, and screw the rails in place (see the Screw-Hole detail). Cut plugs, plug the holes, and sand the

plugs flush with the outside surface of the stiles.

4 For a flush fit against the back side of the front frame, cut the filler strip (L) to size. Glue the strip to the back edge of the stile (A) belonging to the middle frame where shown on the Assembling the Frames drawing.

COMPLETE THE DESK CARCASE

1 Being careful not to mar the surfaces, glue and clamp the drawer unit to the back face of the front frame. Keep the top and bottom edges flush, and keep the outside edge of the front frame flush with the outside surface of the drawer-unit end frame.

2 Glue and clamp the remaining end frame to the front frame, using the corner braces to keep the frames square to each other. Immediately secure the top rail (K) in place to help keep the assemblies square. Drill counterbored holes, and fasten the top rail to the remaining end frame. See the Screw-Hole detail accompanying the drawing titled Assembling the Frames for reference.

3 Now, cut the cleats (M) to size. Drill the mounting holes, and glue and screw them to the end and middle frames where shown on the Exploded View drawing.

4 Scrape off excess glue, and sand the joints smooth.

IT'S TIME TO ADD A TRIO OF DRAWERS

1 Using the Drawer Construction and Exploded View drawings and the Bill of Materials, cut the drawer fronts (N, O, P) to size from ¾"-thick oak.

2 Fit your router with a 5/32" roman ogee bit, and rout along all four edges of each drawer front.

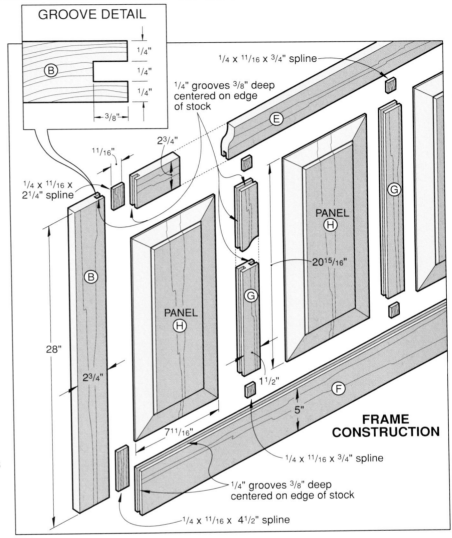

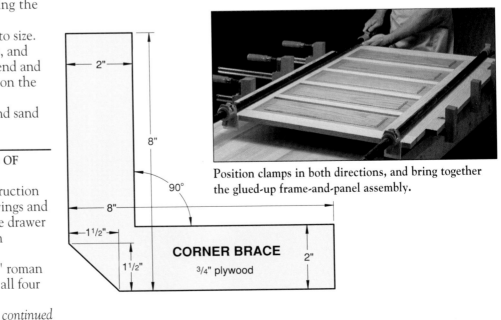

Position clamps in both directions, and bring together the glued-up frame-and-panel assembly.

continued

Down-to-Business Oak Desk with Raised Panels

continued

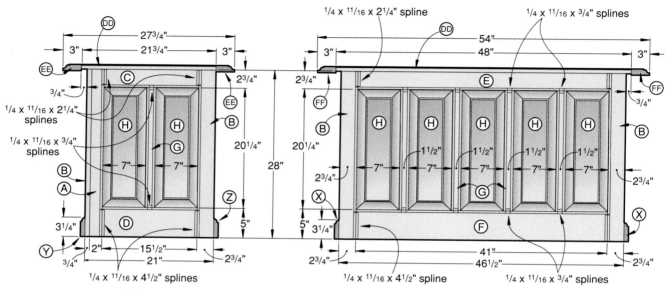

END VIEW

FRONT VIEW

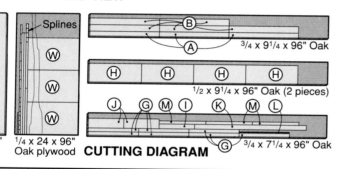

CUTTING DIAGRAM

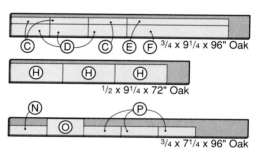

Bill of Materials

Parts	Finished Size			Mat.	Qty.
	T	W	L		
FRAME-AND-PANEL ASSEMBLIES					
A stiles	¾"	2"	28"	RO	3
B stiles	¾"	2¾"	28	RO	5
C top rails	¾"	2¾"	15½"	RO	3
D bottom rails	¾"	5"	15½"	RO	3
E front top rail	¾"	2¾"	41"	RO	1
F bottom top rail	¾"	5"	41"	RO	1
G mullions	¾"	1½"	20¼"	RO	7
H panels	½"	7¹¹⁄₁₆"	20¹⁵⁄₁₆"	RO	11
I top rail	¾"	2"	14¼"	RO	1
J bottom front rails	¾"	4"	14¼"	RO	2
K top rail	¾"	2"	45"	RO	1
L filler strip	¼"	¾"	20¼"	RO	1
M cleats	¾"	1¼"	18¾"	RO	3

Parts	Finished Size			Mat.	Qty.
	T	W	L		
DRAWERS					
N top front	¾"	4"	15"	RO	1
O middle front	¾"	7"	15"	RO	1
P bottom front	¾"	11½"	15"	RO	1
Q sides	½"	3"	20"	RO	2
R sides	½"	6"	20"	RO	2
S sides	½"	9¾"	20"	RO	2
T front & back	½"	3"	12¾"	RO	2
U front & back	½"	6"	12¾"	RO	2
V front & back	½"	9¾"	12¾"	RO	2
W bottoms	¼"	19½"	12¾"	OP	3
BASE TRIM					
X* sides	¾"	3¼"	22½"	RO	2

Parts	Finished Size			Mat.	Qty.
	T	W	L		
Y* front	¾"	3¼"	48"	RO	1
Z* back	¾"	3¼"	17¼"	RO	1
AA* end	¾"	3¼"	2¼"	RO	1
BB* insides	¾"	3¼"	21"	RO	2
CC* inside	¾"	3¼"	30"	RO	1
TOP TRIM					
DD top	¾"	21¾"	48"	P	1
EE trim	1⅛"	3"	54"	RO	2
FF trim	1⅛"	3"	27¾"	RO	2

*Initially cut these parts oversized. Then, trim each to finished size according to the how-to instructions.

Material Key: RO—red oak, OP—oak plywood, P—fir plywood.

Supplies: #17X1¼" brads, #8X1¼" flathead wood screws,#8X1¾" flathead wood screws. 22¾X49" plastic laminate, contact cement, stain, clear finish.

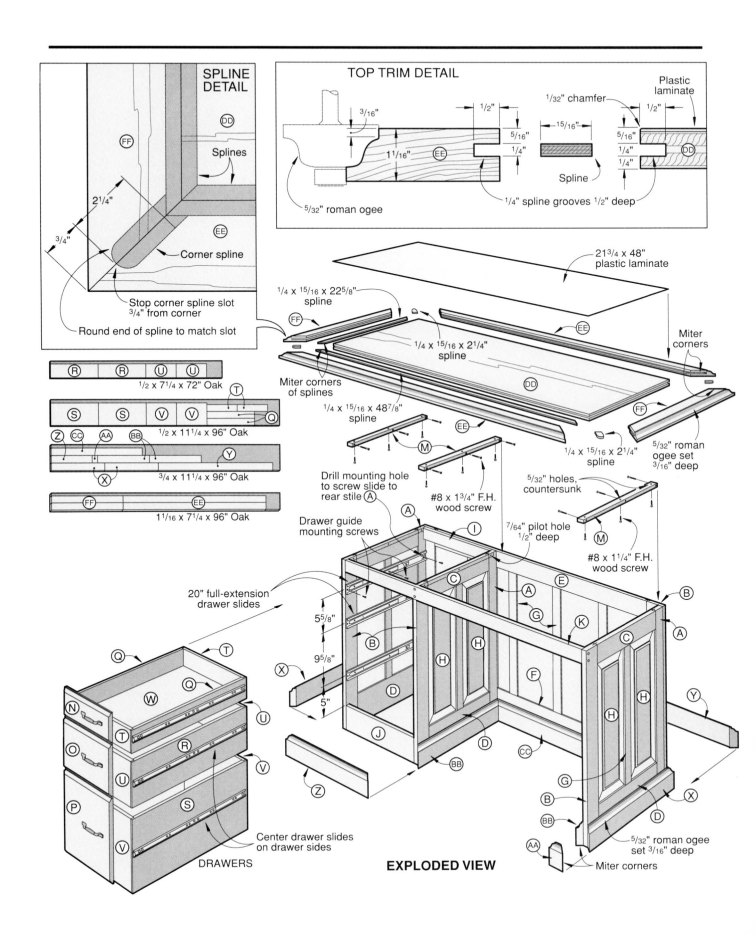

SPLINE DETAIL

DD

FF

Splines

2 1/4"

3/4"

Corner spline

EE

Stop corner spline slot 3/4" from corner

Round end of spline to match slot

TOP TRIM DETAIL

3/16"

1/2"

1/32" chamfer

Plastic laminate

1/2"

5/16"

15/16"

5/16"

DD

1 1/16"

EE

1/4"

1/4"

1/4"

5/32" roman ogee

Spline

1/4" spline grooves 1/2" deep

21 3/4 x 48" plastic laminate

1/4 x 15/16 x 22 5/8" spline

FF

EE

Miter corners

1/4 x 15/16 x 2 1/4" spline

DD

Miter corners of splines

1/4 x 15/16 x 48 7/8" spline

EE

M

FF

1/4 x 15/16 x 2 1/4" spline

5/32" roman ogee set 3/16" deep

R   R   U   U
1/2 x 7 1/4 x 72" Oak

T

S   S   V   V
1/2 x 11 1/4 x 96" Oak

Q

Z CC   AA   BB

Y

X
3/4 x 11 1/4 x 96" Oak

5/32" holes, countersunk

M

#8 x 1 1/4" F.H. wood screw

FF   EE
1 1/16 x 7 1/4 x 96" Oak

Drill mounting hole to screw slide to rear stile A

#8 x 1 3/4" F.H. wood screw

7/64" pilot hole 1/2" deep

A

I

Drawer guide mounting screws

A

C

E

A

B

20" full-extension drawer slides

5 5/8"

G

K

B

Q   T

9 5/8"

X

B

H

H

C

A

Q

N

W

5"

D

F

H

Y

T

U

J

D

CC

H

O

R

U

G

V

BB

B

P

S

X

V

Center drawer slides on drawer sides

AA

D

5/32" roman ogee set 3/16" deep

Miter corners

Z

DRAWERS

EXPLODED VIEW

Down-to-Business Oak Desk with Raised Panels

continued

3 From ½" oak, cut the drawer sides (Q, R, S), and fronts and backs (T, U, V). Next, from ¼" oak plywood, cut the drawer bottoms (W) to size.

4 Cut or rout ¼" grooves ¼" deep and ¼" from the bottom edge of the ½" fronts and backs (T, U, V) and sides (Q, R, S). Next, machine ½" rabbets ¼" deep along the front and back ends of each drawer side. See the Drawer Construction drawing for reference.

5 Glue and clamp each drawer (minus the fronts—N, O, P). Check each corner for square, and adjust clamps accordingly. You'll position and add the drawer fronts later after the drawers have been installed on the slides.

6 For mounting the pulls later, drill a pair of mounting holes centered on the front of each drawer where shown on the Drawer Construction drawing.

7 Using the dimensions on the Exploded View drawing, mark the drawer-slide locations (centerlines) on the inside face of the drawer unit. See the Buying Guide *opposite* for our source of hardware, and review the directions supplied with the slides for detailed mounting instructions. Drill the pilot holes, and screw the slides in place.

To mount the back end of each slide to the back stiles (A), you'll have to drill a mounting hole through the metal slides and into the stiles. The existing rear-most hole in the slide comes too close to the front edge of the rear stile (A). Screws driven this close to the edge can split the stile.

8 Drill the mounting holes, and fasten the mating portion of each drawer slide centered on the drawer sides (Q, R, S) and flush

with the front end of the drawer box. Check the fit of all three drawers in the drawer unit, and adjust the slides if necessary.

NEXT, ADD THE BASE TRIM

1 Using ¾" oak, rip two 96"-long pieces and one 48"-long piece to 3½" wide for the base trim. See the Cutting Diagram for reference.

2 Using a ⁵⁄₃₂" roman ogee bit mounted in your router, rout an ogee along one edge of all three trim pieces. See the Top Trim detail accompanying the Exploded View drawing for reference. Sand the routed ogee smooth.

3 Miter-cut the base trim pieces (X, Y, Z, AA, BB, CC) to length. Glue and clamp the pieces to the desk base where shown on the Exploded View drawing.

4 With the drawers in place on the slides, and leaving a ⅝" gap between the top edge of trim piece Z and the bottom edge of the bottom drawer front P, drill pilot holes in the back face of P, and fasten the bottom drawer front to the bottom drawer assembly. Leaving an equal gap (⅛"), fasten the two remaining drawer fronts to their respective drawers.

AND NOW FOR THE DESKTOP

1 From ¾" fir plywood, cut the desktop substrate (DD) to size.

2 Cut a piece of plastic laminate (we used Formica #302, Russet Oxide) to the size of the substrate plus 1" in length and width. Using

SCREW-HOLE DETAIL

⁵⁄₃₂" hole, countersunk

¾" ¼"

½"

1"

#8 x 1¼" F.H. wood screw

⅜" plug ⁵⁄₁₆" long

K

B

⅜" hole ¼" deep

⁷⁄₆₄" pilot hole ¾" deep

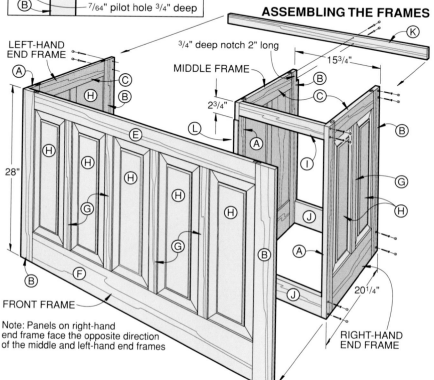

ASSEMBLING THE FRAMES

LEFT-HAND END FRAME

¾" deep notch 2" long

MIDDLE FRAME

15¾"

2¾"

28"

20¼"

FRONT FRAME

RIGHT-HAND END FRAME

Note: Panels on right-hand end frame face the opposite direction of the middle and left-hand end frames

contact cement, center and adhere the plastic laminate to the top of the substrate.

3 Fit your router with a flush-trimming bit, and rout the edges of the laminate flush with the edges of the substrate.

4 Rout a $\frac{1}{32}$" chamfer along the top four edges of the laminate where shown on the Top Trim detail accompanying the Exploded View drawing.

5 Rip and miter-cut the desktop trim pieces (EE, FF) to size.

6 Fit your router with a $\frac{1}{4}$" slotting cutter. Rout $\frac{1}{4}$" grooves along the edges of the plywood substrate and along the inside edges of the trim. See the Top Trim detail for reference. Then, rout $2\frac{1}{4}$"-long stopped-spline grooves along the mitered ends of the trim where shown on the Spline detail accompanying the Exploded View drawing.

7 From $\frac{1}{4}$" stock, cut $\frac{15}{16}$"-wide splines to the lengths listed on the Exploded View drawing. Round the ends of the splines that fit between the mitered ends of the trim. Glue and spline the trim pieces to the plywood substrate.

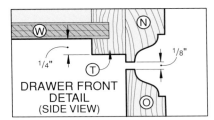

DRAWER FRONT DETAIL
(SIDE VIEW)

1/4"   1/8"

W   N
T   O

SAND AND FINISH YOUR GOOD-LOOKING DESK

1 Mask the laminate top. Finish-sand the trim. Finish-sand the base unit.

2 Remove the drawer slides from the drawer sides.

3 Stain as desired (we used WOODKOTE Danish Walnut). If you use the same pulls we did, don't forget to stain the wood on the drawer pulls. Add the finish (we applied several coats of Minwax fast-dry satin poly-urethane).

4 Reattach the slides and add the pulls. If you want file holders (see the Buying Guide), cut the hanging holders to length and install them along the top edges of the bottom drawer. Position the desktop on the base unit where located on the End View and Front View drawings. Drive screws through the previously drilled holes in the cleats to secure the two together.

DRAWER CONSTRUCTION

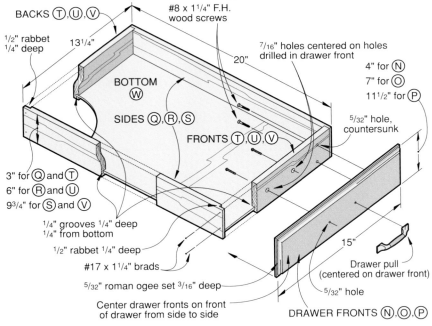

BACKS T, U, V

1/2" rabbet 1/4" deep   13 1/4"

#8 x 1 1/4" F.H. wood screws

7/16" holes centered on holes drilled in drawer front

20"

4" for N
7" for O
11 1/2" for P

BOTTOM W

SIDES Q, R, S

5/32" hole, countersunk

FRONTS T, U, V

3" for Q and T
6" for R and U
9 3/4" for S and V

1/4" grooves 1/4" deep 1/4" from bottom

1/2" rabbet 1/4" deep

#17 x 1 1/4" brads

5/32" roman ogee set 3/16" deep

Center drawer fronts on front of drawer from side to side

15"

Drawer pull (centered on drawer front)

5/32" hole

DRAWER FRONTS N, O, P

High-Styled Raised Panels and Frames

Use our can't-miss guide to make 'em right

You can make a raised panel and frame like this with just your tablesaw and our handy jig.

For centuries, both woodworkers and the general public have viewed raised panels as a hallmark of fine craftsmanship. And with today's power tools and accessories, they're easier than ever to make. In this article we'll share the techniques for making several versions of these classic beauties.

HOW TO BUILD RECTANGULAR PANELS

Although easy to build, the rectangular raised panel and frame shown in the photo *above right* and drawings *opposite* offers the type of clean looks that make it perfect for many woodworking projects. To make such a panel and frame, you first need to build the simple tablesaw jig shown on *page 82*. Once made, this jig will help you safely and accurately cut panel bevels that require minimal cleanup. You'll also use it to cut the grooves that hold the panel in the frame. Now, let's construct this great-looking panel and frame.

FIRST, CUT THE FRAME PIECES

After determining the outside dimensions of your frame, cut the rails and stiles to size. To cut grooves into the ends of the rails, mount a ¼"-wide dado blade into your tablesaw, and position the rails against the jig's upright stop as shown *below*. Always place the face side of the frame pieces against the jig. Adjust the jig for a centered groove and make the ⅜"-deep cut.

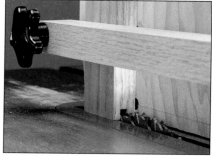

Position the rail against the upright stop and clamp it down before cutting a groove in its end.

To cut grooves along the inside edges of the rails and stiles, remove the upright stop and stock-clamping bar, and use the jig as a fence as shown *right*. To make the spline stock, plane or resaw stock of the same species as the frame pieces. The splines should fit snugly in the grooves. If the splines will be visible in your finished frame (as with a cabinet door), make them a little long and trim them flush after assembling the frame.

NOW, MAKE THE PANEL

Before you start cutting your panel to size, spend some time examining the grain orientation and color of your stock. For example, if you make a narrow panel from one piece of stock with a cathedral (inverse **V**) pattern, be careful to center the cathedral pattern on the panel. If you use several pieces, cut them from the same board for a close color match.

Note: *For dimensional stability we suggest that you make up your raised panels from stock no wider than 8".*

Remove the upright stop and stock-clamping bar from the tablesaw jig to cut grooves along the edges of the rails and stiles for your panel's frame.

If you don't have access to ½" thick stock, or the means to plane thicker stock to ½" thickness, you can make the panel from ¾" stock. However, the face of the panel will be ¼" higher than its surrounding frame—generally an undesirable look, unless you level the panel's front by either of the following two methods.

First, you can rabbet the back side of the panel as shown in the example at *right*. This leaves a square groove around the inside perimeter of the frame, on the back side of the panel.

For a decorative alternative to this square rabbet, try backcutting the panel with a small (2" diameter with ¼" shank) panel-raising bit such as the model shown right. See the Buying Guide on *page 81* for a source for this bit.

HERE'S HOW TO CUT THE BEVELS

After cutting your panel to its finished size, adjust your tablesaw's fence 1¾" from the blade. Cut ⅛" kerfs, ⅛" deep along all four sides of the panel's face as shown in the illustration on *page 78, left*.

Using the Panel End View drawing *below, center*, as your guide, lay out the profile of the bevel along one edge of the panel. Now, set this panel against the fence of your jig as shown in the photo on *page 78, bottom left*. Sight along the blade, and use the

continued

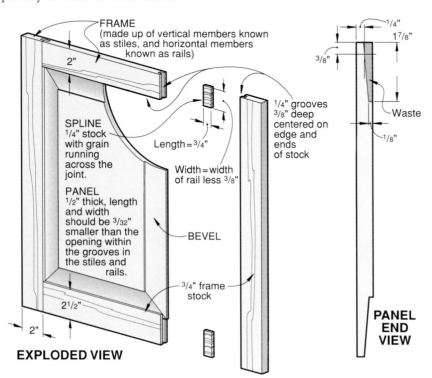

FRAME
(made up of vertical members known as stiles, and horizontal members known as rails)

2"

SPLINE
¼" stock with grain running across the joint.

PANEL
½" thick, length and width should be 3/32" smaller than the opening within the grooves in the stiles and rails.

Length = ¾"

Width = width of rail less 3/8"

¼" grooves 3/8" deep centered on edge and ends of stock

BEVEL

¾" frame stock

2½"

2"

EXPLODED VIEW

¼"
1 7/8"
3/8"

Waste

1/8"

PANEL END VIEW

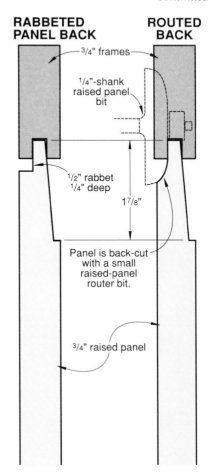

RABBETED PANEL BACK   **ROUTED BACK**

¾" frames

¼"-shank raised panel bit

½" rabbet ¼" deep

1 7/8"

Panel is back-cut with a small raised-panel router bit.

¾" raised panel

High Styled Raised Panels and Frames

continued

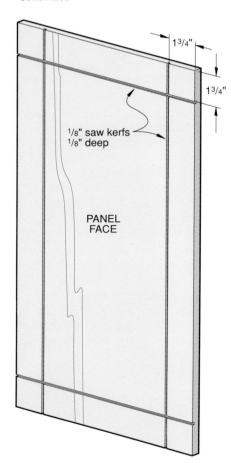

1¾"

1¾"

⅛" saw kerfs
⅛" deep

PANEL
FACE

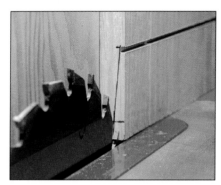

Sight along the blade to adjust the jig and blade for the bevel cut. Test this cut in scrap stock. (We removed the stock-clamping bar for clarity.)

layout lines to adjust the fence as well as the angle and height of the blade. *Note: Test the following cuts in scrap stock of the same thickness as your actual workpiece.*

Now, clamp your panel faceside out into the tablesaw jig and cut the bevels as shown in the photo on *page 76, top left*. Make the end-grain cuts first. These deep cuts require a sharp, 24-tooth-ripping blade. If you have a saw of less than 1½ hp you may need to use a thin-kerf blade to maximize your saw's power. Move the panel through the blade at a consistent speed, slowing down only if the blade slows.

AND NOW FOR THE FINISHING TOUCHES

Because the jig holds the panel firmly during the bevel cuts, you should notice few, if any, sawtooth marks. Remove marks on the top and bottom bevels with 100-grit sandpaper and a hardwood sanding block. Finish-sand the top and bottom bevels with a block and 150-grit abrasive. Now, repeat this procedure on the side bevels. Doing it this way gives you maximum control over stock removal. Be careful not to sand away the ridge at the intersection of the two bevels.

Dry-clamp the panel and frames to check for fit. Disassemble the pieces and apply stain to both sides of the panel. This way, any seasonal contraction of the panel will not reveal unfinished areas. Then, glue and clamp the frame assembly, allowing the panel to float within the frame. Sand the rails and stiles flush. Finish-sand and stain the frame, and apply your clear finish.

A ⅜" round-nose router bit helps you create a panel with a decorative flair such as this one.

ADD A LITTLE PIZZAZZ TO YOUR PANEL

You can dress up the panel described in this section by routing grooves in the face of the panel with a ⅜" round-nose bit (also known as a core-box bit). These grooves take the place of the ⅛" saw kerfs described earlier. After cutting the grooves to a depth of ⅛" according to the drawing *below*, cut the bevels with your tablesaw. This results in a panel like the one *above*.

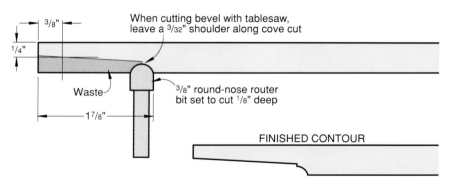

3/8"

1/4"

When cutting bevel with tablesaw, leave a 3/32" shoulder along cove cut

Waste

1⁷⁄₈"

⅜" round-nose router bit set to cut ⅛" deep

FINISHED CONTOUR

Frames with cope-and-stick joinery look great and go together in a jiffy.

COPE-AND-STICK JOINERY

Nearly all commercially produced raised panels have frames with cope-and-stick joinery, such as the example *above*. To make cope-and-stick frames, you'll need a matched rail-and-stile router bit set like the set shown *above right*. Such sets cost $100 or more, but offer you several time-saving and aesthetic advantages.

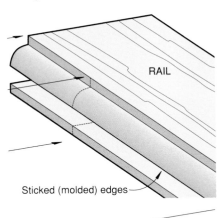

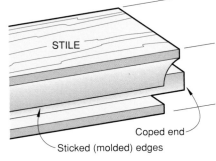

As shown in the drawing *above*, cope-and-stick frames do not require splines because the coped ends fit snugly into the stiles and provide

Two-piece rail-and-style router bit sets such as these make simple work of cope-and-stick joinery.

ample gluing surfaces. And the bead along the inside of the frame provides a nice transition from the frame to the panel.

HOW TO RAISE PANELS WITH ROUTER BITS

If you have a router that accepts ½"-shank bits, you may be interested in raising your panels with router bits such as the versions *below*. We prefer the wide models (3½" in diameter) because they cut 1½"-wide bevels—nearly as wide as the bevels you cut with a tablesaw. Although these bits cost $50 or more, they offer you several advantages. First, you can cut

With raised-panel bits such as these you can cut curved bevels that require no sanding.

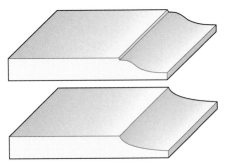

bevels with curved profiles as shown *below center*. Second, these bevels require no sanding.

Typically, these bits are designed for use with ⅝" or ¾" stock. With either bit, the panel will be higher than the surrounding frame unless you rabbet or back-cut the back of the panel as described on *page 77*.

An elegant arched top adds even more appeal to the basic raised panel and its surrounding frame.

HOW TO BUILD ARCHED-TOP PANELS AND FRAMES

As you can see in the drawing on *page 80* and photo *above*, arched-top panels and frames look terrific and assemble in much the same way as rectangular panels and frames. In this section we'll concentrate on the special requirements of this raised panel type, starting with design.

1 Grab your compass and lay out the arch. You can lay out the arch for your panel in just a few minutes with a pencil, compass, straightedge, and a sheet of paper larger than the finished panel and its frame. First, determine the width of the panel and its height measured from the top of the

continued

High-Styled Raised Panels and Frames

continued

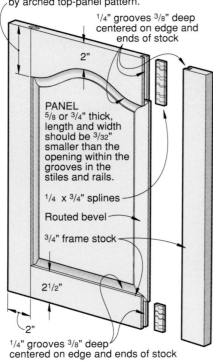

Overall width of upper rail is determined by arched top-panel pattern.

¼" grooves ⅜" deep centered on edge and ends of stock

2"

PANEL
⅝ or ¾" thick, length and width should be ³⁄₃₂" smaller than the opening within the grooves in the stiles and rails.

¼ x ¾" splines

Routed bevel

¾" frame stock

2½"

2"

¼" grooves ⅜" deep centered on edge and ends of stock

LAYING OUT A TEMPLATE FOR ARCHED-TOPPED PANELS

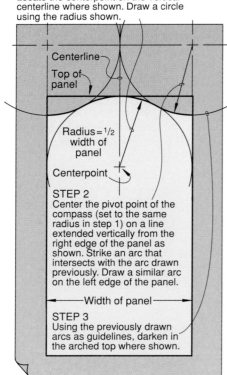

STEP 1
Locate the centerpoint on the vertical centerline where shown. Draw a circle using the radius shown.

Centerline

Top of panel

Radius = ½ width of panel

Centerpoint

STEP 2
Center the pivot point of the compass (set to the same radius in step 1) on a line extended vertically from the right edge of the panel as shown. Strike an arc that intersects with the arc drawn previously. Draw a similar arc on the left edge of the panel.

—Width of panel—

STEP 3
Using the previously drawn arcs as guidelines, darken in the arched top where shown.

Use a paper or plywood template to transfer the arch to the panel and top rail. Be careful to center the arch on the panel.

planned arch to the bottom of the panel. For example, if the finished frame in the drawing *above left* has outside dimensions of 12x18", then the panel should measure 8²¹⁄₃₂x14⁵⁄₃₂". We determined this by subtracting the width of the rails and stiles and adding ¾" because about ⅜" of each edge of the panel is contained in the rails and stiles. Then, we subtracted ³⁄₃₂" from the width and height to allow for contraction and expansion of the panel caused by changes in humidity.

On your sheet of paper, lay out a rectangle according to your height and width figures for the panel. Then, follow the three-

step procedure *left* to lay out the arch. Now, transfer this arch to your panel and your top rail as shown in the photo *above*. Note that we marked two lines ⅜" from both sides of the template to help us center it on the top rail.

Projects with multiple raised panels, such as a kitchen-cabinet installation, may require arched-top panels of varying widths. For aesthetic reasons, the height of the arches should be the same from panel to panel. The information *opposite* shows how to handle this situation.

2 Cut your parts and put it all together. With a bandsaw, cut the arched portion of the panel and top rail, staying just outside the layout

centerpoints for mounting the backboard to the wall.

7 Drill the mounting holes where marked. (See the Buying Guide at the end of the article for our source of brass coat hooks and thin stock.) For ease in driving the softer brass screws later, drive #6x½" steel screws into the hook mounting holes to prethread the holes. Remove the steel screws.

8 Finish-sand the backboard smooth and set it aside for now.

CUT THE WILDLIFE AND BACKGROUND TO SHAPE

1 Make two photocopies of your favorite pattern.

2 Plane or resaw one piece of walnut, oak, cherry, and maple to ¼" thick by 5x9" for the hummingbird or duck. Or, see the Buying Guide for our source of thin stock. One piece of maple and another piece of walnut is all that's necessary for the panda bear.

3 Temporarily join the four layers of ¼"-thick stock face-to-face with double-faced tape.

4 Using Spray adhesive, adhere one of the full-sized photocopied patterns onto the top piece of ¼" stock. Scrollsaw the parts to shape.
continued

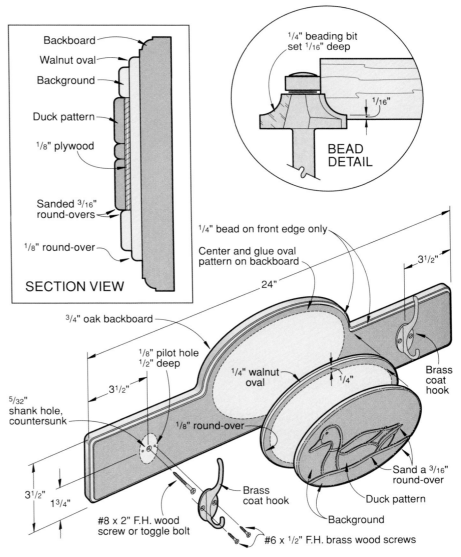

Backboard
Walnut oval
Background
Duck pattern
1/8" plywood
Sanded 3/16" round-overs
1/8" round-over

SECTION VIEW

1/4" beading bit set 1/16" deep
1/16"

BEAD DETAIL

1/4" bead on front edge only
Center and glue oval pattern on backboard
3/4" oak backboard
1/8" pilot hole 1/2" deep
3½"
24"
1/4" walnut oval
1/4"
Brass coat hook
3½"
5/32" shank hole, countersunk
1/8" round-over
3½"
1¾"
#8 x 2" F.H. wood screw or toggle bolt
Brass coat hook
Sand a 3/16" round-over
Duck pattern
Background
#6 x 1/2" F.H. brass wood screws

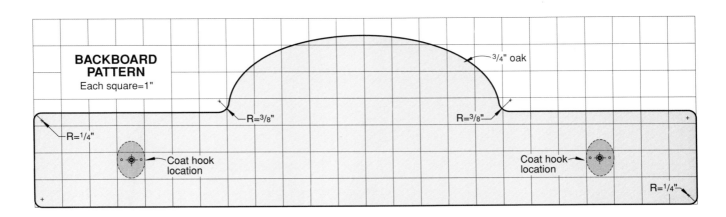

BACKBOARD PATTERN
Each square=1"

3/4" oak
R=3/8"
R=3/8"
R=1/4"
Coat hook location
Coat hook location
R=1/4"

Wild Kingdom Coatrack

continued

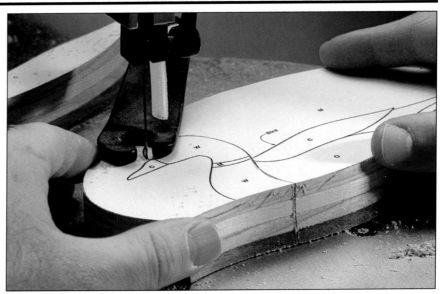

We used a No. 8 (.047x.017"
w/11.5 TPI) blade as shown in the
photo *right*.

5 Separate the parts. Now, using the
wood key, temporarily assemble
the design of your choice on the
second pattern copy, or choose
pieces that match to your liking.
You'll have enough pieces for four
separate hummingbird or duck
patterns, or two panda bears. Hand-
sand a ³⁄₁₆" round-over along the front
edges of the parts. See the Section
View drawing for reference. Be sure
to wear a dust mask. We also wore
rubber finger pads (sold at office
supply stores) to protect our fingers
when rounding-over the edges. Do
not sand all the way to the back
surface. Doing so creates voids
between the parts when gluing them
together.

6 Position the body parts (not the
background pieces) on a piece of
⅛" plywood or other thin stock.
Trace around the perimeter of the
figure. Remove the parts and cut the
pattern to shape, cutting slightly
inside the marked outline.

7 Apply woodworker's glue or epoxy
to the backing, and lay the parts
into position. If using woodworker's
glue, weight the parts with a flat
heavy object such as a clothes iron
or scrap plywood weighted with a
paint can.

8 After the glue dries, round-over
the edges of the backing by
sanding to make it even less visible.

ADD THE WALNUT OVAL

*Note: If you're crafting the panda bear,
you can skip Steps 1, 2, 3, and 4
below. The bear doesn't require the
walnut oval.*

1 Cut a piece of ¼" walnut to 5½"
wide by 9" long. Adhere the
second photocopy to it.

**HALF-SIZED
PATTERNS**
Enlarge 200% on
photocopy machine
for full-sized patterns

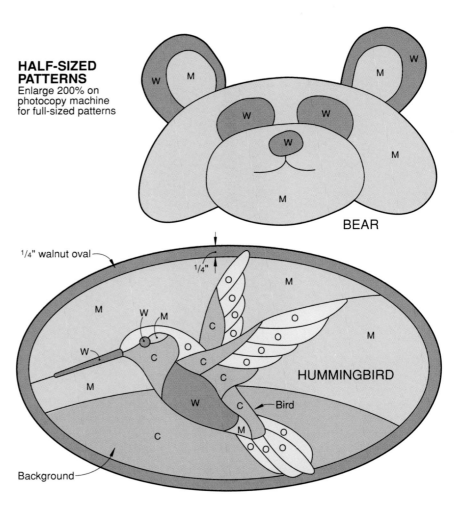

BEAR

HUMMINGBIRD

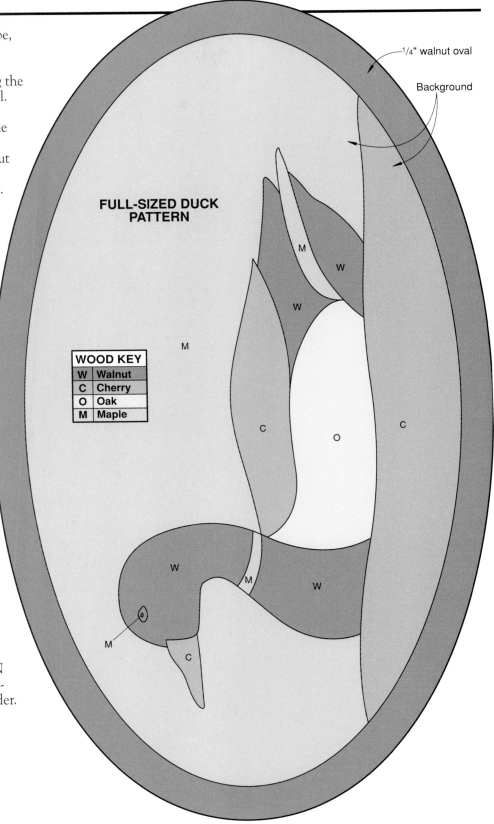

2 Cut the walnut oval to shape, cutting slightly outside the marked outline and sand to it.

3 Sand a ⅛" round-over along the entire front edge of the oval. Next, finish-sand the oval.

4 Position the pieces, and glue and clamp the pattern and background pieces to the walnut oval. Leave an even ¼" of the walnut exposed along all edges.

5 Center and glue the oval/pattern assembly to the backboard where shown on the Exploded View drawing.

6 Apply a clear finish (we used aerosol lacquer). Fasten the backboard to the wall with wood screws if you can hit studs. Or use toggle bolts if you can't. Screw the coat hooks to the backboard.

BUYING GUIDE

• **Thin stock and coat hooks.** One piece of walnut, oak, cherry, and maple ¼"-thick by 5x9" (enough for the wildlife pattern lamination), one piece of ¼" walnut 5½" wide by 10" long for the oval, and two coat hooks needed per coatrack, Stock No. 88163. For current prices, contact The Woodworkers' Store, 21801 Industrial Blvd., Rogers, MN 55374-9514, or call 800/279-4441 or 612/428-3200 to order.

¼" walnut oval

Background

FULL-SIZED DUCK PATTERN

WOOD KEY	
W	Walnut
C	Cherry
O	Oak
M	Maple

For the Very Young

Childhood may be fleeting, but the projects we've gathered here are designed to last for generations. Youngsters will express immediate delight in our personalized dragon pull toy, train puzzle, and rocking snail, while plans for a teddy bear rocking chair and a hardwood-crafted crib will provide you with tomorrow's heirlooms today.

The One-and-Only Teddy Bear Chair

A gift to treasure

The children we've shown this little rocker to just can't resist it. We're not sure if it's the bear cutout in the backrest, the paw armrests, or the smooth rocking action that attracts them to it. But we do know this is one of the most usable pieces you'll ever have the opportunity to present to some lucky young recipient.

continued

Scrollsawed kerfs and round-overs accent the bear-paw armrests.

The One-and-Only Teddy Bear Chair

continued

Note: *Because of space limitations, we can't provide full-sized patterns for this project. However, to enable you to build the project, we've included gridded patterns. To enlarge these patterns, see the instructions on page 160.*

BEGIN CONSTRUCTION WITH THE ARCH-TOPPED BACKREST

1 From ¾" stock (we used cherry), cut one piece to 7x13" and a second piece to 7x10" for the backrest top rail (A). With the bottom edges flush and an even 1½" overhang on each end where shown on the Backrest drawing, glue and clamp the two pieces.

2 To form the backrest uprights (B), cut two pieces of ¾"-thick cherry to 1⅝x18¼" and two pieces to 1⅝x25¼". With the bottom ends and edges flush, glue and clamp the pieces face-to-face.

3 Scrape the excess glue from one edge of each laminated upright (B), and joint or plane the scraped edge flat. Rip and then joint the opposite edge of each upright for a 1½" finished width.

4 Miter-cut the bottom end of each laminated upright where shown on the Backrest drawing. Mark the centerpoints, and drill two counterbored mounting holes through each upright for the seat and two for the armrests.

5 Glue and clamp the uprights to the backrest top rail.

6 Using trammel points, mark a pair of arcs on the backrest top rail where shown on the Backrest drawing. Bandsaw and sand the top rail to shape.

7 Rout a ¾" round-over along the back outside edge of the backrest frame. If you don't have a ¾" round-over bit, a ½" will do. See the Exploded View drawing for reference. Rout ¼" round-overs along the remaining three edges, except where the seat will attach where shown on the drawing.

Rout a pair of ¼" slots ½" deep in the seat blank to house the bottom of the bear's feet. For photo clarity we moved the model's right hand away from the router.

NOW, CONSTRUCT THE SEAT

1 Edge-join enough ¾" stock to form a blank 15½" wide by 13⁹⁄₁₆" long for the seat blank (C).

2 Mark the outline, leg notch locations, and ¼" slots on the chair blank, using the Seat on the Part View drawing for reference.

3 Fit your router with a ¼" straight bit. Position and clamp a straightedge to the seat blank so the ¼" router bit is positioned directly over the marked slots. Rout a pair of ¼" slots ½" deep as shown in the photo *above*.

4 Bandsaw the seat (C) to shape, and rout ⅛" round-overs on all edges except at the corners.

5 Dry-clamp the seat to the backrest assembly. (We cut a pair of 90° plywood corner braces to clamp the seat squarely to the uprights.) Using the previously drilled mounting holes in the uprights for reference, drill a pilot hole centered top to bottom into the seat notch. Drive drywall screws through the uprights and into the seat.

Position the bear cutout on the assembled backrest, and mark the slot locations as shown.

NOW FOR THE BEAR CUTOUT

1 Edge-join enough ¼"-thick stock to form a panel measuring 11x17" for the bear cutout (D). Transfer the bear outline and interior cuts to the 11x17" blank. Drill ⅛" holes at the ends of each marked slot.

2 Using the ⅛" holes as blade-start holes, cut the decorative slots. Scrollsaw or bandsaw the bear's exterior outline to shape.

continued

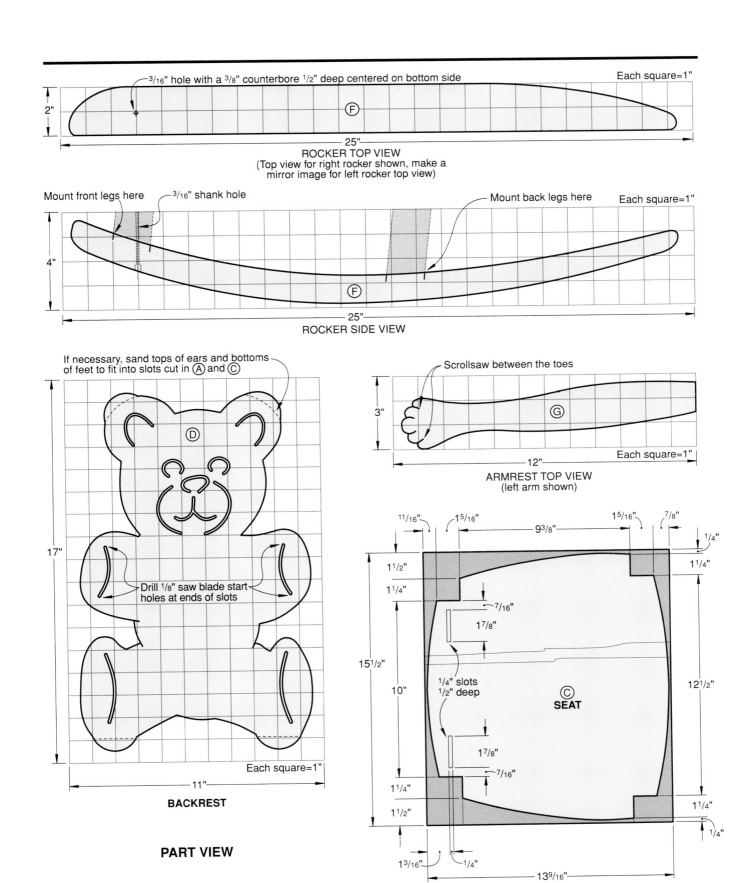

3/16" hole with a 3/8" counterbore 1/2" deep centered on bottom side

Each square=1"

2"

Ⓕ

25"

ROCKER TOP VIEW
(Top view for right rocker shown, make a
mirror image for left rocker top view)

Mount front legs here

3/16" shank hole

Mount back legs here

Each square=1"

4"

Ⓕ

25"

ROCKER SIDE VIEW

If necessary, sand tops of ears and bottoms
of feet to fit into slots cut in Ⓐ and Ⓒ

Scrollsaw between the toes

Ⓓ

3"

Ⓖ

12"

Each square=1"

ARMREST TOP VIEW
(left arm shown)

17"

Drill 1/8" saw blade start
holes at ends of slots

Each square=1"

11"

BACKREST

PART VIEW

11/16"   1 5/16"   9 3/8"   1 5/16"   7/8"

1/4"

1 1/2"   1 1/4"

1 1/4"

7/16"

1 7/8"

15 1/2"

10"

1/4" slots
1/2" deep

Ⓒ
SEAT

12 1/2"

1 7/8"

7/16"

1 1/4"

1 1/2"

1 1/4"

1/4"

1 3/16"   1/4"

13 9/16"

The One-and-Only Teddy Bear Chair

continued

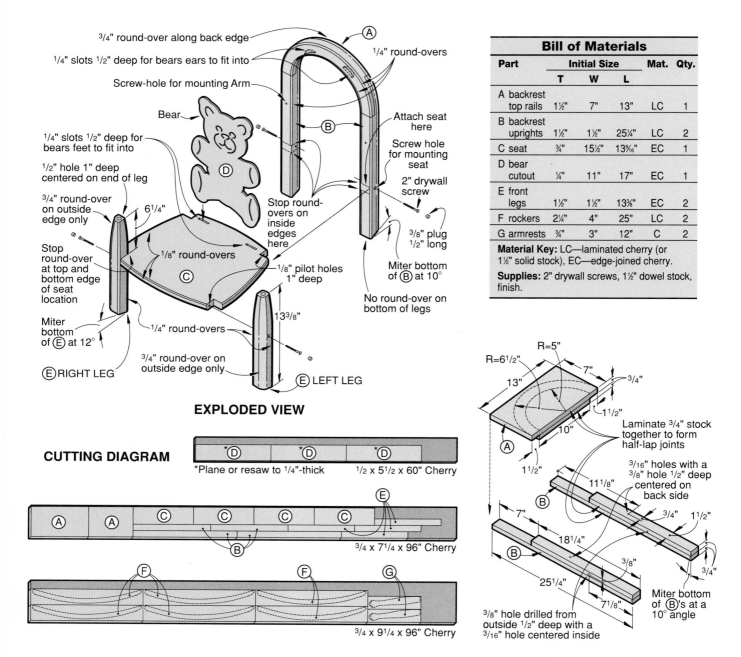

EXPLODED VIEW

- 3/4" round-over along back edge
- 1/4" slots 1/2" deep for bears ears to fit into
- Screw-hole for mounting Arm
- Bear
- 1/4" slots 1/2" deep for bears feet to fit into
- 1/2" hole 1" deep centered on end of leg
- 3/4" round-over on outside edge only
- 6 1/4"
- Stop round-over at top and bottom edge of seat location
- Miter bottom of (E) at 12°
- (E) RIGHT LEG
- 1/8" round-overs
- (C)
- 3/4" round-over on outside edge only
- 1/4" round-overs
- (E) LEFT LEG
- 13 3/8"
- 1/8" pilot holes 1" deep
- Stop round-overs on inside edges here
- 1/4" round-overs
- (A)
- (B)
- (D)
- Attach seat here
- Screw hole for mounting seat
- 2" drywall screw
- 3/8" plug 1/2" long
- Miter bottom of (B) at 10°
- No round-over on bottom of legs

Bill of Materials

Part	Initial Size			Mat.	Qty.
	T	W	L		
A backrest top rails	1½"	7"	13"	LC	1
B backrest uprights	1½"	1½"	25¼"	LC	2
C seat	¾"	15½"	13⁹⁄₁₆"	EC	1
D bear cutout	¼"	11"	17"	EC	1
E front legs	1½"	1½"	13¾"	EC	2
F rockers	2¼"	4"	25"	LC	2
G armrests	¾"	3"	12"	C	2

Material Key: LC—laminated cherry (or 1½" solid stock), EC—edge-joined cherry.

Supplies: 2" drywall screws, 1½" dowel stock, finish.

CUTTING DIAGRAM

- *(D) *(D) *(D)
- *Plane or resaw to 1/4"-thick   1/2 x 5 1/2 x 60" Cherry
- (A) (A) (C) (C) (C) (C) (E)
- (B)
- 3/4 x 7 1/4 x 96" Cherry
- (F) (F) (G)
- 3/4 x 9 1/4 x 96" Cherry

BACKREST

- R=6½"
- R=5"
- 13"
- 7"
- 3/4"
- 1½"
- 10"
- (A)
- 1½"
- Laminate 3/4" stock together to form half-lap joints
- 3/16" holes with a 3/8" hole 1/2" deep centered on back side
- 11 1/8"
- (B)
- 3/4"
- 1½"
- 7"
- (B)
- 18 1/4"
- 3/8"
- 3/4"
- 3/4"
- 25 1/4"
- 7 1/8"
- Miter bottom of (B)'s at a 10° angle
- 3/8" hole drilled from outside 1/2" deep with a 3/16" hole centered inside

3 Position the bear cutout on the backrest assembly where shown in the photo on *page 90*. Mark the start and stop marks on the front face of the backrest top rail (A) for the slots needed to house the ear tabs.

4 Using your router fitted with a ¼" slotting-cutter, rout two ½"-deep slots, centered from face-to-face, between the start and stop marks on the backrest top rail.

5 Remove the seat from the uprights, fit the bear cutout in place, and reattach the seat.

LET'S ADD THE FRONT LEGS

1 Using the same laminating and trimming method used to form the uprights, build a pair of 1½x1½x14" front leg blanks (E).

2 Miter-cut the bottom ends of the front legs where shown on the Exploded View and Front Leg drawings. Crosscut the top ends for a 13⅜" finished length.

3 Draw diagonals on the top end of each leg to find center. Then, drill a ½" hole 1" deep where marked. (We used a brad-point bit to center the hole directly over the marked centerpoint and to eliminate bit wander.)

4 Transfer the full-sized leg top patterns to the leg blanks. Cut the legs to shape and sand smooth.

5 Rout a ¾" round-over (again, a ½" will do) along the outside corner of each leg (E). See the Exploded View drawing for reference. Next, rout ¼" round-overs along the other three edges except on the inside edge where the seat will attach later.

LAMINATE AND CUT THE ROCKERS TO SHAPE

1 Cut six pieces of ¾"-thick stock to the sizes shown on the Rocker Lamination drawing for the two rocker blanks (F). Glue and clamp the two laminations (three boards each) together, with the edges and ends flush.

2 Joint or plane the top edge flat. Enlarge and transfer the full-sized

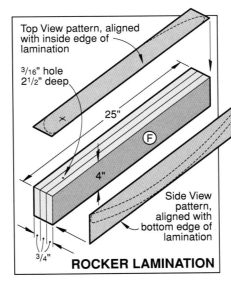

Top View pattern, aligned with inside edge of lamination

³⁄₁₆" hole 2½" deep

25"

F

4"

¾"

ROCKER LAMINATION

Side View pattern, aligned with bottom edge of lamination

patterns (top and side) to each lamination. Note that you'll need a right and left top view pattern. Check that the patterns align with each other. Also, note that the

inside edge of each rocker is straight while the outside edge is curved.

3 Working from the top surface of the rocker blank, drill a ³⁄₁₆" shank hole 2½" deep into each blank where marked. (We'll drill the rear hole in each rocker later.)

4 To bandsaw the rockers to shape, cut the top pattern to shape first. Using double-faced tape, adhere the back piece of scrap cut from each rocker back end to its original position. (Taped back in place, the scrap keeps the blank from rocking when cutting the side view pattern. Now, bandsaw the side profile of each rocker to shape. Remove the taped-on scrap parts, and sand the rockers smooth. Rout ½" round-overs on the bottom edges of each rocker and sand ⅛" round-overs along the top.

continued

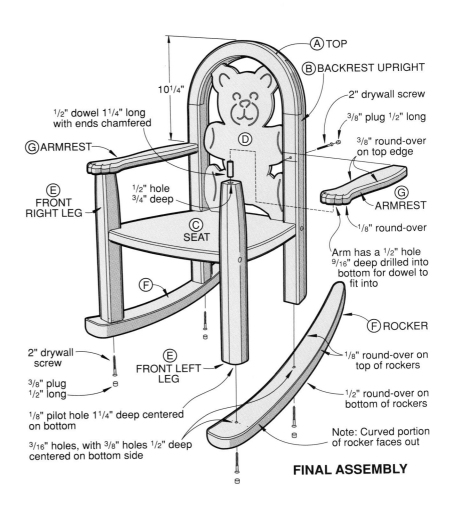

10¼"

½" dowel 1¼" long with ends chamfered

Ⓖ ARMREST

Ⓔ FRONT RIGHT LEG

½" hole ¾" deep

Ⓒ SEAT

Ⓕ

2" drywall screw

³⁄₈" plug ½" long

⅛" pilot hole 1¼" deep centered on bottom

³⁄₁₆" holes, with ³⁄₈" holes ½" deep centered on bottom side

Ⓔ FRONT LEFT LEG

Ⓐ TOP

Ⓑ BACKREST UPRIGHT

2" drywall screw

³⁄₈" plug ½" long

³⁄₈" round-over on top edge

Ⓓ

Ⓖ ARMREST

⅛" round-over

Arm has a ½" hole ⁹⁄₁₆" deep drilled into bottom for dowel to fit into

Ⓕ ROCKER

⅛" round-over on top of rockers

½" round-over on bottom of rockers

Note: Curved portion of rocker faces out

FINAL ASSEMBLY

The One-and-Only Teddy Bear Chair

continued

Position and clamp the rockers to the chair assembly. Mark the centerpoints, and drill pilot holes through the rockers and into the bottom of the uprights and legs.

FASTEN THE FRONT LEGS AND ROCKERS

1 To join the front legs squarely to the the seat, cut a plywood spacer 13⅜x15⅝". Cut notches in the corners to match those in the seat. Cut the spacer in two, and tape the pieces back together with duct tape. See the photo *above* for reference.

The tape acts as a temporary hinge when positioning the spacer. If you leave the spacer as one solid piece, you can't remove it once the rockers have been attached.

2 Secure the spacer between the uprights and front legs with a bandclamp as shown in the photo. To clamp the rockers securely to the

uprights, cut two small corner blocks. Clamp the rockers to the seat/uprights as shown in the photo.

3 Using the previously drilled ⁵⁄₁₆" shank hole in each rocker as a guide, drill a ⅜" counterbore ½" deep into the bottom side of each rocker. Fasten the rockers to the front legs with drywall screws.

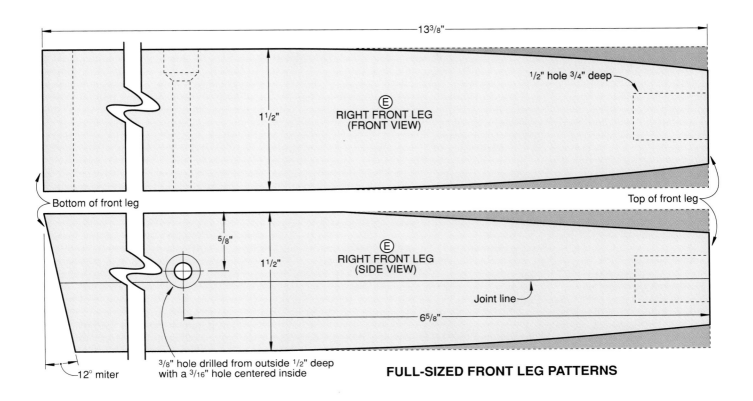

13³/₈"

½" hole ¾" deep

1½"

Ⓔ RIGHT FRONT LEG
(FRONT VIEW)

Bottom of front leg

Top of front leg

5/8"

1½"

Ⓔ RIGHT FRONT LEG
(SIDE VIEW)

Joint line

6⁵/₈"

12° miter

³/₈" hole drilled from outside ¹/₂" deep
with a ³/₁₆" hole centered inside

FULL-SIZED FRONT LEG PATTERNS

4 Mark the centerpoints on the bottom edge of the rockers to screw them to the uprights. Drill ⅛" pilot holes 1½" deep into the bottom end of each upright as shown in the photo. Drill ⅜" plug holes into the rockers, centered over the pilot holes. Finally enlarge the pilot hole in the rockers to ³⁄₁₆". Drive the screws.

5 Plug the ⅜" holes in the bottom of the rockers with extra-long plugs. Sand the plugs flush.

ADD THE BEAR-PAW ARMRESTS AND THEN THE FINISH

1 Cut two pieces of ¾"-thick stock to 3" wide by 12" long for the armrest blanks (G). Stick the arm-rest blanks together face-to-face with double-faced tape.

2 Transfer the full-sized armrest pattern to the top piece.

3 Bandsaw the taped-together armrests to shape. Separate the pieces and remove the tape.

4 Rout ⅜" round-overs along the top edges of the armrests. To accent the paws on the armrests, scrollsaw between the toes. Sand slight round-overs on the areas around the toes where shown in the inset photo on *page 89*.

5 Insert a ½" dowel center into the ½" hole in the top end of a front leg. Hold an armrest in position so the back end of the armrest is flush with the front surface of the

backrest. Push down to transfer the dowel hole centerpoint to the bottom of the armrest. Repeat for the other armrest.

6 Drill a ½" hole ⁹⁄₁₆" deep into the bottom surface of each armrest where indented.

7 Cut two ½" dowels to 1¼" long. Sand a chamfer on each end of each dowel. Glue and dowel the armrest fronts to the front legs, and use drywall screws to fasten the back end of the armrests to the uprights. Plug the holes.

8 Sand the rocking chair. Stain and finished as desired (we used Watco Natural Danish Oil).

Little Red Tote Barn

Farmyard fun for the sandbox set

City kids and country kids alike love to play with toy tractors and farm animals. Here's just the barn for them—one that doubles as a colorful tote box for carrying the complete spread out to the sandbox south 40. There's plenty of room, too, for storing livestock and equipment.

Rip and crosscut Parts A, B, C, D, E, F, and G to the sizes shown in the Bill of Materials. Tilt your tablesaw blade to 45°, and rip the top edge of each Part B, cutting so the width of the good face of the stock is 4¼".

Photocopy the Full-Sized Front Pattern for the barn on *page 98.*

Adhere the pattern to one Part A with spray adhesive or rubber cement. (You also could trace the pattern onto your stock with carbon paper.)

Stack the patterned piece on top of the other Part A, holding them together with double-faced tape. Scrollsaw or bandsaw along the outside pattern line. Then, with a ½" Forstner bit chucked into a drill press, bore through the top piece and ⅛" into the bottom piece, a total depth of ⅜". Separate the two pieces.

Transfer patterns for Parts E and F to the stock. Scrollsaw the loft door trim (E) along the outside pattern line, and the door frame (F) along the inside line. Glue both to the barn front (the piece with the hole through it).

Drill a blade start hole where shown, and scrollsaw the loft-door opening. Then, saw the door opening, guiding on the inside edge of the door frame. Cut the waste in half for the doors (H). Scrollsaw the inside cuts on the door trim (I), and then glue the trim to the doors. Make mirror image doors by flipping one trim piece over before gluing it on.

Sand the edges of the trim flush to the door edges. Cut out the window frames (G). Saw the door latch from ⅛" scrap material.

Assemble Parts A, B, C, and D with glue and brads. Cut a 13" length of ½" dowel, and glue it into place where shown.

For the fences, center a ⅛" wide saw kerf ¼" deep lengthwise on ⅜x¾x37" stock. Cut six 6" lengths for Parts J. Then cut Parts K, lay out the fence pattern on one, and stack-cut.

Sand the barn, and glue on the window frames. Prime the barn and fence parts for painting. Acrylic gesso, available from art supply dealers, makes a great primer for craft projects when thinned slightly with water.

Paint with acrylic artist's colors. (We mixed the traditional barn red by adding a bit of red iron oxide color to bright red acrylic.) Paint the fences white and their bases burnt umber to look like soil.

After the paint dries, attach the barn doors (we used brass dollhouse T-hinges from a crafts shop). Center the door latch above the doors, letting it swing freely, and glue each fence section into a base.

continued

Bill of Materials

Part				Mat.	Qty.
	T	**W**	**L**		
A ends	¼"	6½"	8"	P	2
B sides	¼"	4½"	11½"	P	2
C bottom	¼"	7½"	11½"	P	1
D roof	¼"	2¼"	12"	P	2
E loft door trim	⅛"	1⁷⁄₁₆"	2¾"	P	1
F door frame	⅛"	3"	4½"	P	1
G window trim	⅛"	1¼"	1¼"	P	8
H* doors	¼"	1¾"	2½"	P	2
I* door trim	⅛"	1¾"	2½"	P	2
J** fence base	⅜"	¾"	6"	B	6
K fence	⅛"	1⅝"	6"	P	6
L handle	½" dia. dowel 13⅜"			B	1

*Cut the doors (H) out of front (A) according to the how-to instructions. Use waste cut from the door frame (F) for door trim (I).

**Do not cut fence bases to length until you have cut the groove in accordance with the how-to instructions.

Material Key: P—Baltic birch plywood; B—birch.

FENCE AND BASE

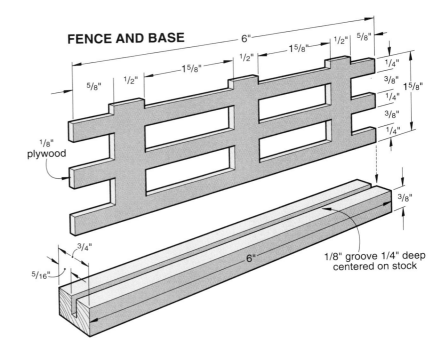

EXPLODED VIEW

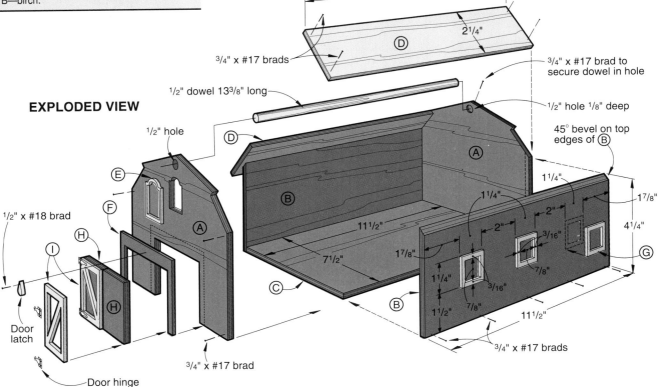

Little Red Tote Barn

continued

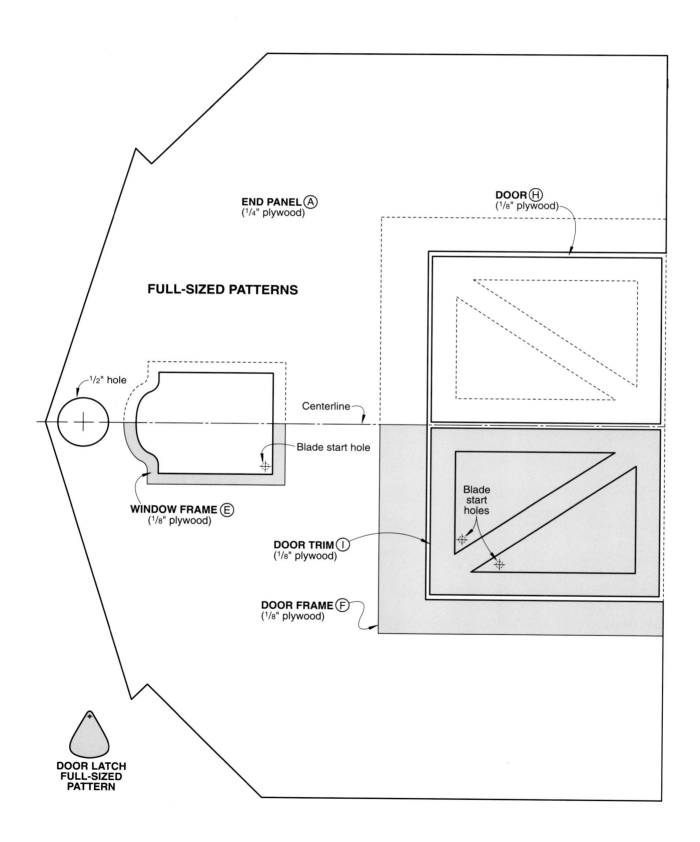

END PANEL Ⓐ
(¹/₄" plywood)

FULL-SIZED PATTERNS

DOOR Ⓗ
(¹/₈" plywood)

¹/₂" hole

Centerline

Blade start hole

WINDOW FRAME Ⓔ
(¹/₈" plywood)

Blade start holes

DOOR TRIM Ⓘ
(¹/₈" plywood)

DOOR FRAME Ⓕ
(¹/₈" plywood)

DOOR LATCH
FULL-SIZED
PATTERN

Keep-on-Recycling Toy Box

Picking up toys is now tons of fun

What better way to teach children the valuable lesson of recycling than with this roll-around toy-box truck? Simply let your kids know that at the end of playtime all the toys go into the roomy open storage areas at the rear of the truck or under the seat. They just might jump at the opportunity to help out.

START WITH THE CHASSIS AND BOX

Note: *To construct this project, you have your choice of several types of sheet goods. AB birch plywood and particleboard work fine. The edges of plywood always require extra effort for a flawless finished appearance.*

Because of its paintability (we found the painted surface of this product smoother than either particleboard or plywood), we used ¾" Medite, a medium-density fiber panel. Medite paints well because it's grainless and free of voids. The edges cut cleanly and require minimal sanding. This material costs about the same as plywood, though it weighs about 20 percent more. Call 503/779-9596 for the Medite dealer nearest you.

If for safety reasons you prefer that the toy box remain stationary and not roll on the wheels, screw through the box sides (B) and into the inside face of the rear wheels (N).

1 Lay out and mark the outlines for the chassis (A), box sides (B), box front (C), box top (D), cab sides (E), cab front (F), and shelf (G) on ¾" sheet goods. (We used a framing square for the straight lines and trammel points to mark the arcs.) See the dimensions on the Parts View drawing for laying out the chassis (A) and cab sides (E). The radius for the box side is shown on the Carcase Assembly drawing. For minimum waste, see the Cutting Diagram.

2 Glue and screw (we used particle-board screws) the chassis (A) and

continued

Keep-on-Recycling Toy Box

continued

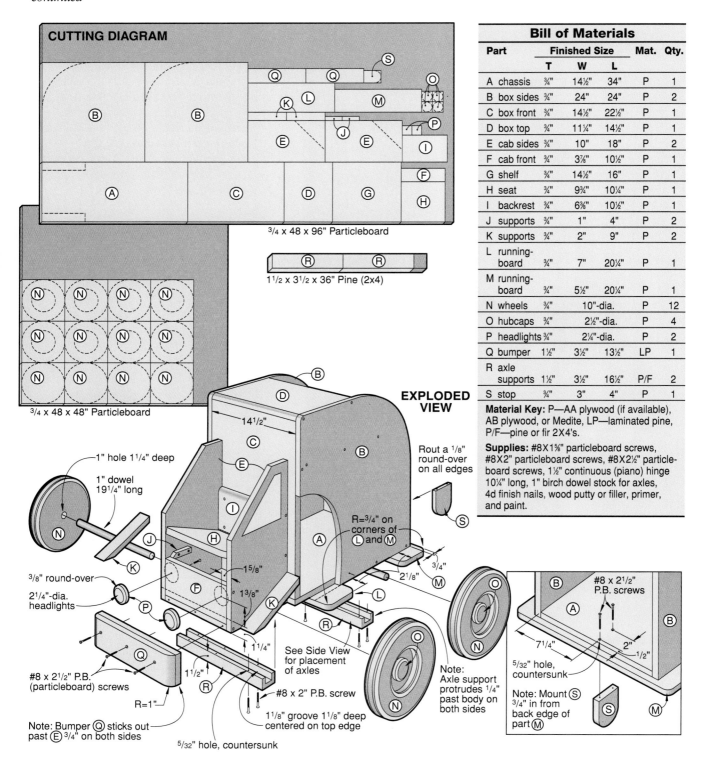

CUTTING DIAGRAM

3/4 x 48 x 96" Particleboard

1 1/2 x 3 1/2 x 36" Pine (2x4)

3/4 x 48 x 48" Particleboard

Bill of Materials

Part	Finished Size			Mat.	Qty.
	T	W	L		
A chassis	3/4"	14 1/2"	34"	P	1
B box sides	3/4"	24"	24"	P	2
C box front	3/4"	14 1/2"	22 1/2"	P	1
D box top	3/4"	11 1/4"	14 1/2"	P	1
E cab sides	3/4"	10"	18"	P	2
F cab front	3/4"	3 7/8"	10 1/2"	P	1
G shelf	3/4"	14 1/2"	16"	P	1
H seat	3/4"	9 3/4"	10 1/4"	P	1
I backrest	3/4"	6 5/8"	10 1/2"	P	1
J supports	3/4"	1"	4"	P	2
K supports	3/4"	2"	9"	P	2
L running-board	3/4"	7"	20 1/4"	P	1
M running-board	3/4"	5 1/2"	20 1/4"	P	1
N wheels	3/4"	10"-dia.		P	12
O hubcaps	3/4"	2 1/2"-dia.		P	4
P headlights	3/4"	2 1/4"-dia.		P	2
Q bumper	1 1/2"	3 1/2"	13 1/2"	LP	1
R axle supports	1 1/2"	3 1/2"	16 1/2"	P/F	2
S stop	3/4"	3"	4"	P	1

Material Key: P—AA plywood (if available), AB plywood, or Medite, LP—laminated pine, P/F—pine or fir 2X4's.

Supplies: #8X1 5/8" particleboard screws, #8X2" particleboard screws, #8X2 1/2" particleboard screws, 1 1/2" continuous (piano) hinge 10 1/4" long, 1" birch dowel stock for axles, 4d finish nails, wood putty or filler, primer, and paint.

EXPLODED VIEW

14 1/2"

Rout a 1/8" round-over on all edges

R=3/4" on corners of L and M

1" hole 1 1/4" deep

1" dowel 19 1/4" long

3/8" round-over

2 1/4"-dia. headlights

3/4"

2 1/8"

#8 x 2 1/2" P.B. (particleboard) screws

R=1"

Note: Bumper Q sticks out past E 3/4" on both sides

5/32" hole, countersunk

1 5/8"

1 3/8"

1 1/4"

1 1/2"

See Side View for placement of axles

#8 x 2" P.B. screw

1 1/8" groove 1 1/8" deep centered on top edge

Note: Axle support protrudes 1/4" past body on both sides

#8 x 2 1/2" P.B. screws

7 1/4"

2"

1/2"

5/32" hole, countersunk

Note: Mount S 3/4" in from back edge of part M

Transfer the full-sized pattern for the dragon's body to posterboard. Cut out the pattern with an X-ACTO knife, and cut it in half where shown.

On a ¾ x3x10" board, mark a line the length of the board 1" from the bottom. Position the front and rear templates for the dragon's body on the board, matching the line on the templates with the line on the board.

Place the name on top of the templates with the first and last letters aligned where shown. Trace around the body templates and the name, adding additional feet

(wheels) to the dragon for names with more than six or seven letters. Space the wheels evenly.

Drill ⁷⁄₃₂" holes where indicated and then scrollsaw the dragon body. Attach 1"-diameter wooden toy

wheels to the body with toy axle pegs glued into the holes. Don't pinch or glue the wheels. Apply a clear finish to the dragon body and wheels, and paint the letters with acrylic paints.

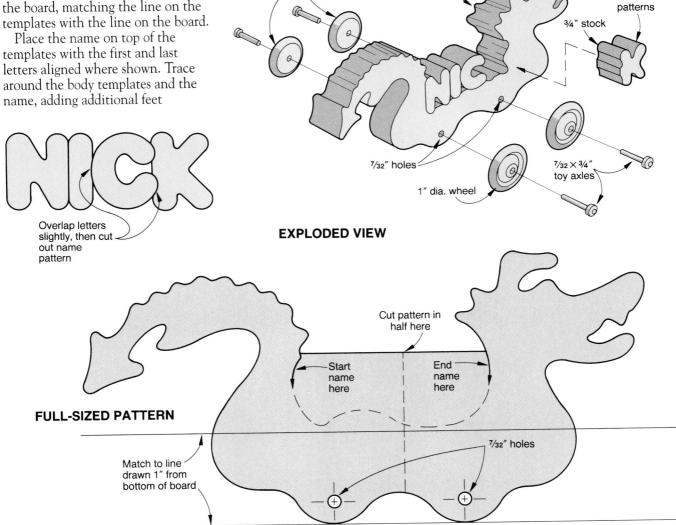

Overlap letters slightly, then cut out name pattern

EXPLODED VIEW

FULL-SIZED PATTERN

Choo-Choo To Go

A toy train that's a puzzle, too

Here's a trainload of play value. After a playtime journey, it's fun to fit the puzzle-like pieces back into the handy carrier.

Note: *To build the train, you'll need 1¹⁄₁₆"-thick maple 5¼x12½", 3¾x 12½", and 1x12½", one piece each size. You'll also need 14 wheels 1¼" dia., two wheels 1¾" dia., toy axle pegs to fit the wheels, ⅛"-thick stock , and ¼" dowel rod.*

Clamp (but don't glue) the three pieces edge to edge with the narrowest piece on the bottom and the widest on top. Draw a vertical centerline on one side.

Photocopy the train patterns. Adhere them to the stock where shown, aligning the straight bottom line of each on a joint. Cut the patterns at the joints with an X-ACTO knife.

Separate the three boards. Bandsaw or scrollsaw along the *red* pattern lines. (Use a ⅛" blade for bandsawing; for scrollsawing, install a No. 9 or No. 11 blade.)

On the top board, lay out the handle according to the Handle Detail. Bore the two 1" holes where shown, backing the stock with scrapwood to prevent tear-out. Cut the handle opening between the holes with a scrollsaw. Saw the outside profile.

Glue the three pieces together. Lay out and bandsaw the rounded corners. Sand the outside and inside edges. Drill the four pilot holes through the carrier where shown. With a ⅛" round-over bit and table-mounted router, round over the inside of the handle opening and all outside edges.

Drill the holes for the axles and couplers through the train pieces where shown. Saw along the black lines on the train pieces. Cut three ¾" lengths of ¼" dowel, and glue them into the ¼" coupler holes. Make eight retainers from ⅛" stock.

Finish-sand all parts. Paint the train with acrylic artist colors, and apply a clear finish. Shorten the toy axle pegs to 1" long, and install the wheels, taking care not to pinch or glue them. Then, install the retainers with #4x⅝" screws, and put the train into the carrier.

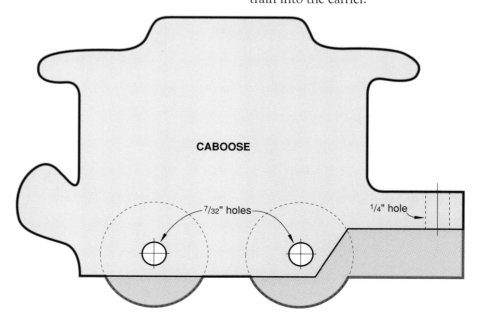

CABOOSE

⁷⁄₃₂" holes

¼" hole

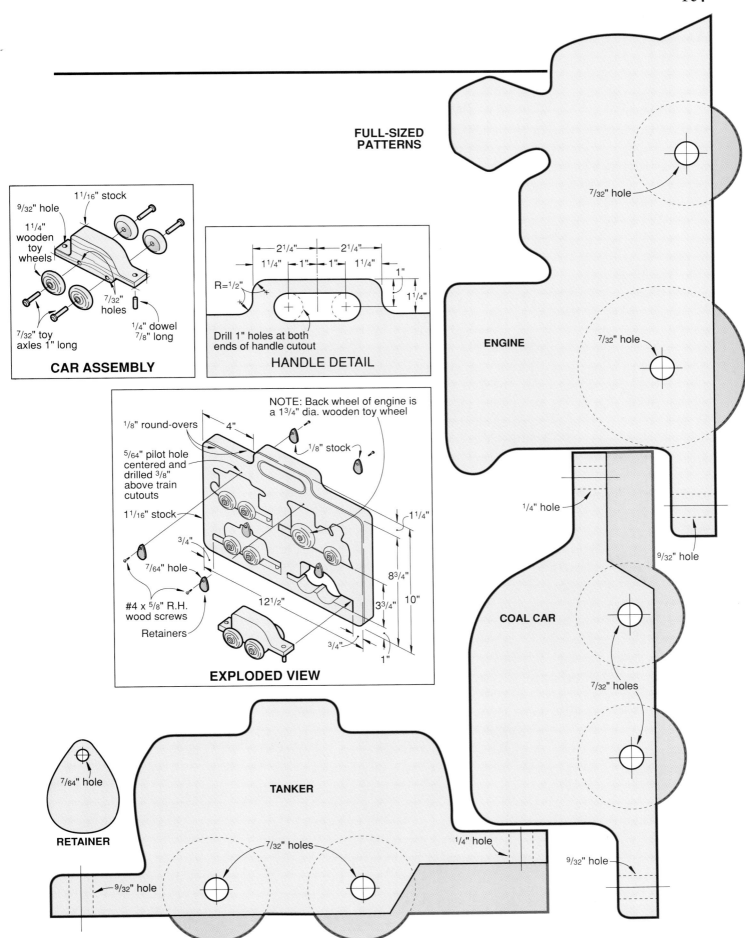

FULL-SIZED PATTERNS

CAR ASSEMBLY

9/32" hole
1 1/16" stock
1 1/4" wooden toy wheels
7/32" holes
7/32" toy axles 1" long
1/4" dowel 7/8" long

HANDLE DETAIL

2 1/4"   2 1/4"
1 1/4"   1"   1"   1 1/4"
1"
1 1/4"
R = 1/2"
Drill 1" holes at both ends of handle cutout

EXPLODED VIEW

NOTE: Back wheel of engine is a 1 3/4" dia. wooden toy wheel

1/8" round-overs
5/64" pilot hole centered and drilled 3/8" above train cutouts
1 1/16" stock
3/4"
7/64" hole
#4 x 5/8" R.H. wood screws
Retainers
4"
1/8" stock
1 1/4"
8 3/4"
10"
3 3/4"
12 1/2"
3/4"
1"

ENGINE

7/32" hole
7/32" hole

COAL CAR

1/4" hole
9/32" hole
7/32" holes
9/32" hole

RETAINER

7/64" hole

TANKER

7/32" holes
1/4" hole
9/32" hole

Smiley the Rocking Snail

Pride of the playroom

We're not sure if our happy-go-lucky snail rocker is a boy or a girl, but we are certain of one thing: Your special little one will fall in love with this perky playroom pal the first time he or she takes it for a test ride. In addition to its winning looks, this project features sturdy construction held together by glue, dowels, and screws.

Note: Because of space limitations, we can't provide full-sized patterns for this project. However, to enable you to build the project, we've included gridded patterns. To enlarge these patterns, see the instructions on page 160.

START WITH THE ROCKERS TO GET THINGS MOVING

1 Cut two pieces of clear pine, spruce, or fir to 6" wide by 31" long for the rocker blanks (A). Plane or joint the *top* edge of each piece.

2 Using double-faced (carpet) tape, adhere the two rocker blanks together face-to-face, with the edges and ends flush.

3 Cut a piece of paper to 6x30", and mark 1" grid lines on it. Lay out the shape of the rocker on the gridded paper. To do this, mark the points where the rocker outline crosses each grid line. (To lay out the curved bottom, we cut a ³⁄₁₆"-thick

continued

CUTTING DIAGRAM

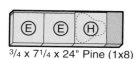

³⁄₄ x 7¹⁄₄ x 24" Pine (1x8)

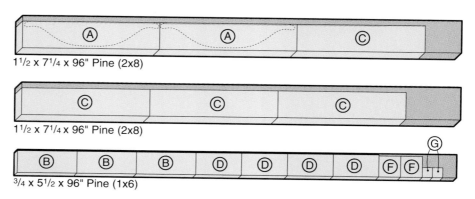

1¹⁄₂ x 7¹⁄₄ x 96" Pine (2x8)

1¹⁄₂ x 7¹⁄₄ x 96" Pine (2x8)

³⁄₄ x 5¹⁄₂ x 96" Pine (1x6)

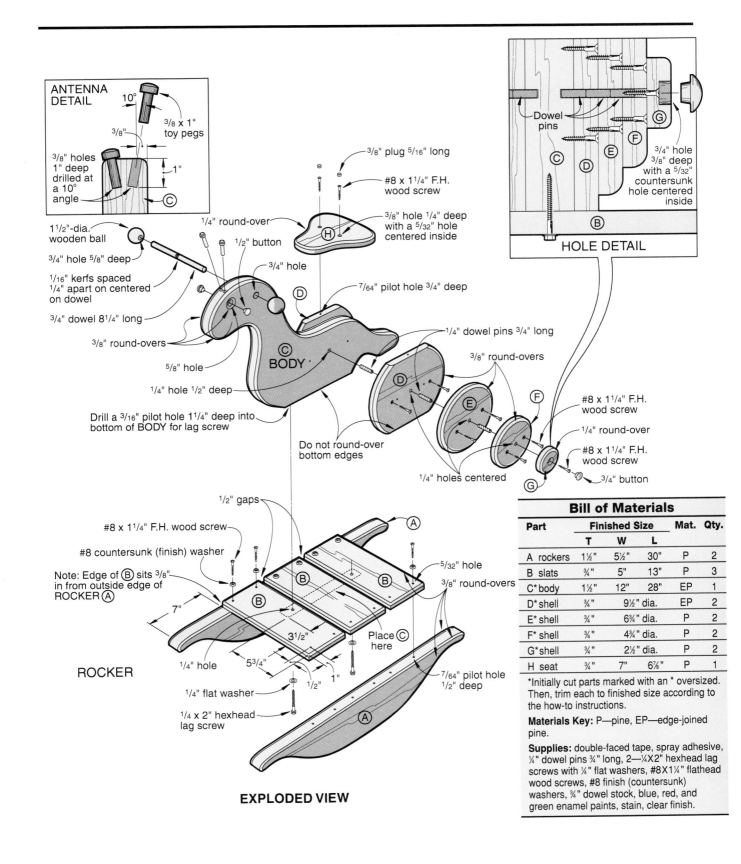

ANTENNA DETAIL

10°
³/₈ x 1" toy pegs
³/₈"
³/₈" holes 1" deep drilled at a 10° angle
1"
C

1¹/₂"-dia. wooden ball
³/₄" hole ⁵/₈" deep
¹/₁₆" kerfs spaced ¹/₄" apart on centered on dowel
³/₄" dowel 8¹/₄" long
³/₈" round-overs
⁵/₈" hole
¹/₄" hole ¹/₂" deep
Drill a ³/₁₆" pilot hole 1¹/₄" deep into bottom of BODY for lag screw

¹/₄" round-over
¹/₂" button
³/₄" hole
C BODY
D

³/₈" plug ⁵/₁₆" long
#8 x 1¹/₄" F.H. wood screw
³/₈" hole ¹/₄" deep with a ⁵/₃₂" hole centered inside
H

7/₆₄" pilot hole ³/₄" deep

Do not round-over bottom edges

HOLE DETAIL
Dowel pins
³/₄" hole ³/₈" deep with a ⁵/₃₂" countersunk hole centered inside
C D E F G
B

¹/₄" dowel pins ³/₄" long
³/₈" round-overs
D E F G
¹/₄" holes centered
#8 x 1¹/₄" F.H. wood screw
¹/₄" round-over
#8 x 1¹/₄" F.H. wood screw
³/₄" button

¹/₂" gaps
#8 x 1¹/₄" F.H. wood screw
#8 countersunk (finish) washer
Note: Edge of B sits ³/₈" in from outside edge of ROCKER A
7"
3¹/₂"
5³/₄"
1"
¹/₄" hole
¹/₂"
¹/₄" flat washer
¹/₄ x 2" hexhead lag screw
ROCKER
A
B B B
5/₃₂" hole
³/₈" round-overs
Place C here
7/₆₄" pilot hole ¹/₂" deep
A

EXPLODED VIEW

Bill of Materials

Part	Finished Size			Mat.	Qty
	T	W	L		
A rockers	1½"	5½"	30"	P	2
B slats	¾"	5"	13"	P	3
C* body	1½"	12"	28"	EP	1
D* shell	¾"	9½" dia.		EP	2
E* shell	¾"	6¾" dia.		P	2
F* shell	¾"	4¾" dia.		P	2
G* shell	¾"	2½" dia.		P	2
H seat	¾"	7"	6⅞"	P	1

*Initially cut parts marked with an * oversized. Then, trim each to finished size according to the how-to instructions.

Materials Key: P—pine, EP—edge-joined pine.

Supplies: double-faced tape, spray adhesive, ¼" dowel pins ¾" long, 2—¼X2" hexhead lag screws with ¼" flat washers, #8X1¼" flathead wood screws, #8 finish (countersunk) washers, ¾" dowel stock, blue, red, and green enamel paints, stain, clear finish.

Smiley the Rocking Snail

continued

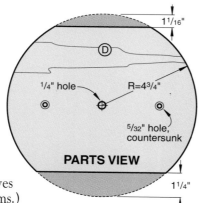

PARTS VIEW

D

1¹/₁₆"

¼" hole   R=4³/₄"

5/32" hole, countersunk

1¹/₄"

ROUTER FENCE

Cut to fit length of router table

1½"-dia. hole

1½"

4"

45°   45°

¾" stock

Center of fence

strip of wood to 1" wide by 36" long. Using a helper to position the flexible strip, we positioned one edge of the strip against the marked points on the gridded paper, and marked the curves for the rocker bottoms.)

4 Using spray adhesive, adhere the paper pattern to the rocker blanks. Center the pattern from right to left and keep the *top* edge of the pattern flush with the planed *top* edge of the taped-together rocker blanks.

5 Use a square to transfer the slat location lines to the planed top edge of the rocker blanks.

6 Bandsaw the rockers to shape (we used a ¼" blade). Sand the bandsawed edges smooth to remove the saw marks. Using a wood wedge, pry the rockers apart. Peel the pattern from the rocker. If necessary, splash a bit of lacquer thinner onto the paper pattern to dissolve the spray adhesive holding it down.

FOR LOTS OF SUPPORT, ADD THE ROCKER SLATS

1 Cut the rocker slats (B) to size.

2 Rout ⅜" round-overs along the top edges of each slat and along all edges of the rockers where shown on the Exploded View.

3 Drill mounting holes through the slats where dimensioned and to the sizes shown on the Exploded View drawing. Sand the rockers and slats smooth.

IT'S TIME FOR THE MAIN BODY SECTION

1 To form the main body section (C), edge-join 1½"-thick stock to form a blank 12" wide by 28" long. **Important:** For additional strength

across the neck, notice how we slanted our pattern on the grid and wood blank.

2 Using the method described under the heading Start with the rockers, repeat the process to transfer the pattern, and cut the body section (C) to shape. Next, cut the mouth kerf where marked.

3 Bore the holes for the eye, handle, shell dowels, and antennae where marked on the body section. See the Antenna detail for reference when drilling the antenna holes.

NOW, BUILD YOUR SNAIL A HOME

1 Mark the diameters on ¾"-thick stock for the shell Parts (D, E, F, G). (We edge-joined narrower stock for the largest shell piece D.) Rip the top and bottom edges of Part D where shown on the Parts View drawing. Bandsaw the remaining pieces to shape, and sand the edges smooth.

2 With the centerpoints used to mark the radii, drill a ¼" hole through shell pieces D, E, and F. Drill a counterbore and screw-mounting hole into the outermost shell Part G to the sizes stated on the Hole detail accompanying the Exploded View.

3 Rout a ⅜" round-over along the outside face of shell pieces D, E, F, body section C, and eye openings where shown on the Exploded View drawing. Do not rout the bottom edge of the body section or along the top and bottom of the large shell Parts D. Rout ¼" round-overs on

Part G. (To keep our fingers safely away from the router bit, we cut a board 4" wide and as long as our router table. Then, we bored a 1½" hole and cut a V-shaped notch to the hole where shown on the Router Fence drawing. As shown *below*, we used this for support when routing the smaller shell pieces.)

FIT YOUR SNAIL WITH A SEAT AND A HANDLE

1 Transfer the full-sized seat pattern and hole centerpoints to ¾" stock. Cut the seat to shape. Rout a ¼" round-over along all edges of the seat (H). Next, drill a pair of mounting holes into the top of the seat where shown and dimensioned on the Seat pattern.

2 Cut a piece of ¾" dowel to 8¼" long for the handle. Locate and mark the center 1½" section of the dowel that will fit inside in the snail's head. Then, use a bandsaw or handsaw to cut three ¹/₁₆" kerfs ⅛" deep and ¼" apart (glue grooves) within the marked area.

3 Apply glue to the kerfs. Next, center and glue the handle into the ¾" hole in the snail's head. Wipe off the excess glue.

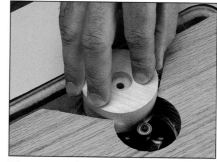

Use a router fence with a V-shaped notch to safely support the round discs when routing.

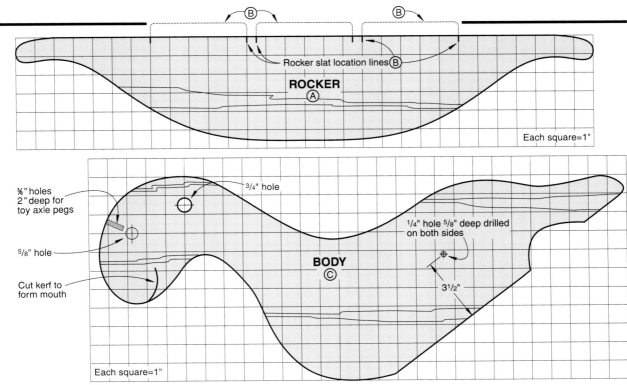

ROCKER
Ⓐ

Rocker slat location lines Ⓑ

Each square=1"

⅜" holes
2" deep for
toy axle pegs

¾" hole

¼" hole ⅝" deep drilled
on both sides

BODY
Ⓒ

⅝" hole

Cut kerf to
form mouth

3½"

Each square=1"

4 Bore a ¾" hole ⅝" deep into a pair of 1½" wooden balls. See the Buying Guide at the end of the article for our source of wooden balls.(To drill the holes, we clamped a ball in a handscrew clamp. Then, we centered the ball under the point of the Forstner bit, and clamped the handscrew clamp to the drill-press table to steady it.)

SAND, FINISH, AND ASSEMBLE

1 Finish-sand all the pieces. Stain the rockers, rocker slats, handle dowel, and main body section.

2 Paint the shell pieces, antennae, handle balls, and wooden buttons. Next, paint the *bottom and edges* of the seat (you'll do the top later). See the introductory photo for our color selections.

To paint the pine pieces, first apply a coat of lacquer sanding sealer—especially to the porous end grain. Let dry, and lightly sand with 220-grit sandpaper. Apply a second coat. The sanding sealer helps seal the wood, allowing the paint to build a more even coat than if painting bare wood. (We supported the pieces on blocks of wood, and

painted one side of each piece. Later, we painted the other side. Next, we applied a second coat, being careful to avoid runs. We used a high-quality spray enamel paint.)

3 Using ¼" dowels to center the pieces, screw the shell pieces (D, E, F, G) to the main body section.

4 Drill the mounting holes and fasten the slats to the rockers. Then, drill the holes and fasten the snail to the slats. Glue the handle balls onto the dowel handle.

5 Screw the seat to shell pieces (D). Plug the holes and sand them flush. Mask the rest of the snail, and paint the top of the seat.

6 Sand the mating surfaces for a good glue joint. Glue the ½" and ¾" wooden buttons in place.

7 Finally, trim the shank portion of two ⅜x2" axle pegs to 1" long for the antenna (see the Antenna detail for reference). Glue the axle pegs into the ⅜" holes in the head. Although the intro photo of our original snail shows the antenna

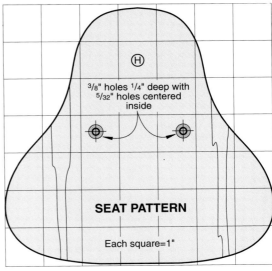

Ⓗ

⅜" holes ¼" deep with
5/32" holes centered
inside

SEAT PATTERN

Each square=1"

protruding from the head, we decided it would be safer that only the head of the peg protruded.

Baby's First Bed

An heirloom in the making

Bill of Materials					
Parts	Finished Size			Mat.	Qty.
	T	W	L		
CORNER POSTS					
A* posts	1½"	1½"	43⁷⁄₁₆"	LA	4
END PANELS					
B top rails	¾"	4⅞"	28¼"	A	2
C rails mdl & btm	¾"	2"	28¼"	A	4
D center slats	⅜"	7"	23¾"	A	2
E outer slats	⅜"	2½"	23¾"	A	8
F* spacers	⅜"	½"	2"	A	76
G* spacers	⅜"	½"	1⅝"	A	8
H* rails top & btm	¾"	2"	49⅞"	A	4
I slats	⅜"	1"	23¾"	A	32
J* spacers	⅜"	½"	1⅛"	A	4
K* spacers	⅜"	½"	⁷⁄₁₆"	A	8

*Initially cut parts marked with an * oversized. Then, trim each to finished size according to the how-to instructions.

Material Key: LA—laminated ash, A—ash.

Supplies: ⅜" dowel pins 2" long, 27½X52½" crib mattress, clear finish.

Few events can match the excitement surrounding the birth of a child or grandchild. And you can add to the exhilaration by presenting baby's parents with this stylish, sturdy, hardwood crib. It features adjustable sides, a teething rail, and a reliable means for raising or lowering the side panel and mattress. And with our step-by-step instructions and hardware Buying Guide you'll beat the stork if you start building right away.

Note: *You'll need 1½"-thick stock for the corner posts. You can buy stock of this thickness, plane thicker stock, laminate thinner stock, or see the Buying Guide for a lumber kit for the entire project.*

OKAY, LET'S START WITH THE FOUR CORNER POSTS

1 Unless you're working with 1½"-thick stock, start by laminating thinner stock to form the 1½"-thick posts. To do this, cut eight pieces of ¾"-thick stock to 1¾" wide by 46" long. Then, glue and clamp the pieces face-to-face, with the edges and ends flush. After the glue dries, scrape the excess from one edge, plane that edge smooth, and then rip the opposite edge for a 1½" finished width. Finally, crosscut the 1½" square posts to length.

2 Cut a ⅛" taper across all four edges of the top end of each post where shown in the Taper detail. (As shown in the photo *below,* we screwed a long auxiliary wooden

continued

Fasten a long auxiliary wooden fence to your miter gauge, angle the blade 10° from square, and angle cut the top end of each corner post. Use a clamp attached to the fence for a stopblock.

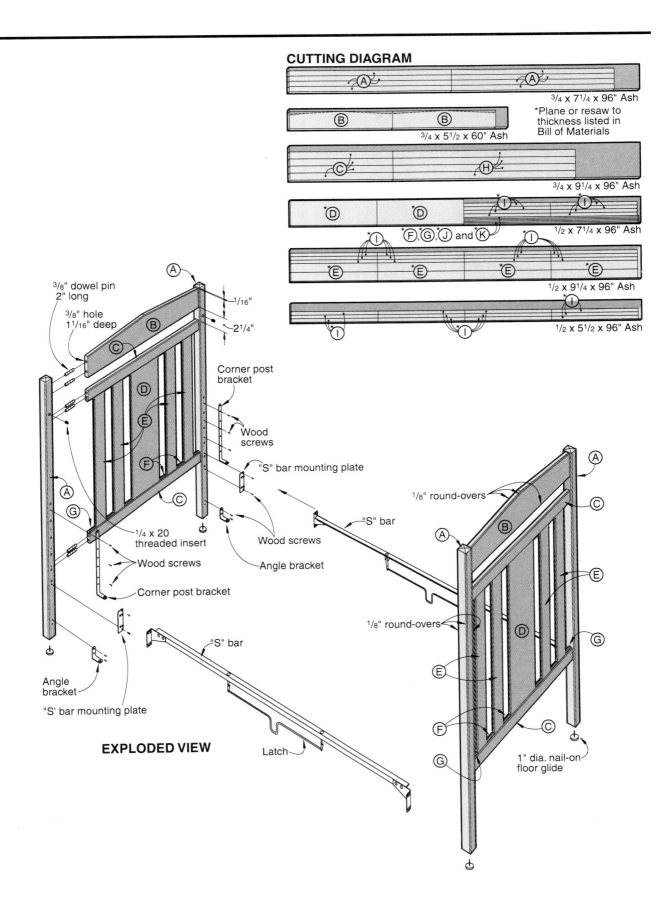

CUTTING DIAGRAM

Ⓐ Ⓐ
³/₄ x 7¹/₄ x 96" Ash

Ⓑ Ⓑ
³/₄ x 5¹/₂ x 60" Ash

*Plane or resaw to thickness listed in Bill of Materials

Ⓒ Ⓗ
³/₄ x 9¹/₄ x 96" Ash

Ⓓ Ⓓ Ⓘ Ⓘ
Ⓕ,Ⓖ,Ⓙ and Ⓚ
¹/₂ x 7¹/₄ x 96" Ash

Ⓘ Ⓘ
Ⓔ Ⓔ Ⓔ Ⓔ
¹/₂ x 9¹/₄ x 96" Ash

Ⓘ
Ⓘ Ⓘ
¹/₂ x 5¹/₂ x 96" Ash

³/₈" dowel pin 2" long

³/₈" hole 1¹/₁₆" deep

1/16"

2¹/₄"

Corner post bracket

Wood screws

"S" bar mounting plate

"S" bar

¹/₄ x 20 threaded insert

Wood screws

Corner post bracket

Wood screws

Angle bracket

Angle bracket

"S' bar mounting plate

EXPLODED VIEW

"S" bar

Latch

¹/₈" round-overs

¹/₈" round-overs

1" dia. nail-on floor glide

Baby's First Bed

continued

fence to our miter gauge, and angled the blade 10° from vertical. Then, we clamped a small handscrew clamp to the fence to act as a stop, and made four cuts across the top end of each corner post.) Using a block and sandpaper, sand the mitered ends smooth.

3 Using the Corner Posts drawing for reference, mark all the hole centerpoints. Remember that you're making two pairs of posts, with each pair having a left and right member. Mark the holes accordingly, and label the posts in each pair *left* or *right* to avoid confusion. See the Exploded View drawing for further reference. Drill all the holes to the sizes stated on the Corner Post drawing.

4 Rout ⅛" round-overs along all four edges (not the ends) of each corner post.

IT'S TIME TO BUILD THE END PANELS

1 From ¾"-thick stock, cut the top rails (B) and the middle and bottom rails (C) to the sizes listed in the Bill of Materials. Using the End Panel drawing for reference, mark the tapered top edge of the top rails. Bandsaw and sand the pieces to shape.

2 Mark the locations and drill the dowel holes in the ends of the top rails (B) and middle and bottom rails (C). See the Dowel detail for dimensions.

3 Cut a ⅜" groove ⅜" deep centered along one edge of the middle and bottom rails (C). See the End Panel drawing for reference.

4 Cut the end panel slats (D, E) to size from ⅜"-thick stock. (We planed thicker stock to size.)

5 Using the Routing the Stopped Round-Overs drawing for reference, clamp start- and stop-blocks to your router-table fence, and

rout stopped round-overs along each edge of each slat where shown on the End Panel drawing.

6 Rout ⅛" round-overs along all edges of the rails (B, C).

7 To make the spacers (F, G, J, K), cut four pieces of stock to ⅜" thick by ½" wide by 48" long. Check the fit of the strips in the ⅜" grooves in the rails (C), and sand slightly if necessary. Rout ⅛" round-overs along the top edges of each strip. See the Dowel Hole detail accompanying the End Panel drawing for reference.

8 Crosscut the spacers (F, G) to length (we used a stop for consistent lengths.)

9 Dry-fit the slats (D, E) and spacers (F, G) between the rails (C) to check the fit. If adjustment is needed, trim the outside spacers (G). Then, starting with the end panel center slat (D) and working out, glue and clamp the pieces together, checking for square. Repeat for the other end panel.

10 Glue, dowel, and clamp each end panel assembly and top rail (B) between a pair of matching corner posts (A), checking for square. (We measured diagonally to check for square.)

NEXT, CONSTRUCT THE SIDE ASSEMBLIES

1 Cut the top and bottom side panel rails (H) to size.

2 Rout ⅛" round-overs along all four edges of the bottom rails (H) and bottom edges of the top rails (H). Rout ¼" round-overs along the top edges of the two top rails.

3 Mark the locations, and drill the bushing holes ⅝" from one end of the top and bottom rails (H) to the sizes shown on the Guide-Rod Hole detail. Mark the centerpoint for the other bushing holes 48⅝" from the center of the holes just drilled. Now, drill the second set of bushing holes in the top and bottom rails.

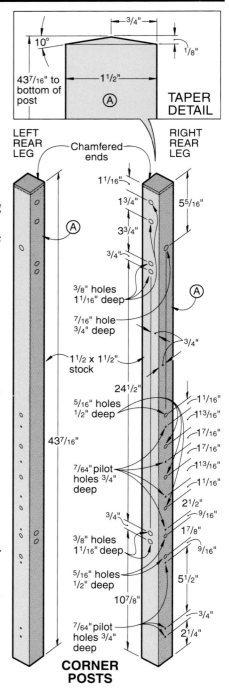

(**Important:** For smooth sliding of the side panels on the guide rods later, the hole centerpoints must be 48⅝" apart.)

4 Cut or rout a ⅜" groove ⅜" deep centered along the top edge of the bottom rails and along the bottom edge of the top rails.

continued

END PANEL

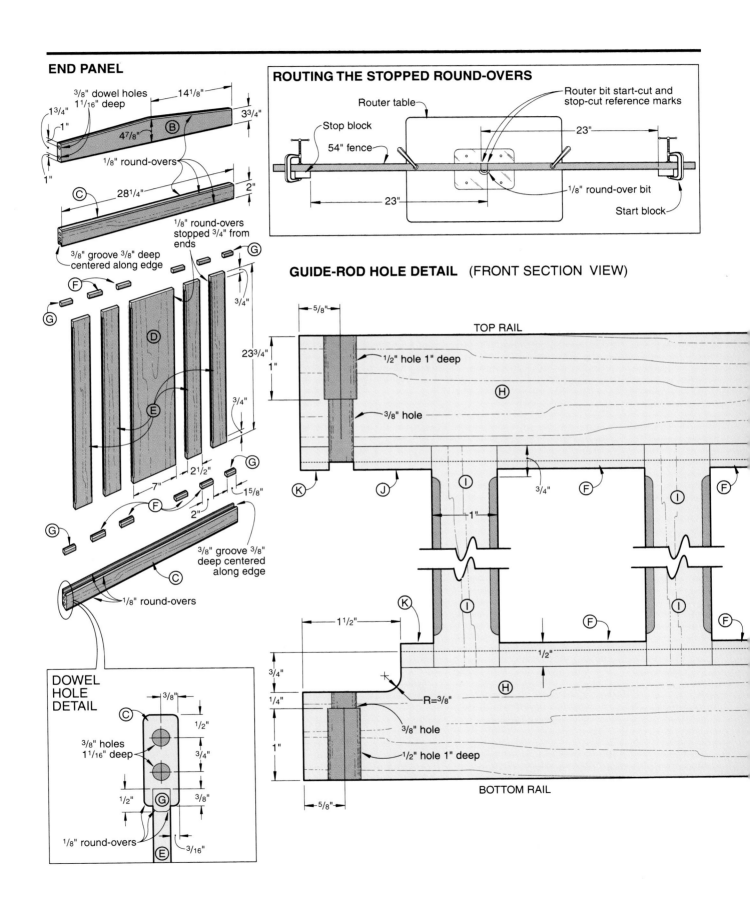

ROUTING THE STOPPED ROUND-OVERS

Router table

Stop block

54" fence

Router bit start-cut and stop-cut reference marks

23"

23"

1/8" round-over bit

Start block

3/8" dowel holes 1 1/16" deep

14 1/8"

3 3/4"

1 3/4"

1"

4 7/8"

B

1/8" round-overs

1"

C

28 1/4"

2"

1/8" round-overs stopped 3/4" from ends

3/8" groove 3/8" deep centered along edge

G

F

G

G

3/4"

D

23 3/4"

E

3/4"

G

7"

2 1/2"

G

F

2"

1 5/8"

C

3/8" groove 3/8" deep centered along edge

1/8" round-overs

G

GUIDE-ROD HOLE DETAIL (FRONT SECTION VIEW)

5/8"

TOP RAIL

1"

1/2" hole 1" deep

H

3/8" hole

K

J

I

3/4"

F

I

F

1"

K

I

I

1 1/2"

F

F

3/4"

1/2"

1/4"

H

R=3/8"

1"

3/8" hole

1/2" hole 1" deep

5/8"

BOTTOM RAIL

DOWEL HOLE DETAIL

3/8"

C

1/2"

3/8" holes 1 1/16" deep

3/4"

1/2"

G

3/8"

1/8" round-overs

E

3/16"

Baby's First Bed

continued

5 Using the Guide-Rod Hole detail, mark the ⅜"-radiused notches on the top ends of both bottom rails (H). Cut the notches to shape, and drum-sand smooth.

6 So that the top rails can receive the plastic teething rail later, tilt your tablesaw blade to 45° and position the blade where shown on the Cutting the V-Grooves drawing *below*. Make a cut along each surface of both top (not the bottom) rails where shown on the drawing.

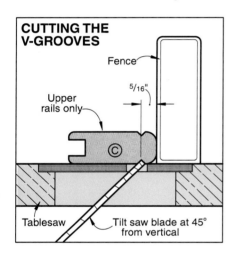

CUTTING THE V-GROOVES

Fence

Upper rails only

⁵/₁₆"

Tablesaw

Tilt saw blade at 45° from vertical

7 Repeat the process described under the heading It's time to build the end panels to machine the slats (I) and spacers (F, J, K). We recommend cutting a few extra slats and spacers. See the Bill of Materials for sizes and the Side Panel drawing for reference.

8 Dry-clamp the pieces to check the fit; trim if necessary. Starting at the center and working toward the ends, glue and clamp each side panel, checking for square. For a smooth sliding action of the side panels on the guide rods later, the panels must be square and the bushing holes aligned.

ASSEMBLE THE PIECES, AND ADD THE HARDWARE

1 Considering the young tender hands that will be in contact with

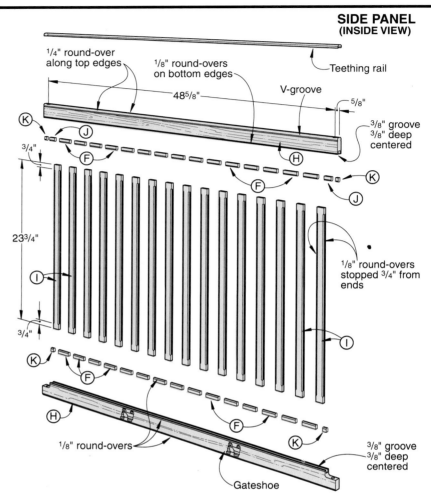

SIDE PANEL (INSIDE VIEW)

¼" round-over along top edges

⅛" round-overs on bottom edges

Teething rail

V-groove

48⅝"

⅝"

⅜" groove ⅜" deep centered

23¾"

¾"

¾"

⅛" round-overs stopped ¾" from ends

⅛" round-overs

Gateshoe

⅜" groove ⅜" deep centered

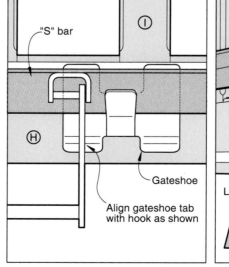

GATESHOE

"S" bar

Gateshoe

Align gateshoe tab with hook as shown

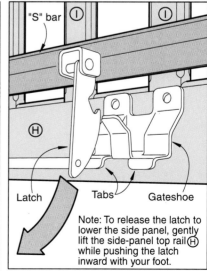

"S" bar

Latch

Tabs

Gateshoe

Note: To release the latch to lower the side panel, gently lift the side-panel top rail (H) while pushing the latch inward with your foot.

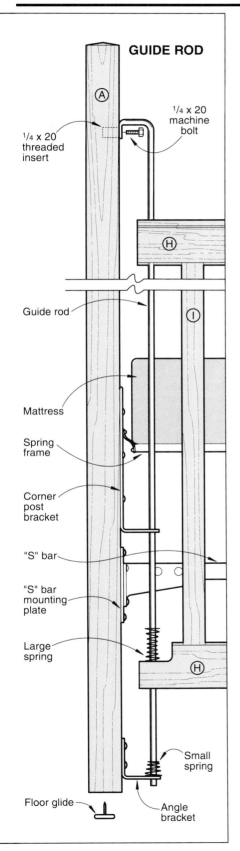

GUIDE ROD

¼ x 20 threaded insert

Ⓐ

¼ x 20 machine bolt

Guide rod

Ⓘ

Mattress

Spring frame

Corner post bracket

"S" bar

"S" bar mounting plate

Large spring

Ⓗ

Small spring

Floor glide

Angle bracket

the parts, finish-sand the end and side panels. Apply the finish. (We applied Minwax fast-drying satin polyurethane, rubbing with 0000 steel wool between coats.)

2 Tap the plastic bushings into the holes into the top and bottom side panel rails (H).

3 Slide a plastic teething rail onto the top edge of each top rail (H).

4 Using the Guide Rod Assembly drawing and following the assembly instructions supplied with the crib hardware, work from the bottom up to attach the angle brackets, "S" bar mounting plates, and corner post brackets to the posts. For further reference, see the Exploded View drawing.

5 Drive a threaded insert squarely into the ⁷⁄₁₆" hole in each corner post where shown on the Exploded drawing.

6 To join the end assemblies, attach the "S" bars to the "S" bar mounting plates already fastened to the corner posts. Slide the guide rods through the side panels, springs, and angle bracket where shown in the drawing at *left*. (We attached both side panels to one end panel. Then, we added the second end panel to the end/side panel assembly.)

7 Carefully position the assembled crib on its side on a blanket. Drill the mounting holes and attach a pair of gateshoes to the bottom rail, centering the latch hook on the inside tab of each gateshoe. See the Gateshoe drawing *opposite* for reference. Carefully turn the crib over, and add a pair of gateshoes to the opposite bottom rail.

8 As shown in the photo *above right*, fasten the mattress spring to the four corner posts. Then, you'll need to purchase and add a crib mattress. (We purchased a standard 27½ x52½" crib mattress at a local department store.)

Fasten the mattress spring frame to each corner post bracket and then add the crib mattress.

9 Add floor glides to the bottom of the crib if desired.

BUYING GUIDE

- **Crib hardware.** Spring frame, 2—"S" bars with release latches, 4—"S" bar mounting plates, 4—angle brackets, 4—corner post brackets, 4—gateshoes, 4—steel guide rods, 8—plastic bushings, 2—plastic teething rails, 4—¼ x20 machine bolts, 4—¼ x20 threaded inserts, 4—1"-dia. floor glides. Kit No. 80953. For current prices, contact Wood-workers' Store, 21801 Industrial Blvd., Rogers, MN 55374-9514, or call 612/428-2199 or 800/279-4441 to order. (Mattress not included or available through the Woodworkers' Store.)

- **Hardwood kit.** All the individual pieces shown in the Cutting Diagram cut slightly oversized in length and width from the thicknesses stated. Available in cherry or oak. Stock No. W59CR. For current prices, contact Heritage Building Specialties, 205 North Cascade, Fergus Falls, MN 56537, or call 800/524-4184 to order.

Special Mementos and Gifts

Whether presented for the holidays, a birthday, or any other occasion, a gift of wood, crafted by hand, is special indeed. Here we've brought together a group of our favorites—from picture frames to clocks to a jewel of a perfume vial—that will be given with pride and received with delight.

Autumn Leaves

Scrollsaw a fall fantasy for your wall

Putting together our wreath of scrollsawed fall foliage is almost as much fun as jumping into a pile of autumn leaves! What's more, the colors of the season will warm your home all season long.

1 Refer to the chart of blank sizes *opposite*, and cut four blanks for each part letter. (For stock, we resawed ¾" pine to ¼" thick.)

2 Photocopy the five full-sized leaf patterns, and trace each to its corresponding set of blanks. Note the grain direction.

3 Drill blade start holes where shown for leaves A and B. Cut all Parts A, Parts B, and so on. Begin with the inside cuts. Then, cut the outside to shape. (We used a No. 5 blade, .038x.016" with 12.5 teeth per inch for all sawing.)

4 Because the knob on the stem of Part C fits into the notch on Part A, cut both carefully. The most fragile part of the cutting comes at the point where the two stems cross on Part D.

5 Sand all parts. Following label instructions, color the leaves with Delta's Home Decor gel wood stains and pickling gels, available in craft shops. Use the colors indicated on the patterns or your own. (Washes of thinned acrylic artist's colors also work.)

6 To begin assembly, draw diagonal lines to locate the center on a 20" square of card-board or heavy paper. Draw one circle 18" in diameter (9" radius) and one 2½" (1¼" radius) around the center. Lay waxed paper on the cardboard so you don't glue the wreath to it.

7 Glue Parts A and B together. Then, place Part C inside the arc, fitting the stem into the notch on Part A, where shown in the detail drawing. Adjust as necessary, and glue. Complete the four assemblies, and arrange them on the cardboard as shown in Step 1 of the assembly drawings on *page 121*.

8 Place Parts D in position as shown in Step 2. Adjust as necessary, lightly mark the overlap on Parts A, B, and C, and then glue Parts D into place. After the glue dries, glue a Part E to the back of each Part D (Step 3).

continued

Autumn Leaves

continued

Blanks	
Part	**Dimensions**
A	¼X3½X5½"
B	¼X3½X4½"
C, E	¼X3X4"
D	¼X4½X7½"

9 Let the glue dry thoroughly, and spray on clear polyurethane. Attach a hanger to the back.

BUYING GUIDE

• **Patterns.** For information about other designs, send a SASE to Susan Evarts, 115 Kensington Ave. No. 8, Meriden, CT 06450. Please, no telephone requests.

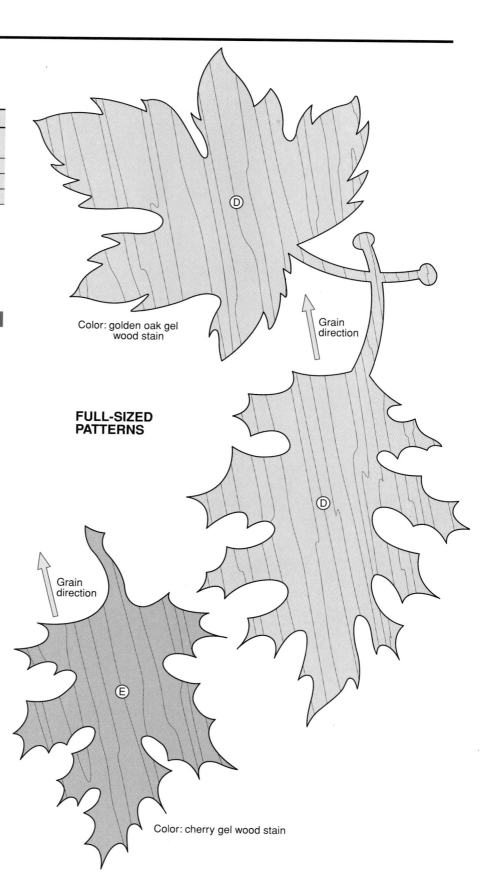

Color: golden oak gel wood stain

Grain direction

FULL-SIZED PATTERNS

Grain direction

Color: cherry gel wood stain

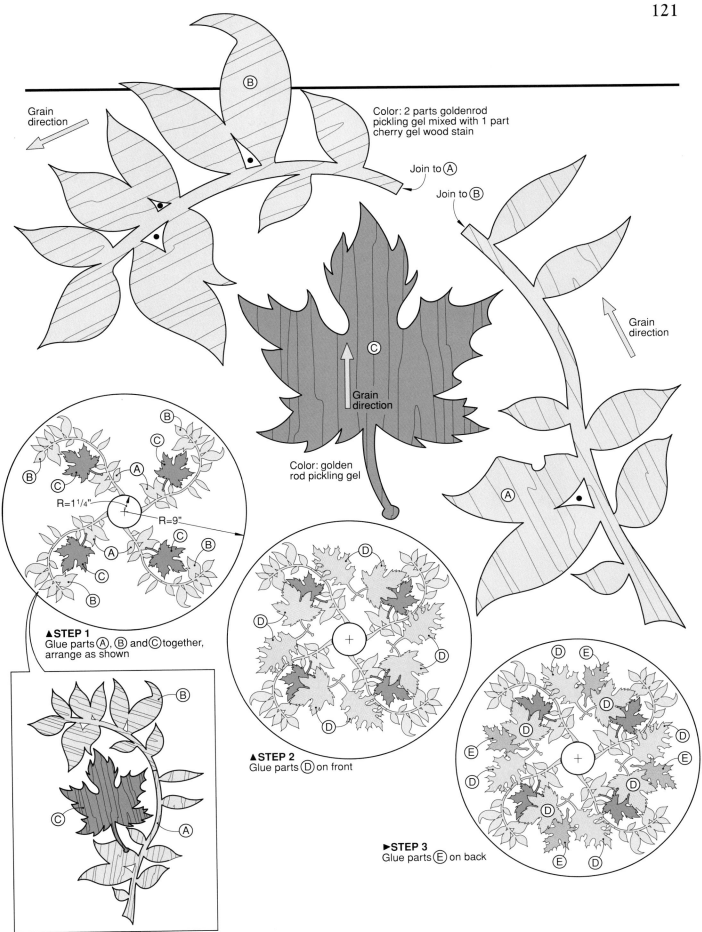

Grain direction

Color: 2 parts goldenrod pickling gel mixed with 1 part cherry gel wood stain

Join to (A)

Join to (B)

Grain direction

(C)

Grain direction

Color: golden rod pickling gel

R=1¼"

R=9"

▲STEP 1
Glue parts (A), (B) and (C) together, arrange as shown

▲STEP 2
Glue parts (D) on front

►STEP 3
Glue parts (E) on back

Echoes of Antiquity

A classic clock for all time

Do ordinary clocks leave you uninspired? Then how about giving this columned beauty a try? Imitating the lines of Greek and Roman architecture, our elevated timepiece offers plenty of room underneath for the swinging pendulum. Use our instructions to turn your own columns, or purchase preturned ones through our Buying Guide.

Note: *You'll need some thin stock for this project. You can either resaw or plane thicker stock to the thicknesses listed in the Bill of Materials. For our*

source of the clock movement, hands, dial, and turned columns, see the Buying Guide at the end of the article.

START WITH THE CLOCK MOVEMENT ENCLOSURE

1 Cut a piece of ½"-thick maple to 4" wide by 14" long. Tilt your tablesaw blade 45° from vertical, and bevel-rip one edge of the 14"-long piece. Reposition the tablesaw fence, and rip the opposite edge at 45° for a 3¾" finished width.

2 From the 14"-long strip, crosscut a piece to 3⅛" long for the front (A). See the Movement Enclosure

drawing for reference. Mark the centerpoint, and drill a 5⁄16" shaft hole in the front piece.

3 With a beveled edge against the fence, reset the blade to 90°, and rip the opposite edge of the remaining 10" strip to 2½" wide.

4 Cut a ⅛" rabbet ⅜" deep along the square-cut edge of the 10" piece, and then crosscut the two side pieces (B) to length.

5 Cut a 2¾ x3½" spacer block from ¾" stock. As shown in the photo *below*, glue and clamp the front piece (A) to the sides (B). Use masking tape to align the mitered joints and the spacer block to keep the pieces square.

6 From ⅛"-thick stock (we planed thicker stock to size), cut the enclosure back (C) to fit the rabbeted opening. For mounting the back to the enclosure later, drill four 3⁄32" shank holes where shown on the Movement Enclosure drawing. Hold the back piece in place in the rabbeted back of the enclosure (A, B), and use the shank holes as guides to drill 1⁄16" pilot holes ¼" deep into the back rabbeted edge of each side piece.

7 Then, from ¼"-thick stock, cut the bottom (D) to size.

8 Mark the pendulum slot location on the top face of the bottom piece where dimensioned on the Movement Enclosure drawing. Bore
continued

Secure the mitered joints together with masking tape when gluing the pieces. The spacer holds the pieces square.

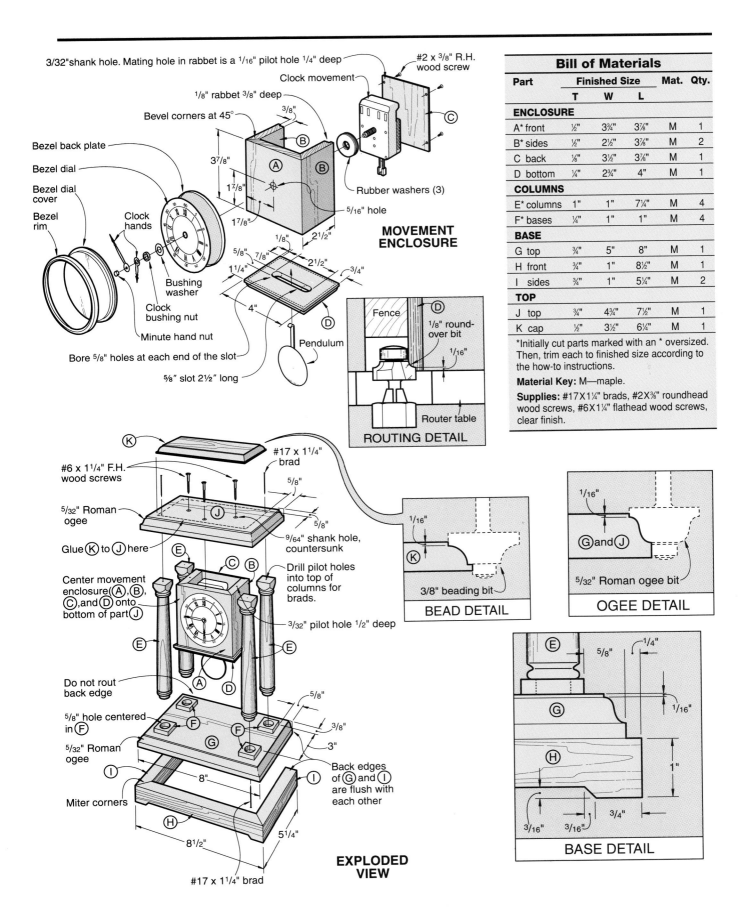

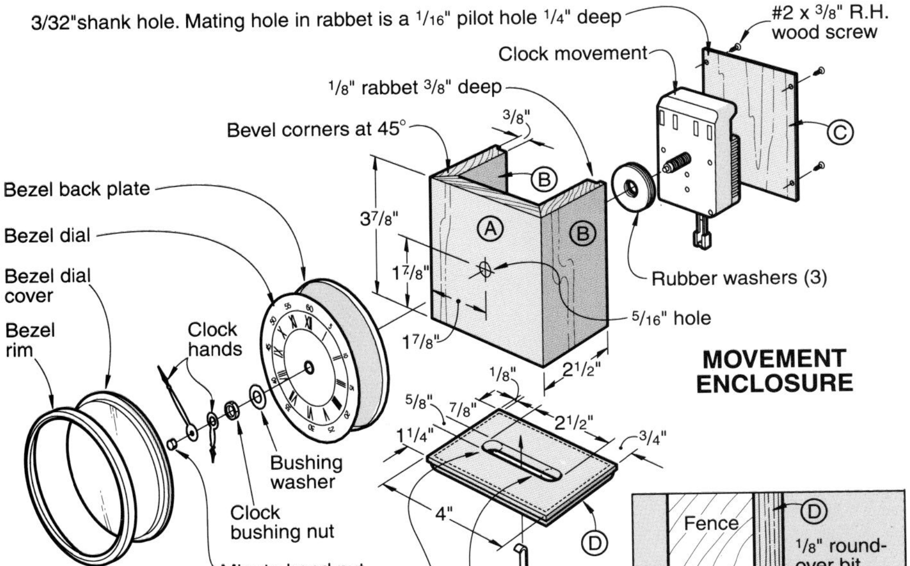
3/32"shank hole. Mating hole in rabbet is a 1/16" pilot hole 1/4" deep
#2 x 3/8" R.H. wood screw
Clock movement
1/8" rabbet 3/8" deep
3/8"
Bevel corners at 45°
B
C
Bezel back plate
3 7/8"
A
B
Bezel dial
1 7/8"
Rubber washers (3)
Bezel dial cover
Bezel rim
Clock hands
5/16" hole
1 7/8"
2 1/2"
MOVEMENT ENCLOSURE
1/8"
5/8"
7/8"
2 1/2"
1 1/4"
3/4"
Bushing washer
Clock bushing nut
4"
D
Minute hand nut
Pendulum
Bore 5/8" holes at each end of the slot
5/8" slot 2 1/2" long

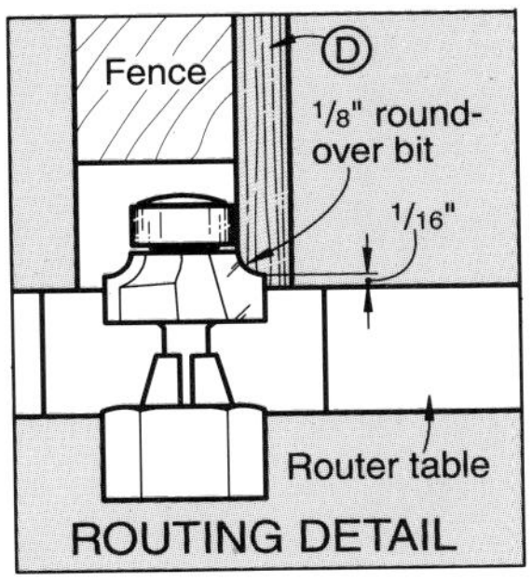
Fence
D
1/8" round-over bit
1/16"
Router table
ROUTING DETAIL

Bill of Materials

Part	Finished Size T	W	L	Mat.	Qty.
ENCLOSURE					
A* front	½"	3¾"	3⅞"	M	1
B* sides	½"	2½"	3⅞"	M	2
C back	⅛"	3½"	3⅞"	M	1
D bottom	¼"	2¾"	4"	M	1
COLUMNS					
E* columns	1"	1"	7¼"	M	4
F* bases	¼"	1"	1"	M	4
BASE					
G top	¾"	5"	8"	M	1
H front	¾"	1"	8½"	M	1
I sides	¾"	1"	5¼"	M	2
TOP					
J top	¾"	4¾"	7½"	M	1
K cap	½"	3½"	6¼"	M	1

*Initially cut parts marked with an * oversized. Then, trim each to finished size according to the how-to instructions.

Material Key: M—maple.

Supplies: #17X1¼" brads, #2X⅜" roundhead wood screws, #6X1¼" flathead wood screws, clear finish.

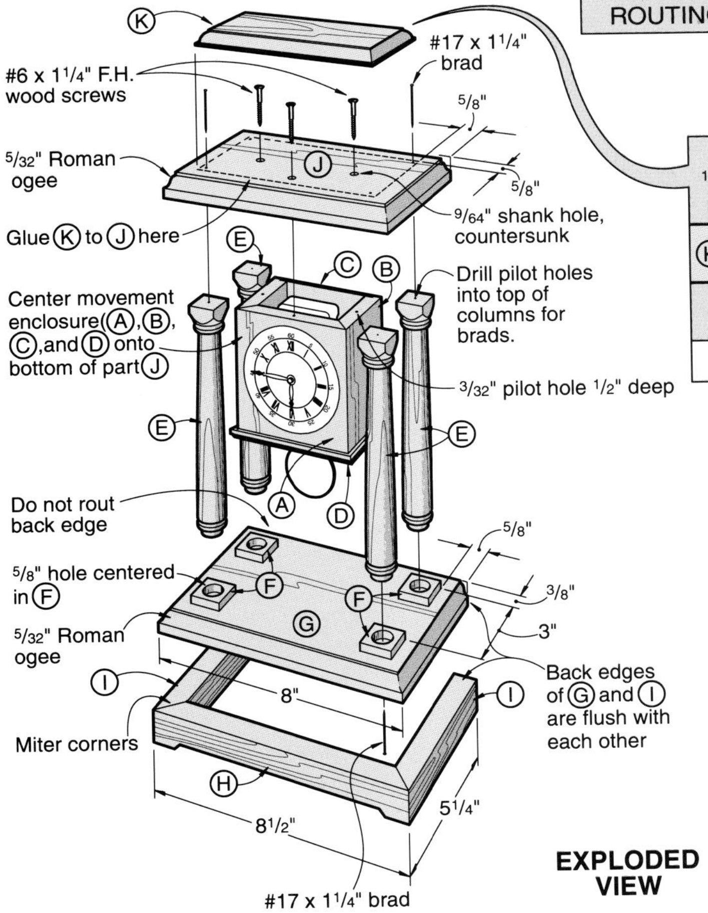
K
#17 x 1 1/4" brad
#6 x 1 1/4" F.H. wood screws
5/8"
5/32" Roman ogee
J
5/8"
9/64" shank hole, countersunk
Glue K to J here
E
C
B
Center movement enclosure A, B, C, and D onto bottom of part J
Drill pilot holes into top of columns for brads.
3/32" pilot hole 1/2" deep
E
E
Do not rout back edge
A
D
5/8"
5/8" hole centered in F
F
F
3/8"
5/32" Roman ogee
G
3"
I
8"
I
Back edges of G and I are flush with each other
Miter corners
H
5 1/4"
8 1/2"
#17 x 1 1/4" brad
EXPLODED VIEW

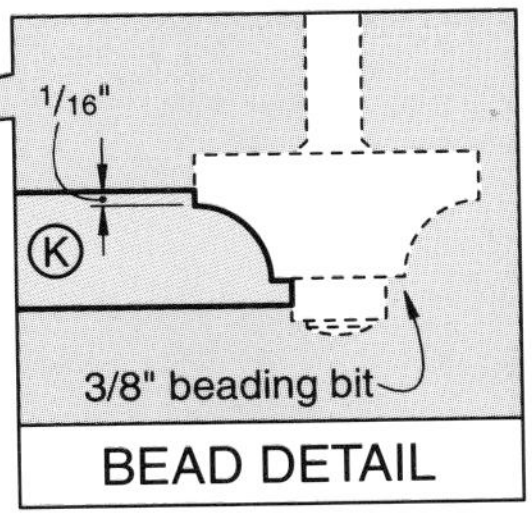
1/16"
K
3/8" beading bit
BEAD DETAIL

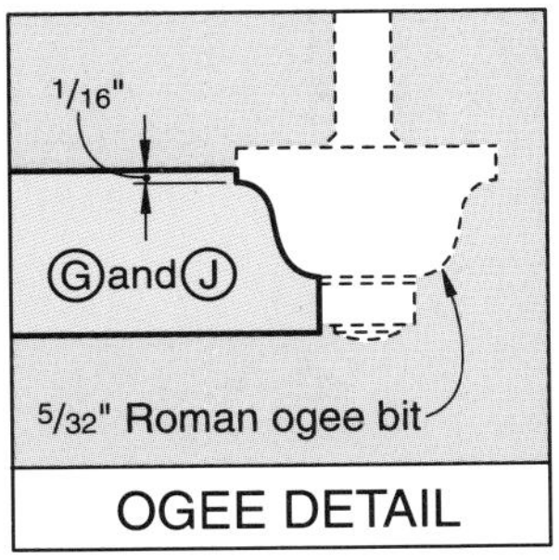
1/16"
G and J
5/32" Roman ogee bit
OGEE DETAIL

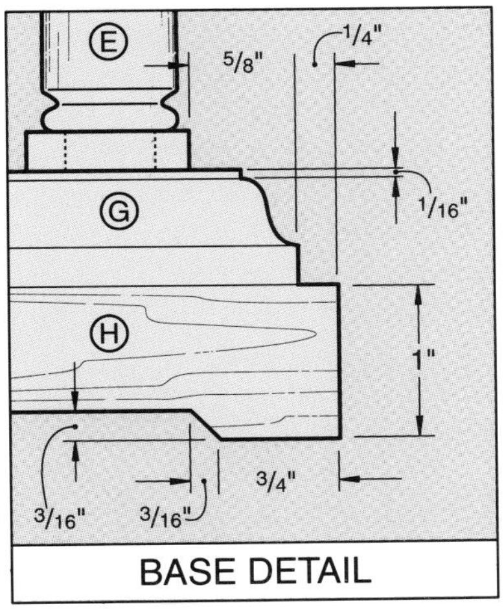
E
5/8"
1/4"
G
1/16"
H
1"
3/16"
3/16"
3/4"
BASE DETAIL

Echoes of Antiquity

continued

CUTTING DIAGRAM

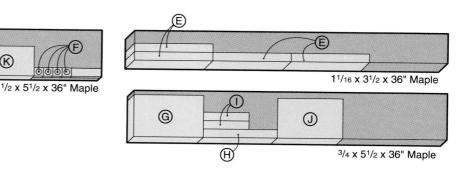

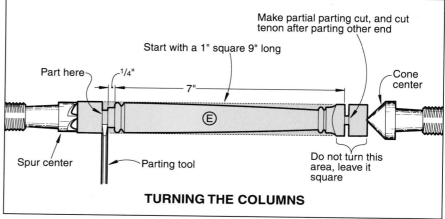

COLUMN
(FULL-SIZED PATTERN)

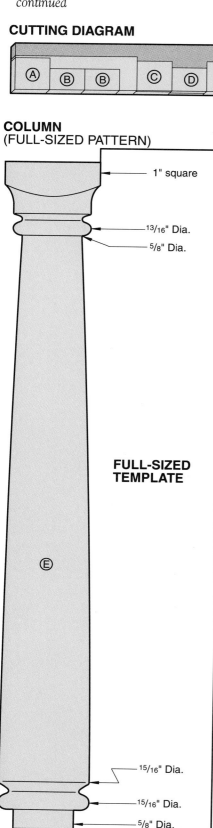

1" square

13/16" Dia.

5/8" Dia.

FULL-SIZED TEMPLATE

E

15/16" Dia.

15/16" Dia.

5/8" Dia.

1/2 x 5 1/2 x 36" Maple

1 1/16 x 3 1/2 x 36" Maple

3/4 x 5 1/2 x 36" Maple

Make partial parting cut, and cut tenon after parting other end

Start with a 1" square 9" long

Part here

1/4"

7"

Cone center

Spur center

Parting tool

E

Do not turn this area, leave it square

TURNING THE COLUMNS

a ⅝" hole at each end of the marked opening. Then, cut between the holes to finish forming the slot. (We used a scrollsaw. You could also use a coping saw.) Sand the slot smooth.

9 Using the Routing detail accompanying the Movement Enclosure drawing for reference, rout along all four edges of the bottom piece.

TURN (OR BUY) THE COLUMNS

1 Cut four pieces of 1 1/16"-thick maple to 1" square by 9" long for the columns (E). Mark diagonals on each end to find centers, and then mount one of the pieces between centers on your lathe.

2 Turn the column to the shape shown on the full-sized Column drawing at *left* (we used a small skew and the full-sized template at *left*) and where indicated on the drawing titled Turning the Columns *above*.

3 Sand the column smooth and apply the finish. (For best results, we prefer to finish turned

pieces on the lathe.) Use a parting tool where shown *above* to separate the ends. Repeat for the other three columns.

4 Cut a piece of ¼"-thick stock to 1" wide by 8" long for the column bases (F). Mark centerpoints 1½" apart (center-to-center), and then bore a ⅝" hole at each centerpoint. (We found it easier to bore the holes in a long strip rather than trying to safely hold and bore each hole in a 1x1" piece.) Cutting equally on both sides of each hole, crosscut the column bases (F) to length from the 8"-long strip.

ADD THE BASE AND TOP

1 Cut the base top (G) to size.

2 Mount a 5/32" Roman ogee bit into your table-mounted router. As shown in the Ogee detail accompanying the Exploded View drawing, rout an ogee around the front and side edges (not the back edge) of the base top (G).

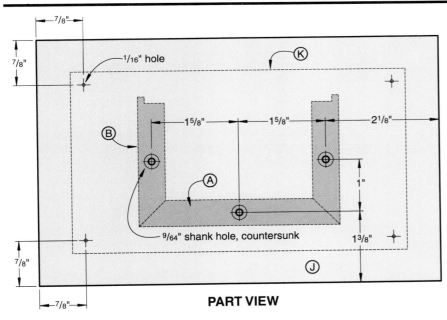

PART VIEW

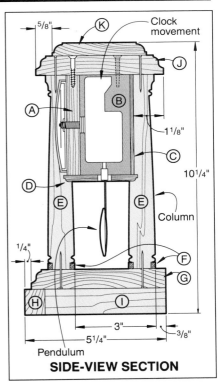

SIDE-VIEW SECTION

3 Referring to the dimensions on the Exploded View drawing, use a square and lightly mark the locations of the column bases (F) on the top surface of the base top. Glue the column bases onto the base top (G). Now, drill a ¹⁄₁₆" pilot hole centered in each column base and through the base top.

4 Cut the base front piece (H) to size, miter-cutting both ends. Using the Base detail accompanying the Exploded View drawing for reference, mark the outline and cut the notch across the bottom edge of the front piece.

5 Cut the base sides (I) to size, miter-cutting the ends.

6 Glue and clamp the base pieces (H, I) to the base top (G). Check that the miter joints are tight.

7 Cut the top pieces (J, K) to size. Using the Part View *above* for dimensions, mark all the hole centerpoints on the top piece (J). Drill the pilot and shank holes to the sizes listed.

8 Using your table-mounted router, rout a ⁵⁄₃₂" Roman ogee along all edges of the top piece (J). Switch to a ³⁄₈" beading bit, and rout a ³⁄₈" bead along all edges of the smaller cap piece (K). Sand the pieces smooth.

See the Bead detail accompanying the Exploded View drawing for reference.

ASSEMBLE THE PARTS, AND ADD THE MOVEMENT

1 Sand the movement enclosure, base, and top pieces smooth.

2 Center and lightly clamp the movement enclosure (A, B) to the bottom surface of Part J, centering the pieces over the drilled screw holes. Using the previously drilled holes in J as guides, drill pilot holes into the top edges of the movement enclosure. Screw the enclosure to the bottom of Part J.

3 For securing the column tops to Part J, position the columns between the base and top, and center the column tops under the ¹⁄₁₆" holes in J. Glue and nail the columns between the base top (G) and top piece (J).

4 Center, and then glue the cap piece (K) to the top of Part J where shown on the Exploded View drawing.

5 Finish-sand the assembly, and add a clear finish.

6 Adhere the bezel dial to the front face of the bezel back plate.

Add a dab of silicone sealant to the back surface of the bezel back plate. Stick the back plate to the front surface of the enclosure front (A), with the 12 o'clock position directly at the top and the shaft holes aligned.

7 Position the rubber spacers between the movement and back face of the front piece (A). Use the spacers to center the pendulum in the slot and prevent the minute hand from rubbing against the back face of the bezel dial cover. Install the movement where shown on the Movement Enclosure drawing.

BUYING GUIDE

• **Clock and columns.** Quartz pendulum clock movement with bezel, hands, four 7¼"-long maple columns, and dial. Kit No. 4C-P. For current prices, contact Schlabaugh & Sons, 720 14th Street, Kalona, IA 52247, or call 800/346-9663 or 319/656-2374 to order.

A Welcome Sign That Says It All

Glad to see you!

Welcome signs don't come much more inviting than this. The open door and friendly folks beckoning just seem to say, "Come on in!" It's also a call to some scrollsaw fun.

Note: *You'll need ⅜- and ¾"-thick stock for the welcome sign. You can plane or resaw thicker stock to make the ⅜" material. Contrasting woods add interest. (We cut ours from ¾" oak and ⅜" oak and walnut.) Use a fine, plain-end scrollsaw blade. If your machine doesn't accept such blades, check with your tool dealer for a blade-holder adapter.*

Photocopy the full-sized patterns *opposite*. Trace the *red* outside pattern line and cut-out line onto a ⅜x8½x9½" piece of walnut. Refer to the Exploded View drawing, and then trace the roof trim, window shutters, female figure, and shrubs onto the same piece of walnut.

Transfer the house outline (marked in *green*), the window and door lines, and the male figure to a ⅜x5½x5½" piece of oak. Trace the plaque outline and *yellow* letters onto a piece of oak ¾x2½x8½". Trace carefully so the edges of the stacked pieces will match after cutting.

Drill the two ₁⁄₁₆"-blade start holes where shown on the large walnut piece. Complete the inside cuts first, and then the outside cut. (We used a scrollsaw with a No. 7 blade, .043x.016" with 12 teeth per inch.) Continue cutting out the pieces, drilling blade start holes where indicated. Cut out the house door. Follow the pattern lines carefully—

you'll have less sanding to do if the edges line up after sawing.

Round over the front edge of the ¾"-thick plaque with a ⅛" round-over bit in a table-mounted router. Sand slight round-overs on the front edge of the trees, the house sides, the chimney, the window shutters, and the roof trim. Do the same on both sides of the shrubs and people. Sand the front surfaces smooth.

Glue the plaque and house to the large backpiece with woodworker's glue. Next, glue on the roof trim. When the glue has dried, sand the outside edges of the joined pieces, using a disc or belt sander. Hand-sand where the machine won't reach.

Apply a little glue to the left edge of the door, and place it into the opening so it's standing slightly ajar. Then, glue the shrubs, shutters, and people into place. Spray on clear lacquer or polyurethane varnish.

EXPLODED VIEW

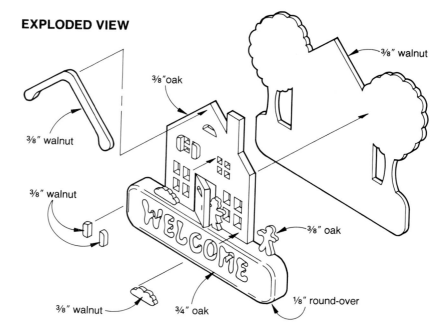

FULL-SIZED PATTERN

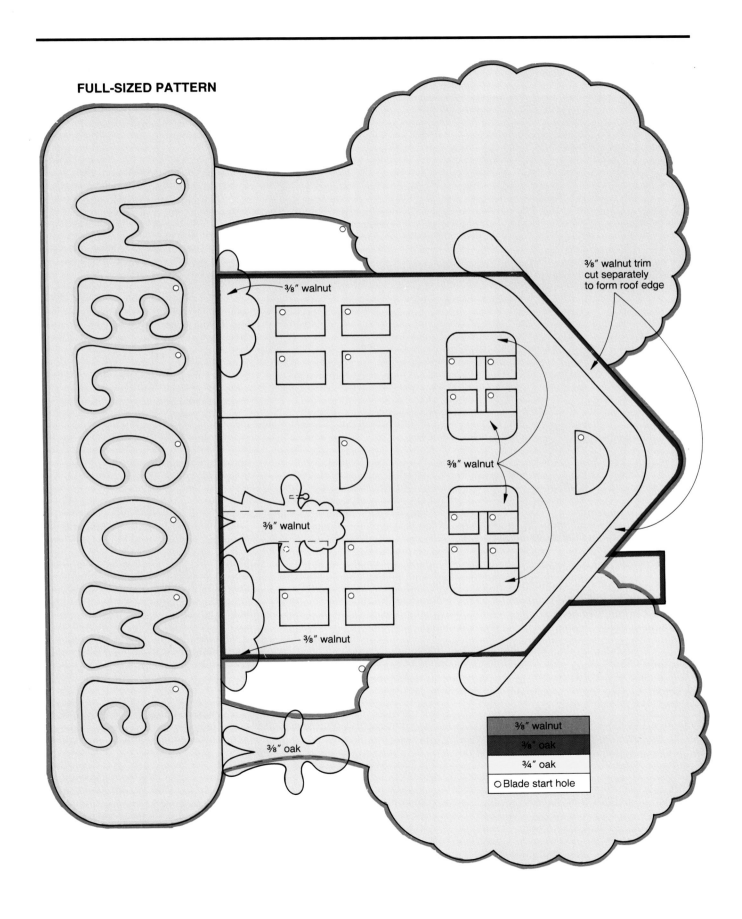

⅜" walnut

⅜" walnut trim
cut separately
to form roof edge

⅜" walnut

⅜" walnut

⅜" walnut

⅜" oak

⅜" walnut
⅜" oak
¾" oak
○ Blade start hole

Olympian Display

Heroic setting for a favorite photo

Make a snapshot something special by displaying it in imposing surroundings—a Greek temple. This stately project goes together easily, and it's just the right size for a standard 3½x5" photographic print.

Note: *To build the frame, you'll need stock ¾" and 1" thick. You could substitute 1¹⁄₁₆" stock for the 1" material. We used maple, but whatever turns up in your scrapwood pile will work.*

Rip and crosscut the base to ¾x2x7¼". On 1x2x7¾" material, lay out the triangular top, and mark the center for the 1" hole where shown.

See the Bottom View of Top and Top View of Base drawings, and mark the location of the ¾" holes on both pieces. Bore the holes ¼" deep with a Forstner bit chucked into a drill press.

Change to a 1" bit, and bore the hole through the face of the top piece. Back it with scrapwood to prevent tear-out.

Fit your table-mounted router with a ¼" straight bit, and adjust the fence to center the bit side-to-side on the top piece. Now, rout a ¼"-deep groove connecting the ¾" holes. (We clamped stop-blocks to the fence 6⅜" from either side of the bit.) For a clean job, make several light cuts.

Next, make the dowel carrier shown in the Column Routing drawing. Nail two ¾x1¼x12" pieces of scrapwood to a ¾x3x12" piece (we used plywood). Leave a ¾" gap between the narrow pieces.

Place a ¾x10" dowel into the channel on the jig. Hold it in place with hotmelt glue at each end. Adjust the router-table fence to center the bit under the dowel, and rout the ¼x¼" lengthwise groove. Cut two 3⅞" lengths from the dowel for the columns.

Change to a ⅜" piloted rabbeting bit, and rout the top of the base (the side with the holes) ³⁄₁₆" deep on both ends and both sides. Again, take several light cuts.

Bandsaw the top. Sand all parts, and then apply a clear finish to the base and top. Paint the columns black with white spatters to simulate marble. (For grooved, prepainted columns, see the Buying Guide, *below.*)

Drill the ⁵⁄₃₂" holes through the base where shown, and countersink them on the bottom. Place a column into each base hole, with the groove facing the center. Secure the columns with a 1" drywall screw from the bottom.

Sandwich your photograph between two ⅛x3½x5" acrylic sheets and slide them into the column grooves. Finally, set the top onto the columns.

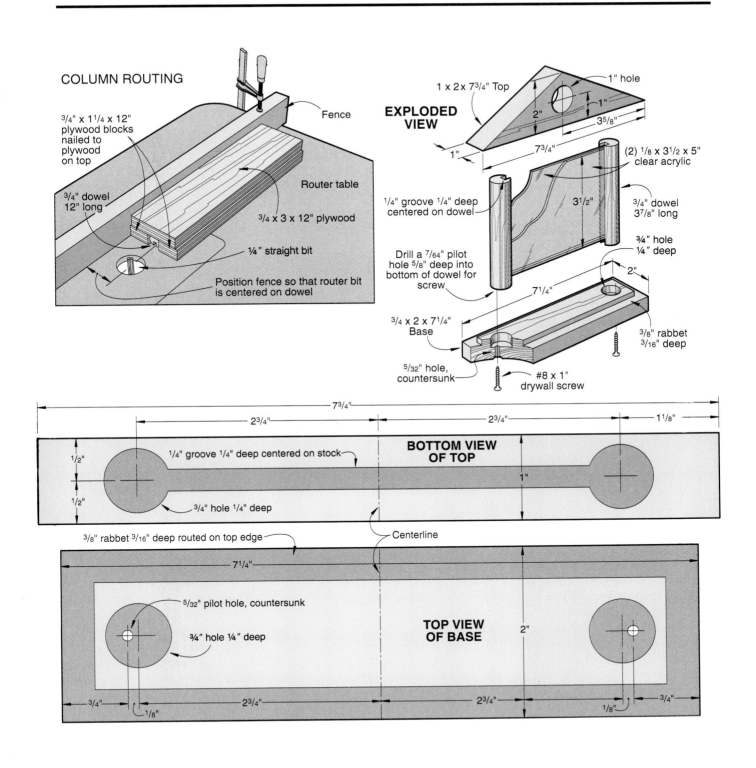

COLUMN ROUTING

3/4" x 1 1/4 x 12" plywood blocks nailed to plywood on top

Fence

Router table

3/4" dowel 12" long

3/4 x 3 x 12" plywood

1/4" straight bit

Position fence so that router bit is centered on dowel

EXPLODED VIEW

1 x 2 x 7 3/4" Top

1" hole

2"

1"

3 5/8"

1"

7 3/4"

(2) 1/8 x 3 1/2 x 5" clear acrylic

1/4" groove 1/4" deep centered on dowel

3 1/2"

3/4" dowel 3 7/8" long

Drill a 7/64" pilot hole 5/8" deep into bottom of dowel for screw

3/4" hole 1/4" deep

2"

7 1/4"

3/4 x 2 x 7 1/4" Base

3/8" rabbet 3/16" deep

5/32" hole, countersunk

#8 x 1" drywall screw

7 3/4"

2 3/4"

2 3/4"

1 1/8"

BOTTOM VIEW OF TOP

1/2"

1/2"

1/4" groove 1/4" deep centered on stock

3/4" hole 1/4" deep

1"

3/8" rabbet 3/16" deep routed on top edge

Centerline

7 1/4"

5/32" pilot hole, countersunk

3/4" hole 1/4" deep

TOP VIEW OF BASE

2"

3/4"

2 3/4"

1/8"

2 3/4"

1/8"

3/4"

A Picture-Book Box

A frame that speaks volumes

When they see this great frame, family and friends will figure you wrote the book on setting up a great photo display. Our frame for two photos, resembling a leather-bound book, goes together so easily that you just might want to build a library of them.

Cut two backs (A) to the size shown in the Bill of Materials. Rout ½" rabbets ¼" deep on both ends and one edge of each, a ¼" rabbet ¼" deep on the other edge.

Cut a ¼" rabbet ½" deep along each edge of a ¾ x4x36" board. Then, rip ½" from each edge, forming L-shaped stock. Miter-cut to length for Parts B and C.

Lay the backs (A) beside each other, rabbeted sides facing up, narrow rabbets to the inside. Glue two sides (C) and the top (B) into place, *but not the bottom.*

With the glue dry, position each bottom (B), and center a ⁵⁄₆₄" hole ⅞" deep ⅛" from each end. Enlarge the holes through part B to ⅛". Countersink them for #4x¾" flat-head wood screws.

On the inside edge of each assembly, sand the edges of Parts A and C flush. Cut spine (D) to size, and sand to the profile shown.

Finish-sand, rounding over where shown. Apply a clear finish, except to the backs of the frames and the rounded spine.

Fasten the frames and spine together with double-faced tape as shown. Mask the finished wood. Apply adhesive to a 10x15" piece of leather and the frame (we used 3M Spray Trim Adhesive, No. 08074, from an auto-supply store). Stretch the leather over the frame, working out the wrinkles and rolling it with a rolling pin to ensure a tight bond.

Trim the leather flush to the edges with a sharp utility knife. Now, remove each bottom, and insert your photo, the mat, and a 4⅛x6⅞" piece of ⅛" glass.

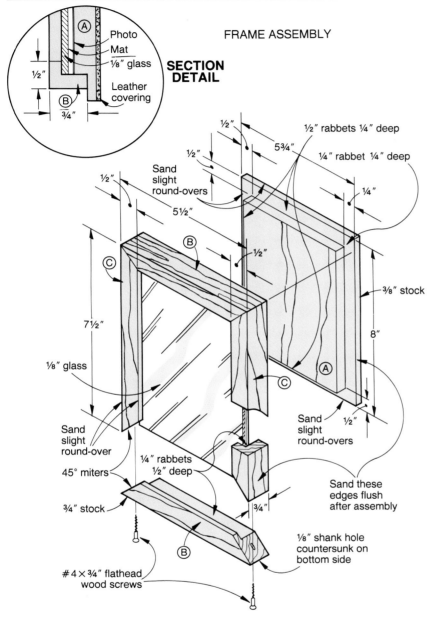

SECTION DETAIL

Photo
Mat
1/8" glass
Leather covering

1/2"
3/4"

FRAME ASSEMBLY

1/2"
5 3/4"
1/2"
1/2"
1/2" rabbets 1/4" deep
1/4" rabbet 1/4" deep
1/4"

Sand slight round-overs

5 1/2"
1/2"

Ⓑ
Ⓒ
Ⓐ
Ⓒ

3/8" stock

8"

7 1/2"

1/8" glass

Sand slight round-over

45° miters

3/4" stock

1/4" rabbets 1/2" deep

3/4"

1/2"

Sand slight round-overs

Sand these edges flush after assembly

1/8" shank hole countersunk on bottom side

Ⓑ

#4 × 3/4" flathead wood screws

Bill of Materials

Part	Finished Size			Mat.	Qty.
	T	W	L		
A back	3/8"	5 3/4"	8"	M	2
B* top and bottom	3/4"	1/2"	5 1/2"	M	4
C* sides	3/4"	1/2"	7 1/2"	M	4
D spine	1/4"	1 3/4"	8"	M	1

*Initially cut these parts oversized. Then, trim each to finished size according to the how-to instructions.

Material Key: M—maple.

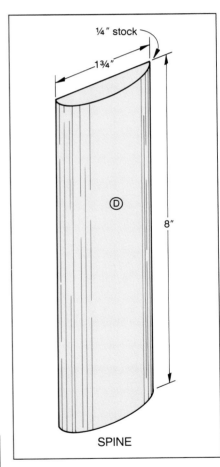

1/4" stock
1 3/4"
Ⓓ
8"

SPINE

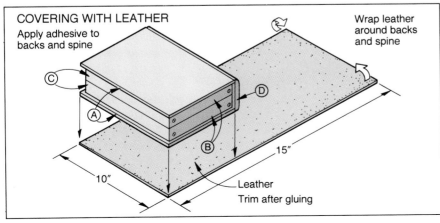

COVERING WITH LEATHER

Apply adhesive to backs and spine

Wrap leather around backs and spine

Ⓒ
Ⓓ
Ⓐ
Ⓑ

15"
10"

Leather
Trim after gluing

One-Stop Chopping

This cutting board packs a knife

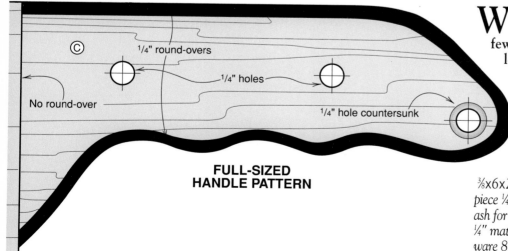

© 1/4" round-overs

1/4" holes

No round-over

1/4" hole countersunk

**FULL-SIZED
HANDLE PATTERN**

Whether slicing open a couple of hoagie rolls, cutting up a few mushrooms, or serving a loaf of nutbread, any cook will love this little cutting board. As a bonus, it features a slot that holds a knife securely in place with magnets.

Note: *You'll need stock ⅜x6x24", ⅜ x5x18", and a contrasting piece ¼x3¼x12". We resawed and planed ash for the ⅜" stock, and cherry for the ¼" material. Our knife slot fits a Farberware 8" bread knife. Modify the cavity to fit your knife, if necessary.*

Joint one edge of each piece of stock. For Part A, rip the 18"-long piece 3¼" wide from the jointed edge. Crosscut the cut-off piece to 12" long for Part B.

Crosscut the ¼"-thick stock in half for Parts C and the 24"-long piece for Parts D. Ensure that the sawed end of each piece is square to the jointed edge. Mark the square end on each.

Now, start by assembling the handle. Lay Part A on the workbench, with the jointed edge away from you. Lay one Part C on top of it at the right end, jointed edge away from you, square end to your left. Align the top edges flush, then glue and clamp.

Glue the remaining Part C to the opposite face of Part A, aligning the square ends of both Parts C. (We used a try square to align the top and bottom corners.)

Trace the Full-Sized Handle pattern onto Part C. Align the pattern's top with the edge and its front with the square end. Bandsaw along the pattern line.

Back the handle with scrapwood, and drill the three ¼" holes where shown with a drill press. Countersink the hanging hole for appearance. Glue ¼" dowels into the other two holes. Saw the dowel ends off flush. Round over the handle edges where shown with a ¼" round-over bit and a table-mounted router. Then, sand all surfaces smooth.

With the handle completed, build the cutting board. Lay one Part D on the workbench with the jointed edge away from you and the square end to your right.

Glue the handle assembly into position where shown by aligning the top edges of Parts A and D, and butting the end of Part D against Part C. Now, glue Part B to Part D where shown.

Mark and bore the three magnet holes where shown on the inside face of the remaining Part D. (We used ¾"-diameter magnets ³⁄₁₆" thick that we bought at a crafts store.) Epoxy-glue the magnets into the holes.

Glue the remaining Part D in place. Saw the end of the board square, and then bandsaw the rounded corner. Sand the end and top edge smooth, and then rout ¼" round-overs along both sides of the end and top. Bevel-rip the bottom to 45°. Sand, and finish with Behlen's Salad Bowl finish.

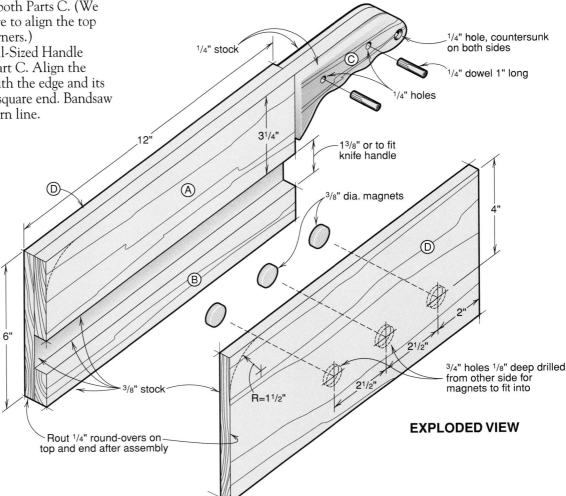

1/4" stock

1/4" hole, countersunk on both sides

1/4" dowel 1" long

1/4" holes

12"

3¼"

1³⁄₈" or to fit knife handle

D

A

B

3/8" dia. magnets

4"

D

2"

6"

3/8" stock

R=1¹⁄₂"

2¹⁄₂"

2¹⁄₂"

3/4" holes 1/8" deep drilled from other side for magnets to fit into

Rout 1/4" round-overs on top and end after assembly

EXPLODED VIEW

Wheat-Motif Bread Box

The best thing since sliced bread

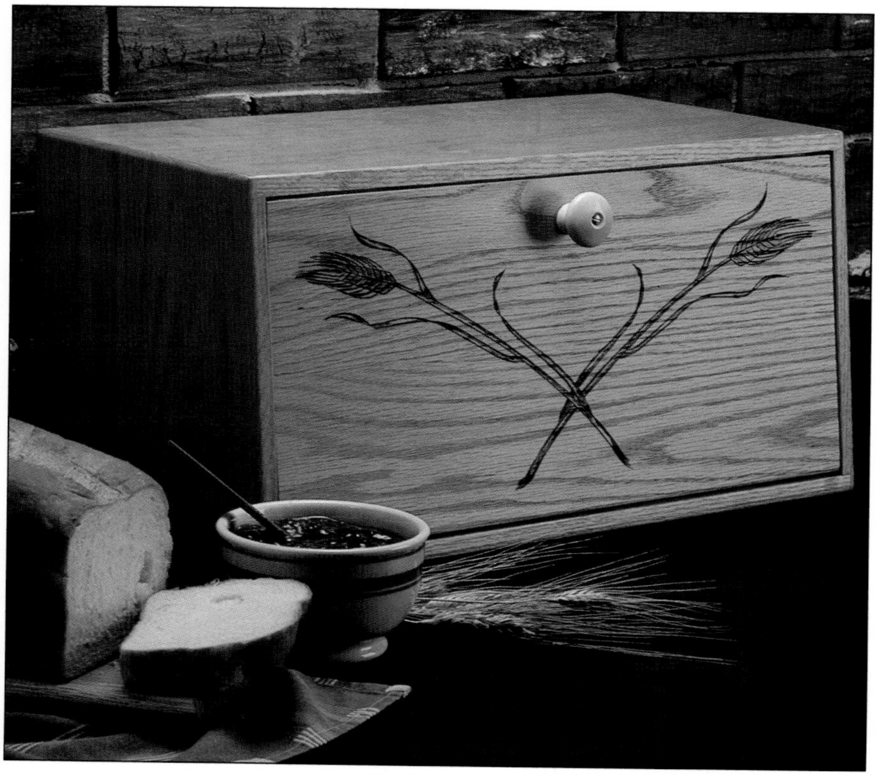

If you're looking for an easy, satisfying kitchen project, look no further. This simple oak bread box goes together as easily as a ham-on-rye sandwich. Its generous capacity and sturdy construction mean that your handiwork will be appreciated now and for years to come.

Bill of Materials					
Part	Finished Size			Mat.	Qty.
	T	W	L		
A* top	½"	9"	18"	O	1
B* bottom	½"	10"	18"	O	1
C sides	½"	10"	9½"	O	2
D* door	½"	8½"	17⁷⁄₁₆"	O	1
E back	¼"	9"	18"	OP	1
F stop	½"	½"	17½"	O	1

*Initially cut parts marked with an * ⅝" wider than listed above. Then, rip each to finished size according to the how-to instructions. The piece ripped from A will make Part F.

Material Key: O—oak, OP—oak plywood.

Cut Parts A, B, C, D, and E to size. Adhere the two sides (C) together with double-faced tape, making sure the edges align and the good side of each faces out.

Then, refer to the Bread Box Cross Section drawing, and lay out the 5° angle on the front edge. Bandsaw, sand to the line, and separate the pieces.

Now, tilt your tablesaw blade to 5° (you can use a side for your guide), and bevel-rip the front edge of the top (A), bottom (B), and the top edge of the door (D) to finished width. Cut the top with the inside face widest, the door and the bottom with their outside faces widest.

Rout ½" rabbets ¼" deep along the top and bottom inside edges of each side (C). With a tablesaw and ¼" dado set, cut a groove ¼" deep ¼" from the back inside edge of Parts A, B, and C.

Dry-assemble the top (A), bottom (B), and back (E), and then the sides (C). For assembly, apply glue to all parts except the back (E), which floats in the grooves to allow for expansion. Check for square, and clamp.

Rout ¼" round-overs on all outside edges of the box and the outside bottom edge of the door, but not the inside edges of the door opening. Trim the piece cut from the top to 17½" for the door stop (F). Glue it ½" from the front inside edge of the top, beveled side parallel to the box side angle.

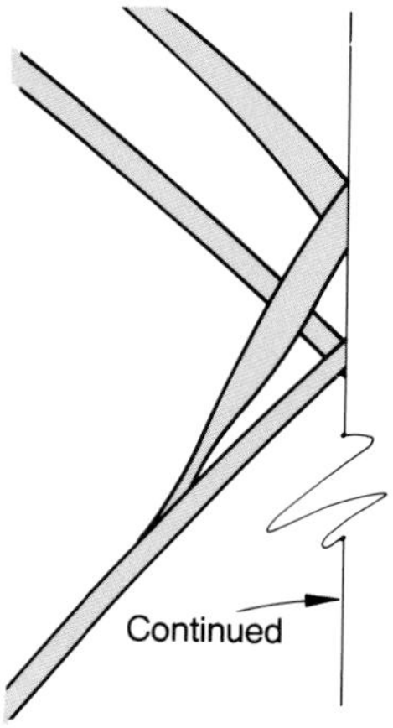

With double-faced tape, tack the piece that you cut from the door edge inside the bottom of the opening to hold the door flush. Then, drill a ⁵⁄₆₄" hole through each side into the door edge where shown. Drill a ⅛" hole for the knob where shown.

Remove the temporary stop, and sand the bread box and door. Center the wheat pattern on the door, and woodburn it.

Cut two 6d finish nails to 1¼" long (from the top of the head), and push them into the drilled holes for hinges. Set them, fill the holes, and finish the breadbox as desired (we used several coats of satin polyurethane). Attach the knob, and install a rubber foot at each bottom corner.

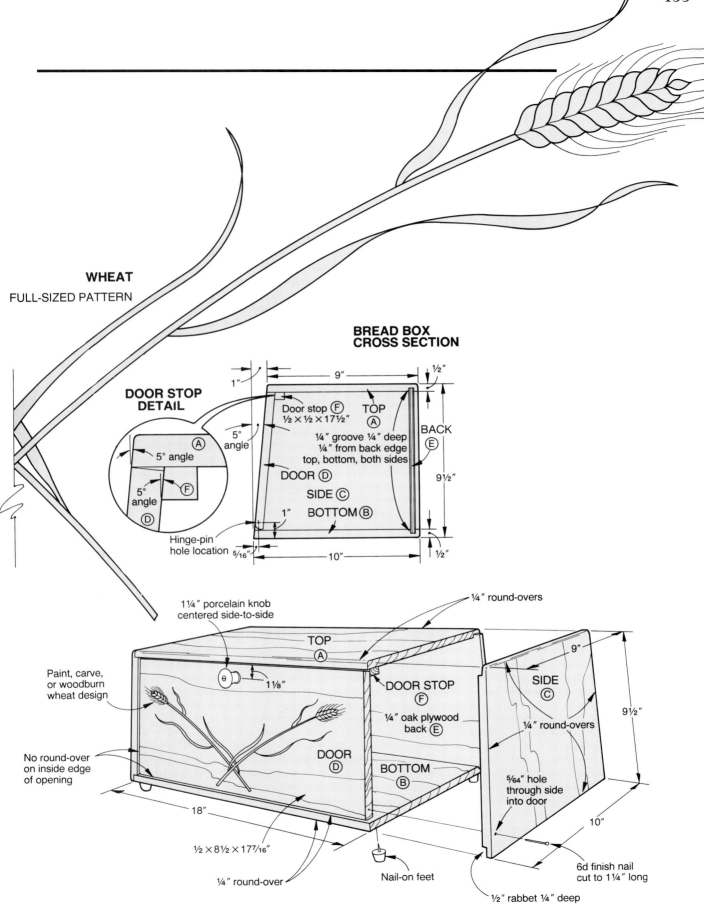

WHEAT
FULL-SIZED PATTERN

DOOR STOP DETAIL

5° angle

5° angle

Ⓐ

Ⓕ

Ⓓ

Hinge-pin hole location

BREAD BOX CROSS SECTION

9"

½"

1"

5° angle

Door stop Ⓕ
½ × ½ × 17½"

TOP
Ⓐ

BACK
Ⓔ

¼" groove ¼" deep
¼" from back edge
top, bottom, both sides

DOOR Ⓓ

SIDE Ⓒ

BOTTOM Ⓑ

9½"

1"

5/16"

10"

½"

1¼" porcelain knob
centered side-to-side

¼" round-overs

Paint, carve,
or woodburn
wheat design

TOP
Ⓐ

θ

1⅛"

DOOR STOP
Ⓕ

¼" oak plywood
back Ⓔ

SIDE
Ⓒ

9"

9½"

¼" round-overs

No round-over
on inside edge
of opening

DOOR
Ⓓ

BOTTOM
Ⓑ

5/64" hole
through side
into door

18"

½ × 8½ × 17 7/16"

¼" round-over

Nail-on feet

10"

6d finish nail
cut to 1¼" long

½" rabbet ¼" deep

Lamination Sensation

For a striking bowl, stack a stylish blank

about 16x24" for the platform. Cut two strips of hardwood that fit into the miter-gauge slots on your tablesaw (⅜x¾x16" fit our saw). Glue and screw these runners to the platform bottom, centering the platform's long dimension on the blade. Cut two pieces of 1x4 stock (actual dimensions ¾x3½") 24" long for the front and back fences.

Tilt the saw blade to 45°. Set the platform runners in the grooves, and cut about ¾ of the way across the platform. Using a framing square, position one of the 1x4 pieces on edge at the back of the platform and perpendicular to the blade kerf line. See the Sliding Table drawing.

Fasten this back fence with glue and #6x1¼" flathead wood screws from the bottom, countersunk. Glue and screw the other fence at the front. Don't place any screws in the saw blade's path.

With the saw still tilted to 45°, cut all the way across the sliding table, kerfing the front and back fences. Wax the runners for smooth operation.

CUT PARTS FOR THE LAYERS

Mark the length on one Part C blank. Align the mark with the upper edge of the kerf in the sliding table's back fence, shown in Cutting the Bevels, *opposite*. Clamp a stopblock to the fence.

To speed things up a bit, bevel Part D at the same time as Part C. Just stack a Part D blank atop one for Part C, align both with the stopblock, and cut them. Saw the other C and D, and then measure, mark, and bevel each Part E.

To cut Parts G, bevel one end of each mahogany piece, using the stopblock to ensure equal lengths.

Th^his bowl won't be the quickest lathe project you've ever done, but it may very well be one of the most eye-catching. Start with a 14-piece blank laminated from three different kinds of wood. We'll show you how to build some jigs to make the job easy and guarantee your success.

BUILD A JIG TO SAW THE BEVELS

Before cutting the parts, plane the ¼" ash and mahogany to uniform thickness. Variations in thickness between these two woods can spoil your lamination.

Next, rip your stock to 6", and then crosscut Parts A and B to 6". Trim stock for Parts C, D, and E to about ½" longer than shown in the Bill of Materials. Mark each piece with its letter. Saw the mahogany board into two 6½" lengths for Parts F and G.

Parts C, D, E, and F are beveled 45° on one end and Part G on both ends. To cut the bevels on the short, thin pieces safely and accurately, use a sliding auxiliary table on your tablesaw.

To build one, start with a piece of ¾" particleboard or plywood

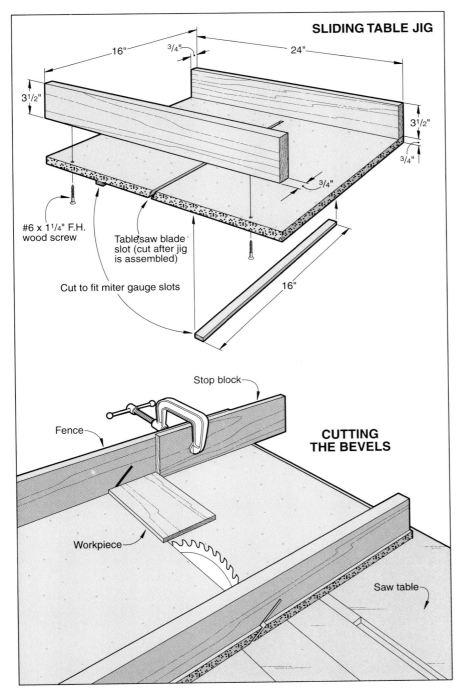

SLIDING TABLE JIG

16"

3/4"

24"

3½"

3½"

3/4"

3/4"

#6 x 1¼" F.H.
wood screw

Table saw blade
slot (cut after jig
is assembled)

Cut to fit miter gauge slots

16"

Stop block

Fence

**CUTTING
THE BEVELS**

Workpiece

Saw table

Next, draw a mark 1¼" (*not* 1½")
from the beveled edge on the long
side of the stock.

Align this mark on the *lower*
edge of the back-fence kerf,
and cut. After you make this
cut, Part G should measure 1½"
from point to point. Cut the
other Part G the same way, and
then set the stopblock to cut
Parts F.

LET'S SEE HOW IT STACKS UP

Build the lamination easily
by taking a few minutes to make
the jig shown *above left* first. On a
piece of ¾x8x8" particleboard or
plywood, mark centers for ¾" holes
where shown. Drill the holes ½"
deep with a drill press.

Glue a 3–3½" length of ¾" dowel
into each hole, setting each
perpendicular to the base. After
the glue dries, wrap each dowel
with plastic food wrap, and lay
another piece on the base. Also,
wrap some around several pieces of
scrapwood about 1x1x6" to use as
clamping bars.

Assemble the lamination upside
down in the numerical order shown
on *page 139*.

Place one Part A facedown in
the lamination jig to begin. Coat
the top surface with glue (we used
an old credit card as a spreader).
Place Part B (layer No. 2) into the
jig, and apply glue to it. Then, lay
Part F on the right side of the
lamination, with the long side
down. Spread some glue on the
beveled edge of Part C, and match
it up to Part F.

continued

Lamination Sensation

continued

Clamp the three layers, ensuring that the joint between Parts C and F remains tight and flush. If necessary, wedge small shims or toothpicks between the dowels and the edge of the layer to keep the joint closed.

Allow the glue to dry, and remove the clamps. Scrape away any dried glue squeeze-out on the face of layer No. 3. Lay Parts D, E, and G in position for layer No. 4, checking the line of the angle on both sides. Adjust as needed, and then remove them and spread glue on layer No. 3.

Place Parts D, E, and G on the glued surface. Apply glue for the next layer, and put the remaining Part A onto the lamination. Clamp, ensuring that the angled design doesn't slip out of alignment as you tighten the clamps. After the glue dries, build layers No. 6 and No. 7, and clamp. Do not add layer No. 8 yet.

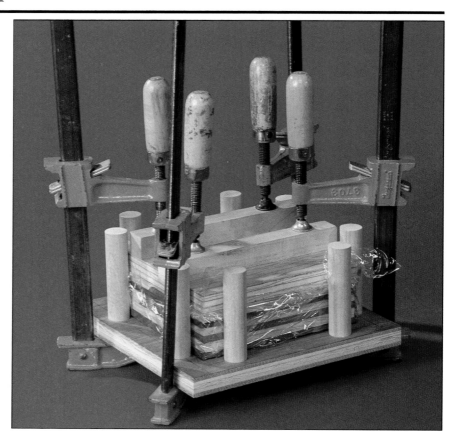

SAW A HOLE, MAKE A BOWL

Draw diagonal lines on one face of the lamination to locate the center. Scribe the largest circle around the center that will fit the blank. Then draw a concentric circle 1½" inside the other.

Bandsaw around the outside line. Drill a ¼" blade start hole inside the smaller circle, and cut around that line with your thickest scrollsaw blade to cut the center from the blank. This will save turning time later.

Place the sawed blank on the remaining Part B, and trace around the outside edge. Bandsaw along the line, and glue the piece to the bottom of the blank.

TAKE A TURN AT THE LATHE

Attach an auxiliary faceplate of ¾" scrapwood to your 3 or 4" lathe faceplate, and turn the face true.

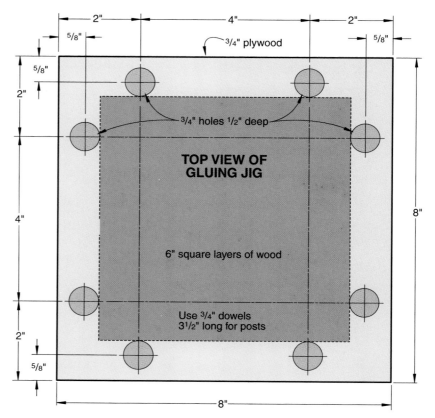

TOP VIEW OF GLUING JIG

2" 4" 2"

5/8" ¾" plywood 5/8"

5/8"

2"

¾" holes ½" deep

6" square layers of wood

4"

Use ¾" dowels 3½" long for posts

2"

5/8"

8"

8"

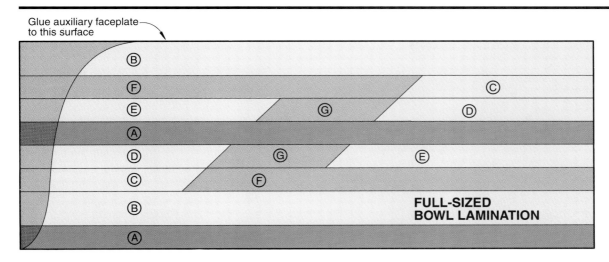

Glue auxiliary faceplate to this surface

FULL-SIZED BOWL LAMINATION

LAMINATION ASSEMBLY FOR STACKED LAMINATED BOWLS

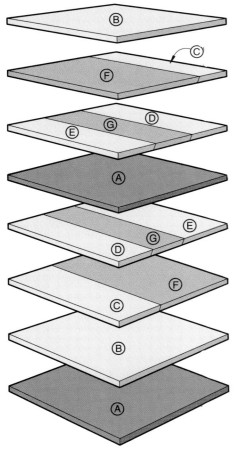

Bill of Materials				
Layer	Finished Size		Mat.	Qty.
A 1, 5	¼"	6" 6"	C	2
B 2, 8	⅜"	6" 6"	A	2
C* 3, 7	¼"	6" 2"	A	2
D* 4, 6	¼"	6" 2¼"	A	2
E* 4, 6	¼"	6" 2¾"	A	2
F* 3, 7	¼"	6" 4¼"	M	2
G* 4, 6	¼"	6" 1½"	M	2

*Initially cut these parts oversized. Then, trim each to finished size according to the how-to instructions.

Material Key: C—cardinal wood, A—ash, M—mahogany.

We first cut our stock to these sizes to make one bowl:

Ash, ⅜X6X13" and ¼X6X17"

Mahogany, ¼X6X13"

Cardinal wood, ¼X6X13"

Scribe a centered circle the size of the faceplate on the bottom of the bowl blank. Glue the auxiliary faceplate inside the circle. (We used yellow woodworker's glue, and clamped the assembly overnight.) Mount the faceplate and blank on your lathe.

With your ½" bowl gouge, turn the outside of the bowl to the profile shown. (Trace the profile onto thin cardboard and cut it out if you'd like a template.) The three woods have different cutting characteristics, so take light cuts for the best results. And, of course, be sure to keep your tools sharp to prevent tear-out.

Reposition the tool rest, and use the same gouge on the inside of the bowl. Turn the bowl to a uniform wall thickness of ³⁄₁₆–¼", checking with your calipers as you work. Remove any waves or ripples with the scraper, and then sand with progressively finer grits from 100 to 400. Sand away any circular sanding marks that remain in the bottom of the bowl.

Finish the bowl with a clear oil or similar. (We used Minwax Wood-sheen natural rubbing oil). After the finish dries, part the bowl from the lathe, angling the point of the parting tool a few degrees toward the top of the bowl to create a slightly dished base. This will prevent the finished bowl from rocking when it's placed on a flat surface. Sand the bottom, sign and date your work, and finish the bottom.

TOOLS AND SUPPLIES
- **Stock**
  See the Bill of Materials
- **Lathe tools**
  3" to 4" faceplate with wooden auxiliary faceplate, ½" bowl gauge, ½" round-nose scraper, parting tool
- **Lathe speeds**
  Roughing: 500–800 rpm
  Finishing and sanding: 1,200–1,500 rpm

Down-Under Desk Clock

It'll grow on you from start to finish

Be ready to field a lot of questions when your friends spot this different-looking desk clock. Turned from the seed pod of an Australian tree, it's sure to draw long looks, even from people who already know what time it is.

WHAT ABOUT THIS ODD POD?

A banksia seed pod doesn't look like something you'd even want to pick up, let alone use for woodturning stock. But looks *can* deceive. Inside the nubby, grayish pod, which slightly resembles a multimouthed creature out of science fiction, you'll discover extraordinary textures and patterns set off by random oval openings.

The otherworldly pods grow on banksia trees, a group of evergreens native to western Australia. Some are shrublike, but bull banksias, the largest, grow to about 30' tall. Their foot-long leaves, shown in the photo *above*, feel like holly and look like coarse, double-edged saw blades.

The trees bear yellow bottle-brush flowers that mature into seed pods as big around as a pop can and half again as long. Years ago, Australian woodturners decided to give the pods a whirl, figuring they would be an intriguing material for decorative turnings. And how right they were.

Now, American turners have discovered this Australian oddity. One of the pioneers of banksia-pod turning in the U.S. is Jerry Brownrigg, professor of technology at Northwestern Oklahoma State University in Alva. His banksia-pod

goblets, urns, bowls, bud vases, and desk clocks never fail to fascinate visitors at woodturning exhibitions.

Turning one of Jerry's banksia-pod desk clocks makes a great introduction to this unusual material. And you'd be hard pressed to come up with a better conversation piece.

CUT THE POD APART

Start by cutting the tapered ends off the pod. Use a bandsaw, or mount the pod between centers on your lathe and remove the ends with your parting tool. Cut as close to the ends as possible.

Pick one of the clock profiles, *opposite*, and divide the pod into shorter pieces—about 3–3½" long for the conical clock, 2–2½" for the flat-back clock. Cut and sand one end flat on each piece.

"Most projects—especially the clocks—look better if you center the pod's distinctive markings in your turning," Jerry comments. To do that, place the pod with the flat end up. Then centerpunch or drill a shallow ⅛"-diameter hole at the pod's core. (Don't worry, you'll know it when you see it.)

Next, attach a 1–2"-thick scrapwood auxiliary faceplate to a 3–4"-diameter lathe faceplate. With the faceplate assembly mounted and the lathe running, find and mark the center. Remove the assembly and drill a ⅛" hole through the mark.

Now, slip a 6d box nail through the hole from the back as shown *opposite, top left.* Apply cyanoacrylate adhesive to the end of the pod with the hole drilled in it. Then, place the hole in the pod over the end of the nail and bring the pod and faceplate together.

Remove the nail, let the glue cure, and install the mounted workpiece on the lathe. Bring the tailstock up to support the pod.

A nail through a hole in the center of the auxiliary faceplate acts as temporary index for mounting the pod.

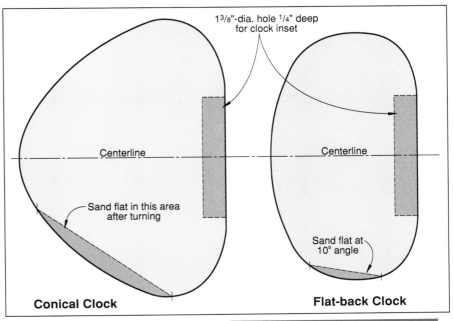

1³/₈"-dia. hole ¹/₄" deep for clock inset

Centerline

Centerline

Sand flat in this area after turning

Sand flat at 10° angle

Conical Clock

Flat-back Clock

IT'S TIME TO TURN A CLOCK

Turn the front of the body (the tailstock end of the pod) to shape. With the lathe running at 1,100–1,400 rpm, Jerry turns the clock body with a ½" bowl gouge, but a spindle gouge would work, too.

You'll encounter a variety of textures, from fuzz (which makes messy dust) to the hard seed-pocket linings. All in all, though, turning the pod isn't much different from turning hardwood. As always, keep your tools sharp.

Turn the side and back profile, leaving a supporting tenon of about ¼ of the pod's diameter at the back. Don't cut too deeply into the sides— leave some of the unusual surfaces showing. "I like to leave some natural outside texture in the turning," Jerry says. "And exposed fuzz, if the pod and design permit, adds interest."

Slide the tailstock back, and replace the tail center with a Jacobs chuck to drill the hole for the clock insert. Reduce the lathe speed to 400–500 rpm. Then, with a 1³/₈" Forstner bit in the chuck, bore the hole ¼" deep into the front of the clock body.

If you don't have a Jacobs chuck for your lathe, remove the faceplate and turning from the lathe. Then,

center it under a 1³/₈" Forstner bit chucked into your drill press. Grip the faceplate with a handscrew clamp, and bore the hole. Remount.

Running the lathe at 1,100–1,400 rpm, sand the turning with 150-, 220-, and 320-grit sandpaper. Slide the tailstock up to support the turning while you complete the back profile. Cut to a small supporting tenon (¼" or so), and then sand the back.

Separate the turning from the waste with a backsaw or coping saw. Sand to match the contour and remove the saw marks.

With a disc sander, sand a flat area 1–1½" wide on the bottom of the clock. Slant the flat-back clock about 10° back from vertical.

Finish the turning with a thin, transparent finish (Jerry uses Waterlox, a tung-oil product available from Craft Supplies USA, 801/373-0917.) Brush it on with a small artist's brush, but don't put it directly on fuzzy areas. Press the clock insert into place to complete the project.

TOOLS AND SUPPLIES

- Stock
  Banksia seed pod (see our Buying Guide source *below*)
- Lathe tools
  3–4" faceplate,
  ½" bowl or spindle gouge,
  parting tool,
  Jacobs chuck for tailstock (optional)
- Lathe speeds
  Boring clock hole: 400–500 rpm
  Turning and sanding:
  1,100–1,400 rpm

BUYING GUIDE

- **Banksia pods.** Banksia seed pods. For current prices, contact One Good Turn, 3 Regal St., Murray, UT 84107.
- **Clock insert.** Quartz clock insert with moon-phase dial and date, order No. 71212. Quartz insert without moon phase dial and date (not shown) No. 71213. For current prices, contact Klockit, P.O. Box 636, Lake Geneva, WI 53147 or call 800/KLOCKIT.

Projects with Porpoise

A desk set that's a shore thing

With your time at such a premium, sometimes it's nice to head into the shop and build a project or two (or, in this case, four projects) in just an evening or two. This simple-to-make desk set fits that description to a T, featuring a pleasing nautical theme.

Note: You'll need some thin stock for these four projects. You can resaw and sand or plane thicker stock to the thicknesses listed on the drawings.

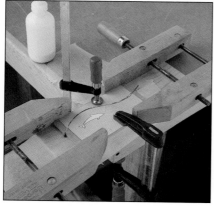

START WITH THE BASE FOR THE LIDDED BOX

1 From ½" cherry, rip a piece to 1¾" wide by 24" long for the box front, back, and sides.

2 Cut or rout a ⅛" groove ¼" deep and ⅛" from the bottom edge along the length of the ½x1¾x24" cherry stock. (We cut ours on the tablesaw.) See the Lidded Box drawing for reference.

3 Miter-cut the box front, back, and sides to the lengths listed on the Lidded Box drawing.

4 From ⅛" stock, cut the box bottom to size. Finish-sand the base pieces; they're easier to sand now than when assembled.

5 Dry-clamp the base pieces to check the fit. The base bottom should be slightly undersized to allow for expansion. Then, glue and clamp the base pieces, checking for square. Position (but don't glue) the bottom in the groove.

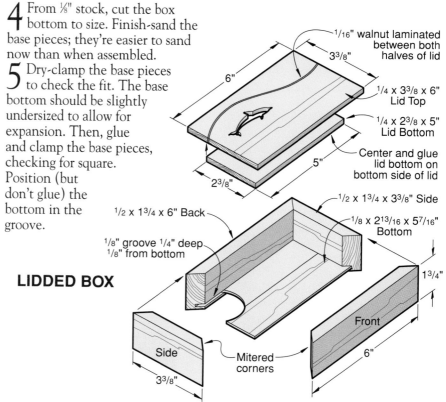

1/16" walnut laminated between both halves of lid

3³⁄₈"

6"

1/4 x 3³⁄₈ x 6" Lid Top

1/4 x 2³⁄₈ x 5" Lid Bottom

5"

Center and glue lid bottom on bottom side of lid

2³⁄₈"

1/2 x 1³⁄₄ x 6" Back

1/2 x 1³⁄₄ x 3³⁄₈" Side

1/8 x 2¹³⁄₁₆ x 5⁷⁄₁₆" Bottom

1/8" groove 1/4" deep 1/8" from bottom

1³⁄₄"

LIDDED BOX

Side

3³⁄₈"

Mitered corners

Front

6"

NEXT, ADD THE DECORATIVE LID

1 To form the lid top blank, cut a piece of ¼" cherry to 4x6½" long. Using carbon paper or a photocopy and spray adhesive, transfer the dolphin and wave patterns to the lid top blank.

2 Bandsaw the lid top in two, cutting through the wave line.

3 Cut a strip of walnut that measures ⅟16x⁵⁄16x7". Glue the strip between the lid top halves as shown in the photo *opposite center*. Keep the ends of the two pieces of cherry aligned. (We placed the laminated lid top on a piece of waxed paper which, in turn, rested on a piece of plywood. The waxed paper kept the pieces from adhering to the plywood, and the plywood allowed us to clamp the lid pieces flat.)

4 After the glue dries, remove the clamps, and trim the ends of the walnut flush with the cherry.

5 Drill a blade start hole, and scrollsaw the dolphin-shaped opening to shape. Remove the paper pattern. Sand the walnut strip flush with the top and bottom of the cherry lid pieces.

6 Measure the length and width of the assembled box base, and cut the lid to the same exact size.

7 Cut the lid bottom to fit snugly inside the base, allowing just enough of a gap to allow the lid to lift off easily. Now, position the lid top facedown on a flat surface, and lay the lid bottom on top of it. Position the box base, also upside down, on the lid and lid bottom, flushing the box with the outside edges of the lid. Slowly lift the base off the lid and trace around the lid

bottom to locate it on the lid. Then, glue and clamp the lid bottom to the bottom surface of the lid top where marked, keeping the adhesive about ½" from the dolphin opening.

MAKE A FISHY PENCIL BOX

1 Cut the pencil box front, back, sides, and bottom to the sizes listed on the Box drawing.

2 Dry-clamp the pieces together to check the fit.

3 Transfer the wave line and dolphin openings to the front piece. Drill a blade start hole and cut the dolphin openings to shape.

4 Glue and clamp the box together. Later, remove the clamps and bandsaw the top edge of the box to shape. Drum-sand the top of the box to remove any saw marks. Sand the pencil box smooth.

continued

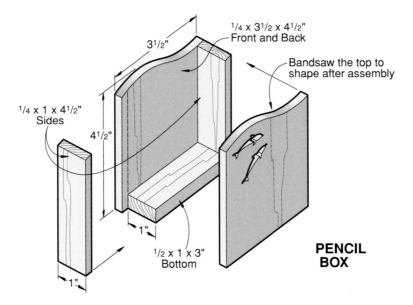

1/4 x 3 1/2 x 4 1/2"
Front and Back

3 1/2"

Bandsaw the top to shape after assembly

1/4 x 1 x 4 1/2"
Sides

4 1/2"

1"

1/2 x 1 x 3"
Bottom

1"

1"

PENCIL BOX

Projects with Porpoise

continued

DO A DOLPHIN LETTER HOLDER

1 Cut the front and back blanks to ¼x3¾x6". Using double-faced tape, adhere the two pieces face-to-face with the edges flush. Transfer the wave line to the top piece of ¼" stock.

2 Cut the wave shape along both edges of the taped pieces and sand them smooth. Using a wood wedge, pry the pieces apart and remove the tape. A splash of lacquer thinner or acetone will dissolve stubborn double-faced tape.

3 Transfer the dolphin pattern to the front piece, drill the blade start hole, and scrollsaw the opening to shape.

4 Cut the bottom to size from ½" stock. Glue and clamp the pieces together with the ends flush.

DIVE INTO THE BUSINESS-CARD HOLDER

Using the dimensions on the Business-Card Holder drawing and the how-to instructions for the letter holder, cut the pieces and assemble the card holder.

Finish-sand all four items. Apply a clear finish (we used Deft aerosol lacquer).

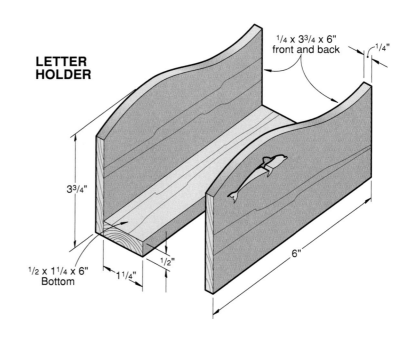

LETTER HOLDER

¼ x 3¾ x 6" front and back

¼"

3¾"

½"

½ x 1¼ x 6" Bottom

1¼"

6"

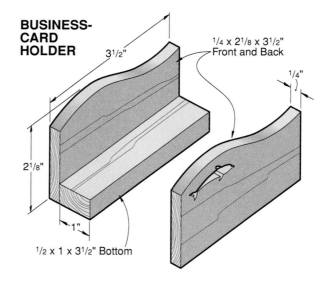

BUSINESS-CARD HOLDER

3½"

¼ x 2⅛ x 3½" Front and Back

¼"

2⅛"

1"

½ x 1 x 3½" Bottom

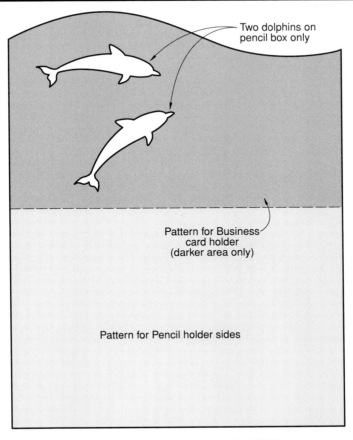

Two dolphins on pencil box only

Pattern for Business card holder (darker area only)

Pattern for Pencil holder sides

FULL-SIZED PATTERNS

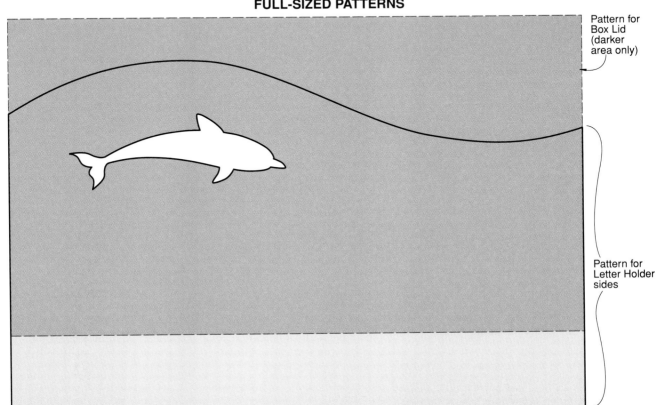

Pattern for Box Lid (darker area only)

Pattern for Letter Holder sides

Ring Around the Wrist Watch

The time is right for turning this project

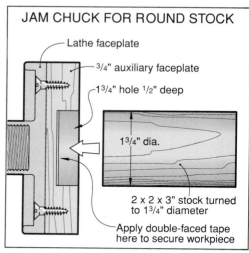

JAM CHUCK FOR ROUND STOCK

Lathe faceplate
¾" auxiliary faceplate
1¾" hole ½" deep
1¾" dia.
2 x 2 x 3" stock turned to 1¾" diameter
Apply double-faced tape here to secure workpiece

Yep, that's real wood around the watch face. And if the thought of wearing a wood-trimmed watch isn't enough to tempt a turner, here's the clincher: You can make four interchangeable wooden bezels for this watch, using your favorite woods.

You can start with almost any scrapwood. A 2x2x3" piece of square stock, a 2" circle or square sawn from ¾"-thick material, or even a glued-up piece will suffice. Exotic woods, burls, or other highly figured pieces can yield spectacular results.

First, round your stock and mount it to turn the backside of the trim ring, or bezel. Here are a couple of ways to start, depending on whether you're using a turning square for spindle-style turning or plank stock for bowl-style turning.

TO START WITH A TURNING SQUARE

Mount the square between centers and round it down to 1¾–2" diameter. Square the tailstock end with a parting tool or skew. Form a flat surface on the end, leaving the smallest possible nubbin under the tail center.

Remove the stock and the drive center from the lathe, and slide the tailstock out of the way. Then, mount a 3" faceplate carrying a ¾"-thick scrapwood auxiliary faceplate. Gouge-cut a straight-sided, flat-bottomed recess about ½" deep in the faceplate to receive the round stock. Check the size frequently to achieve a tight fit—this will be your chuck for turning the backside of the bezel. (This kind of friction-fit fixture is called a *jam chuck*.)

With a chisel or dovetail saw, remove the nubbin from the rounded stock. Slide the stock's squared end into the jam-chuck recess, seating it firmly and squarely, shown *above*. If friction doesn't hold it securely, place double-faced tape in the bottom of the recess.

TO START WITH A FLAT BLANK

For stock sawn from a board or a bowl blank, attach a ¾"-thick scrapwood auxiliary faceplate to your lathe's 3" faceplate. Mount the faceplate and true the surface.

At the center of the auxiliary faceplate, drill an index hole about ⅜" deep to fit an alignment pin such as a 16d nail, a scrap of ⅛" dowel, or a drill-bit shank, shown *opposite, top left*. (We used a twist-drill bit in a Jacobs chuck mounted on the tailstock.) Drill a hole the same size through the center of your stock.

Now, insert the pin to align the holes as you join the workpiece to the faceplate with cyanoacrylate adhesive. Double-faced tape works great for stock up to about ¾" thick, too. Remove the pin. Turn the stock to 1¾–2" diameter, and true the face.

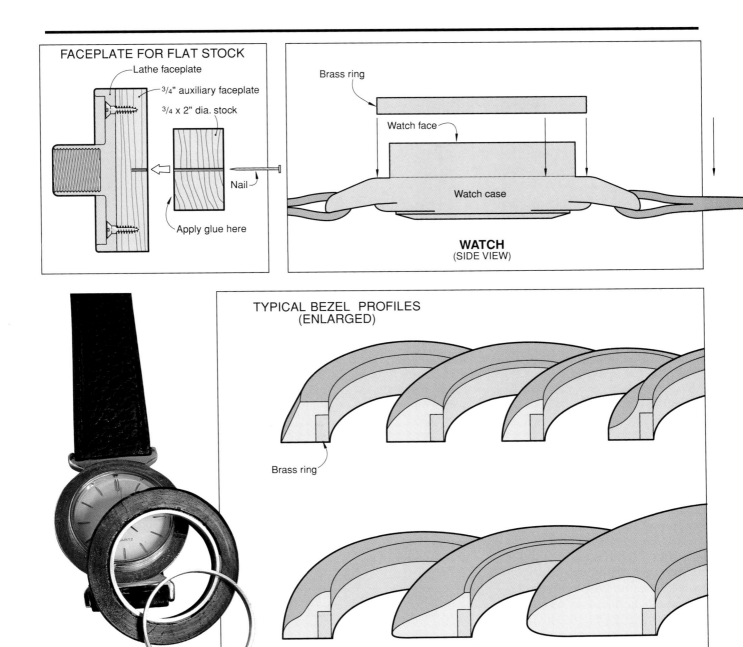

FACEPLATE FOR FLAT STOCK
- Lathe faceplate
- ¾" auxiliary faceplate
- ¾ x 2" dia. stock
- Nail
- Apply glue here

Brass ring
Watch face
Watch case

WATCH
(SIDE VIEW)

TYPICAL BEZEL PROFILES
(ENLARGED)

Brass ring

TURNING THE BEZEL BACK

In the center of the blank, bore a ¾" hole ⅞" deep, or all the way through stock that's less than ⅞" thick (see Step 1 of the Turning the Back drawing). A Forstner bit and Jacobs chuck mounted on the tailstock will do the job, but set your lathe at its slowest speed. You also could bore the hole with a gouge.

Measure the outside diameter of the brass ring. Then, with a small gouge, enlarge the hole in the workpiece to form a seat for the ring (Step 2 of the drawing). Cut deep enough to place the bottom of the ring flush with the bottom of the blank.

Apply instant glue or epoxy to the seating surfaces, and press the ring into place. After the adhesive cures, enlarge the hole to match

the inside diameter of the ring (Step 3). Press the watch into the workpiece to check the fit.

When you achieve a good fit, sand and finish the end of the workpiece. Part the blank off where shown. (We held the end of a short dowel inside the hole to catch the parted-off blank.)

continued

Ring Around the Wrist Watch

continued

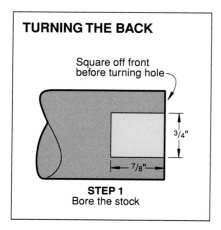

TURNING THE BACK

Square off front before turning hole

3/4"

7/8"

STEP 1
Bore the stock

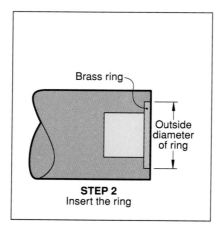

Brass ring

Outside diameter of ring

STEP 2
Insert the ring

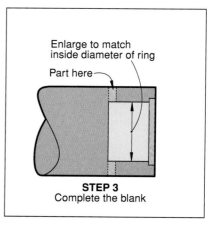

Enlarge to match inside diameter of ring

Part here

STEP 3
Complete the blank

Now, turn the front

To turn the front of the bezel, you first need to construct a chuck fixture like the one shown right. To make one, turn a scrapwood piece round between centers, and true the end at the tailstock. Drill a pilot hole for your screw center into the tailstock end, and attach the piece to the screw center.

Turn a short tenon on the end to fit the bezel blank. The bezel blank must fit snugly over the tenon; check the size as you work. A parting tool works great for this job.

Place the bezel blank over the tenon, seating the blank's bottom firmly against the shoulder on the lathe fixture. Turn the bezel to the desired outside diameter (we made ours anywhere from 1¼ to 1¾" diameter) and thickness (ours varied between ⅛" and ¼").

Turn the top surface of the bezel to one of the typical profiles shown on *page 147* or a design of your own. You'll need miniature-turning tools for coves or beads, but you can use your smallest standard tools for convex forms. Insert the watch face into the hole to check the fit.

Sand the face of the bezel to 320 grit, and finish as desired. Press the bezel onto the watch. If it seems too loose, build up the inside of the brass ring with a thin application of instant glue. If the stem knob interferes with a wide bezel, carve a slight depression in the bottom of the bezel for clearance. To complete the set, turn three more bezels in different woods or styles.

Tools and Supplies

- **Stock**
  Miscellaneous scrapwood (see text)
- **Lathe tools**
  Drive center, tail center
  Screw center

3" faceplate
Gouges ⅜₂", ¼", and ½"
Skew ½"
Parting tools ¹⁄₁₆" and ⅛"
- Lathe speeds
  Turning, sanding:
  1100–1400 rpm

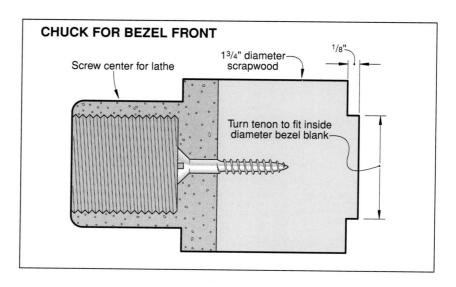

CHUCK FOR BEZEL FRONT

Screw center for lathe

1¾" diameter scrapwood

1/8"

Turn tenon to fit inside diameter bezel blank

Jewel of a Vial

A fanciful flask for perfume

With a fanciful spired stopper, this graceful perfume bottle towers above the ordinary. We think you'll find extraordinary enjoyment in turning the delicate details that give it that exotic look.

Note: Select well-seasoned stock for dimensional stability. Excessive warping after turning could make the stopper or vial inside difficult, if not impossible, to remove. (A few weeks after turning our container, we reamed out the hole in the urn to restore roundness by twisting the drill bit into it by hand.

START WITH THE URN

For your stock, saw a 4½" length from a 1½x1½x10" turning square. Write *top* on the sawed end. Mark the remaining part *bottom* on the sawed end, and set it aside to use later when you turn the stopper.

Locate the center on each end of the urn stock. Bore a ⅝" hole 2½" deep into the top. Drill a pilot hole for your lathe's screw center at the other end. Use a screw that extends ¾" or less into the stock.

Attach the urn stock to the screw center, and mount on the lathe. Support the tailstock end with a revolving cone center in the ⅝" hole. A short tool rest will come in handy for this project.

With a roughing gouge or other large gouge, round down the stock to 1⅜" diameter. Mark the turning ¼" and 3¼" from the tailstock end. With a parting tool, cut in to ⅞" diameter on the waste side of each line.

Following the diameters shown on the Full-Sized Template on *page 150*, turn the outside profile of the urn between the marks, with the top at the tailstock end (Step 1 in the Turning the Urn drawing on *page 150*). Shape it with a gouge or skew, maintaining a slight curve along the side.

Slide the tailstock back, and then complete the bead around the opening. Sand and finish.

Part the urn from the lathe. Make the base slightly concave on the bottom by angling the tool tip slightly toward the top of the urn. Since the bottom will show whenever anyone tips the container to remove the vial inside, sand and finish it carefully.

NOW, LET'S TURN THAT SHOW-STOPPING STOPPER

Mount the remaining part of the turning square between centers, with the bottom at the headstock. Round it to 1" diameter.

At the headstock end, turn a cone tapering to ½" diameter 1" from the end of the stock. Starting there, form a tenon on the bottom of the stopper, shown by Step 1 of the Turning the Stopper drawing on *page 150*. Measure the tenon as you work to ensure that it fits into the hole in the urn. It does not need to be a snug fit; an O-ring holds the stop-per in place. Cut

continued

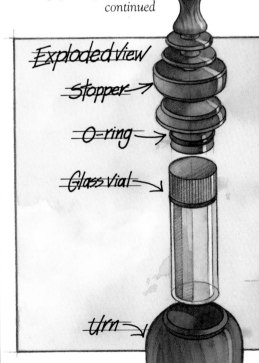

Exploded view
Stopper →
O-ring →
Glass vial →
Urn →

Jewel of a Vial

continued

the O-ring groove ³⁄₃₂" wide and ¹⁄₁₆" deep where shown.

Then rough the turning to approximately the shape shown by the *light tan* area on the drawing. Using the Full-Sized Template, draw pencil lines on the roughed-out turning to layout the features.

Form the profile with small gouges (we used ¹⁄₈" and ¹³⁄₆₄" miniature gouges). A good approach is to bring the finial almost to final form early. Leave it about ¼" diameter at the tip as you turn the stopper. This helps prevent breaking the fragile turning. Further stave off problems by taking light cuts as you develop the shapes.

Note that the sharp-edged discs vary in thickness as well as diameter. Turn square-edged discs of correct diameter and thickness, and then form the curved top and bottom surfaces with your small gouge. Cut the shallow step around the top and bottom of the large bead with a ¹⁄₁₆" parting tool.

Then, carefully complete the finial. Don't damage the fine point on the tip as you separate the waste from the turning.

Finish the stopper to match the urn. Chamfer the bottom about ¹⁄₁₆", and part off the stopper.

Roll a ⅝"-O.D. O-ring (available in the plumbing department at most hardware stores) into the groove around the tenon. Try the stopper's fit in the urn. If it's too loose, try an O-ring made of slightly thicker material or wrap a few strands of black sewing thread into the groove under the O-ring. Fix a lid that's too tight by sanding or filing the groove or changing to an O-ring of smaller-diameter material.

TOOLS AND SUPPLIES

- **Stock**
  **1½x1½x10" turning square
  (We used cocobolo.)**
- **Lathe tools**
  Screw center; Revolving cone tail center; Spindle gouges, ⅛", ¹³⁄₆₄", ½"; Roughing gouge; Skew, ½"; Parting tool, ¹⁄₁₆"
- **Lathe speeds**
  **Roughing: 500–800 rpm
  Finishing and sanding: 1,200–1,500 rpm**

BUYING GUIDE

- **Glass vial.** Vial with screw-on lid, ⅛-oz. size. Drill bit (fits ½" chuck). For current prices, contact Craft Supplies USA, 1287 E. 1120 S., Provo, UT 84601, or call 801/373-0917 to order.

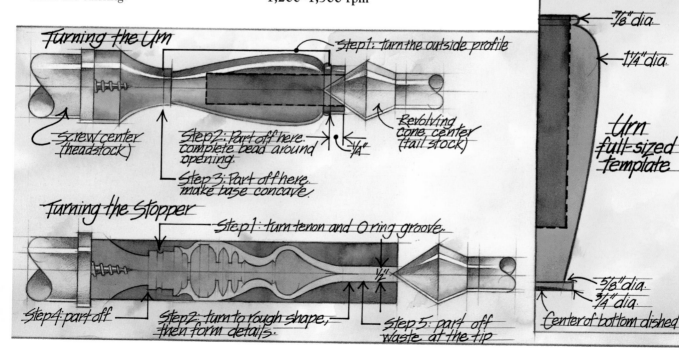

One Sweetheart of a Jewelry Box

It's the perfect gift

You'll surely win your loved one's affection with this unique gift. The lid and trays rotate open to display fine earrings, rings, and necklaces, and they swivel closed, making an eye-pleasing dresser-top showpiece. If you don't get it built by Christmas, keep in mind that the heart-topped container works great for birthdays and Valentine's Day, too.

MARKING THE BASE, TRAYS, AND TOP LAYOUTS

1 From 1¹⁄₁₆"-thick cherry, cut a 7"-square piece for the base (A), two pieces to 5½" square for the trays (B), and one piece of ¾"-thick bird's-eye maple to 5½" square for the lid (C).

2 Mark centerlines on the *bottom surface* of the four blanks where shown on the Parts View drawing. Then, using a combination square,

mark 45° reference lines on the bottom surface of the two trays and lid blanks.

3 Using a compass, mark a 3¼"-radius and 2"-radius circle on the base blank. See the Parts View for reference. Mark 2"-radius and 2½"-radius circles on the tray blanks (B). Mark a 2½"-radius circle on the maple lid blank (C).

continued

One Sweetheart of a Jewelry Box

continued

4 Mark the centerpoints, and drill the pivot holes where shown on the Parts View drawing. For the base pivot hole, drill a ⅝" hole ¼" deep on the bottom side first. Then, drill a ¼" hole centered inside the ⅝" hole.

CUTTING AND SANDING THE PIECES TO SHAPE

1 Fit your bandsaw with a ¼" blade. Following the centerline marked parallel with the grain, bandsaw the base and trays in half.

2 Bandsaw the inner marked circle on the tray and base pieces to cut the interiors to shape.

3 Spread glue on the kerfed areas, and glue the tray and base halves back together, with the top and bottom edges flush.

4 Cutting just outside the outermost marked circle, bandsaw the base, two trays, and lid to shape. Later, sand the outside edge of the base to the marked circumference lines to finish the shaping.

5 Using your largest diameter drum sander, sand the inside of the base and trays, sanding to the inner marked circle.

6 To make the bottom (D) for the base (A), position the base on a piece of ¼"-thick stock (we used plywood). Marking along the inside of the base wall, transfer the shape to the ¼" stock. Cut and sand the base bottom (D) until it fits snugly inside the base and the bottom edges are flush. Glue the bottom in place. Repeat the process for the two trays.

7 Mark the stop-dowel centerpoints on the bottom side of the trays and lid. Drill the holes.

IT'S TIME FOR FINAL MACHINING

1 Cut the pivot dowel to 3¹⁵⁄₁₆" long. Dry-fit (no glue) one end of the dowel into the hole on the bottom side of the lid. Sand the rest of the dowel until the trays rotate easily on it.

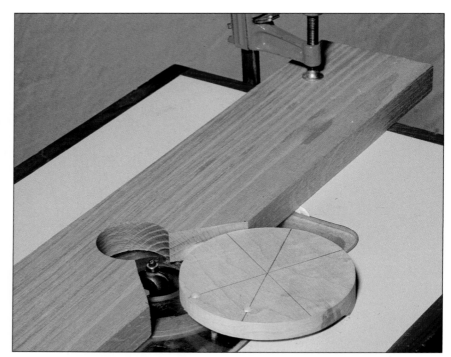

To rout the base and lid coves, fit your router with a V-block fence to help keep your fingers safely away from the rotating router bit.

FULL-SIZED PATTERN

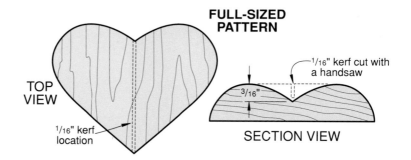

TOP VIEW

1/16" kerf location

1/16" kerf cut with a handsaw

3/16"

SECTION VIEW

2 To sand the edges of the trays and lid flush, use double-faced (carpet) tape to adhere the trays and lid one on top of the other with the outside edges flush and the pivot pin inserted through the pivot pin holes in the trays and into the ¼"-deep hole in the lid.

3 With the assembly upside down and resting on the lid, disc sand the outside edges of the pieces flush. Switch to a palm sander, and sand away any sanding marks left by the disc sander.

4 Use a splash of lacquer thinner or acetone to weaken the double-faced tape joints. Now, separate the parts, and remove the tape and any sticky residue.

5 Cut a V-block router-table fence like that shown in the photo *above*. The fence provides support when routing the base and lid coves and helps keep your fingers safely away from the spinning router bit. Rout a ⅜" cove along the top outside edge of the lid (C). Then, switch bits, and rout a ½" cove along the top

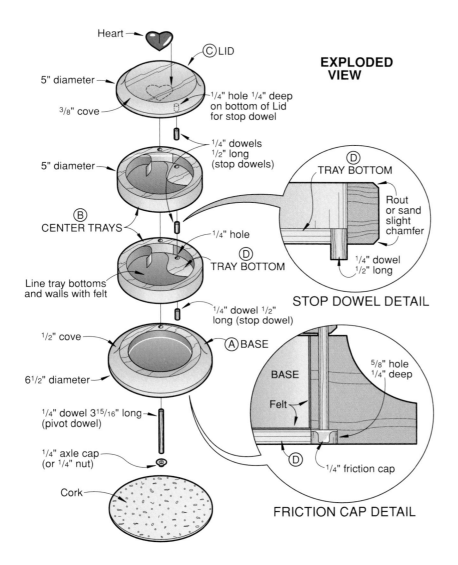

Heart

© LID

5" diameter

3/8" cove

1/4" hole 1/4" deep
on bottom of Lid
for stop dowel

**EXPLODED
VIEW**

5" diameter

1/4" dowels
1/2" long
(stop dowels)

© D
TRAY BOTTOM

Rout
or sand
slight
chamfer

(B)
CENTER TRAYS

1/4" hole

© D
TRAY BOTTOM

1/4" dowel
1/2" long

Line tray bottoms
and walls with felt

1/4" dowel 1/2"
long (stop dowel)

STOP DOWEL DETAIL

1/2" cove

(A) BASE

5/8" hole
1/4" deep

BASE

6 1/2" diameter

Felt

1/4" dowel 3 15/16" long
(pivot dowel)

1/4" axle cap
(or 1/4" nut)

© D

1/4" friction cap

Cork

FRICTION CAP DETAIL

Chiseled and sanded smooth, the painted
wood heart adds an element of romance
to this trayed jewelry box.

Bill of Materials				
Part	Finished Size		Mat.	Qty.
	T	W	L	
A* base	1 1/16"	6 1/2" dia.		C	1
B* trays	1 1/16"	5 1/2" dia.		C	2
C* lid	3/4"	5" dia.		BM	1
D bottoms	1/4"	4" dia.		P	3

*Initially cut parts oversized. Then, trim each
to finish size according to the how-to
instructions.

Material Key: C–cherry, BM–bird's-eye
maple, P–plywood

Supplies: 1/4" friction cap or 1/4" nut, 1/4" dowel
stock, red enamel paint, clear finish, cork.

outside edge of the base (A). To
minimize chip-out when routing
the coves, we did it in three passes,
increasing the depth of cut each
pass.)

6 Sand a 1/32" chamfer along the top
and bottom edges of each tray,
and along the bottom edge of the lid.
See the Stop Dowel detail accompanying the Exploded View drawing
for reference.

7 From 1/4" dowel stock, cut the
three stop dowels to 1/2" long.

Again, see the Stop Dowel detail
for reference. Glue the stop dowels
in place.

OK, LET'S MAKE THE HEART

1 Transfer the full-sized heart
pattern to a piece of 3/8" thick
maple. Using a bandsaw or scrollsaw,
cut the heart to shape, and then sand
the cut edges smooth.

2 For stability, adhere the heart to
one corner of your benchtop or to
a large piece of scrap material. Using

a handsaw, cut a 3/16"-deep kerf down
the middle of the heart where shown
on page 152.

3 Sand or chisel the contours of the
heart to the shape shown on the
drawing and intro photos. Finish-
sand the heart to its final rounded
shape.

4 Seal the heart's top surface (we
used Deft lacquer). Paint the
heart's top surface bright red (we
used a quality enamel aerosol).

One Sweetheart of a Jewelry Box

continued

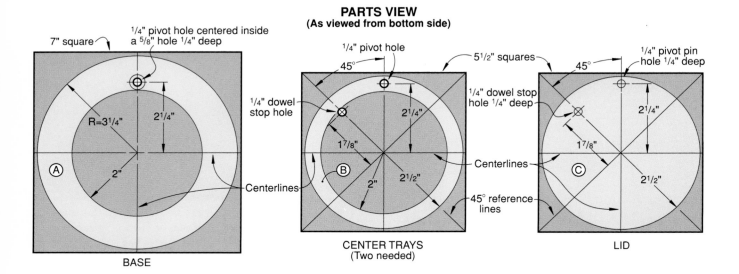

PARTS VIEW
(As viewed from bottom side)

7" square
1/4" pivot hole centered inside a 5/8" hole 1/4" deep
R=3 1/4"
2 1/4"
2"
Ⓐ
Centerlines
BASE

1/4" pivot hole
45°
1/4" dowel stop hole
5 1/2" squares
1/4" dowel stop hole 1/4" deep
2 1/4"
1 7/8"
2"
2 1/2"
Ⓑ
Centerlines
45° reference lines
CENTER TRAYS
(Two needed)

45°
1/4" pivot pin hole 1/4" deep
2 1/4"
1 7/8"
2 1/2"
Ⓒ
LID

ADD THE FINISH AND LINING

1 Finish-sand the base, trays, and lid. Apply a clear finish (again, we used Deft aerosol lacquer) to the individual pieces.

2 Once the finish dries, lightly sand the tray and base interiors. (A roughed-up finish makes for better adhesion when applying the felt jewelry box linings.) Next, cut pieces of felt to fit where shown on the Exploded View drawing. Glue the bottom pieces in place and then the wall pieces.

3 Glue the pivot dowel into the hole in the lid bottom. Slide the dowel through the pivot holes in the trays and base. To align the outside edges of the trays and lid when closed, you may have to sand the side of the stop dowels slightly. Check the alignment, and sand more if necessary.

4 Tap a ¼" friction cap onto the bottom end of the pivot dowel. The cap allows the dowel to swivel when opening the trays. You also can thread a ¼" nut onto the bottom of

the dowel, and secure it with a drop of instant glue.

5 Lightly sand the bottom surface of the base, and adhere ⅟₁₆"-thick cork (we used cork gasket material and adhered it with woodworker's glue). Using an X-ACTO knife, carefully trim the edges of the cork flush with the outside edges of the jewelry box base.

6 Rough-up a small area on the top of the lid, opposite the pivot pin, and glue the heart in place.

Country-Time Plate Rack

A charming addition to any setting

Country charm radiates from this easy-to-build plate rack. That's, in part, due to the simple joinery and pine tongue-and-groove backing strips. Even the cutout apple motif helps make our project the perfect creation for adding real homespun atmosphere to your kitchen or dining area.

Note: Because of space limitations, we can't provide full-sized patterns for this project. However, to enable you to build the project, we've included gridded patterns. To enlarge these patterns, see the instructions on page 160.

To form the cabinet back, we purchased economy-grade tongue-and-groove knotty pine plank paneling at a local home center. Our strips measured ¼" thick by 3½" wide. They came packed in random lengths

measuring 5' to 8' long. The stock is quite inexpensive, but we did have to work around a few knots and defects. You also could use ¼" plywood for the back.

CUT THE MAIN FRAME PIECES FIRST

1 From ¾"-thick pine, cut the sides (A), shelves (B), and upper and lower rails (C) to the sizes listed in the Bill of Materials.

2 Using double-faced tape, adhere the two sides (A) face-to-face with the edges and ends flush. Enlarge and transfer the top and bottom patterns on *page 157*, including the hole centerpoints, to the ends of the taped-together side pieces.

3 Using a bandsaw or scrollsaw, cut the ends of the side pieces to shape. Separate the pieces and remove the tape and residue.

4 Dry-clamp (no glue) the assembly (A, C) to check the fit and for square. Drill the screw-mounting holes through the sides (A) and into the ends of the rails (C) where shown on the Exploded View and Section View drawings. See the Screw-Hole detail accompanying the Exploded View drawing for hole sizes.

5 With the pieces still dry-clamped, rout a ¼" rabbet ¼" deep around the back inside edge of the A/C assembly. See the Exploded View drawing and accompanying Rabbet detail for reference. Remove the clamps and disassemble the unit.

6 Mark the dado locations on the side pieces where dimensioned on the Exploded View drawing. Using your tablesaw or radial-arm saw, cut ¾" dadoes ¼" deep where marked. (We set a stop when cutting each dado to ensure that the dadoes are in the same location on each side piece.)

continued

Country-Time Plate Rack

continued

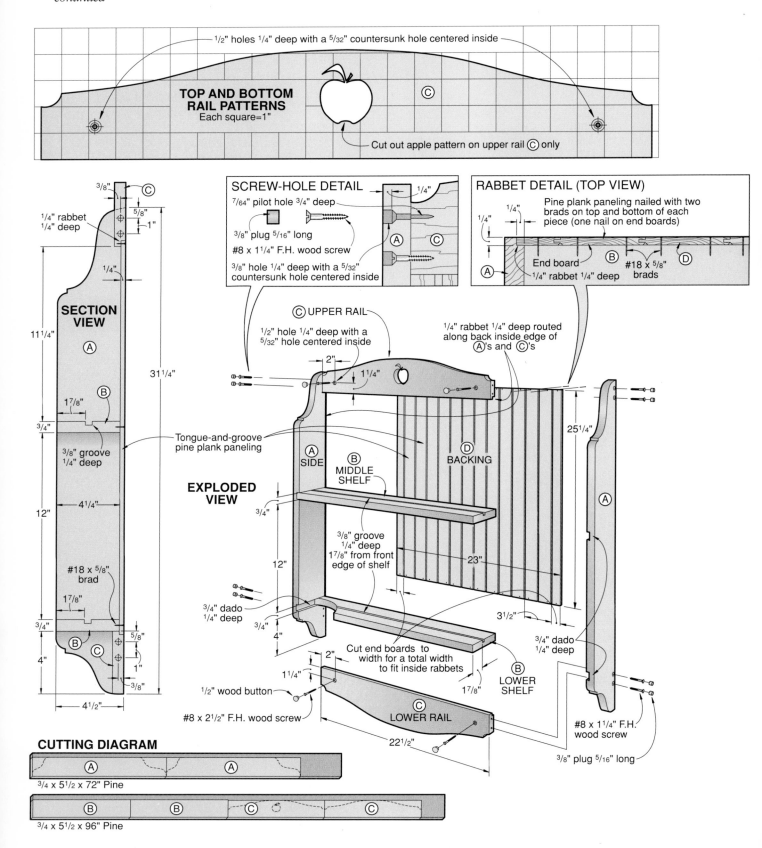

TOP AND BOTTOM RAIL PATTERNS
Each square=1"

1/2" holes 1/4" deep with a 5/32" countersunk hole centered inside

Ⓒ

Cut out apple pattern on upper rail Ⓒ only

SECTION VIEW

3/8"
Ⓒ
5/8"
1"
1/4" rabbet 1/4" deep
1/4"

Ⓐ
11 1/4"

Ⓑ
1 7/8"
3/4"
3/8" groove 1/4" deep
4 1/4"

12"

#18 x 5/8" brad

1 7/8"
3/4"
Ⓑ
Ⓒ
5/8"
1"
3/8"
4"
4 1/2"
31 1/4"

SCREW-HOLE DETAIL

7/64" pilot hole 3/4" deep

1/4"

3/8" plug 5/16" long
#8 x 1 1/4" F.H. wood screw
3/8" hole 1/4" deep with a 5/32" countersunk hole centered inside

Ⓐ
Ⓒ

RABBET DETAIL (TOP VIEW)

Pine plank paneling nailed with two brads on top and bottom of each piece (one nail on end boards)

1/4"
1/4"
1/4"
Ⓑ
Ⓓ
Ⓐ
End board
1/4" rabbet 1/4" deep
#18 x 5/8" brads

Ⓒ UPPER RAIL

1/2" hole 1/4" deep with a 5/32" hole centered inside

2"
1 1/4"

1/4" rabbet 1/4" deep routed along back inside edge of Ⓐ's and Ⓒ's

Tongue-and-groove pine plank paneling

EXPLODED VIEW

Ⓐ
SIDE
Ⓑ
MIDDLE SHELF
Ⓓ
BACKING

3/4"

3/8" groove 1/4" deep 1 7/8" from front edge of shelf

12"
23"

25 1/4"

Ⓐ

3/4" dado 1/4" deep
3/4"
4"

3/4" dado 1/4" deep
3 1/2"

Ⓑ
LOWER SHELF
1 7/8"

Cut end boards to width for a total width to fit inside rabbets

2"
1 1/4"

1/2" wood button

#8 x 2 1/2" F.H. wood screw

Ⓒ LOWER RAIL

22 1/2"

#8 x 1 1/4" F.H. wood screw

3/8" plug 5/16" long

CUTTING DIAGRAM

Ⓐ   Ⓐ
3/4 x 5 1/2 x 72" Pine

Ⓑ   Ⓑ   Ⓒ   Ⓒ
3/4 x 5 1/2 x 96" Pine

7 Cut a ⅜" groove ¼" deep in each shelf (B) where shown on the Section View drawing.

ADD THE SHELVES AND UPPER AND LOWER RAILS

1 Enlarge and transfer the full-sized apple and top outline pattern to the upper-rail blank. Tape the upper and lower rails (C) face-to-face, and cut the outlines to shape. Separate the pieces and remove the tape.

2 Next, drill a blade-start hole, and scrollsaw the apple to shape in the upper rail (you also could use a coping saw).

3 Glue, clamp, and screw the sides (A), shelves (B), and top and bottom rails (C), checking for square. Position the shelves (B) into the dadoes in the side pieces so the back edge of the shelves are flush with the inside edge of the rabbets.

This will leave enough room for installing the pine plank paneling.

4 Cut ⅜"-diameter plugs from ⁵⁄₁₆" stock, and plug the screw-mounting holes. Sand the plugs flush with the outside surface of the side pieces.

5 Working from the center of the rack out, crosscut pieces of the pine plank paneling to fit into the rabbeted back edge of the cabinet assembly. Hold the pieces in place with masking

tape. You'll need to rip the two outside pieces for a good fit. Glue and nail the pieces in place, being sure to wipe off excess glue with a damp cloth. (We used #18x⅝" brads to secure the pine plank paneling in the rabbets and to the back edges of the shelves where shown on the Section View drawing.)

6 For mounting to the wall later, drill and counterbore a pair of mounting holes through the upper and lower rails (C). You'll need to use long screws and hit studs or use toggle bolts to hang the unit. Plug the holes with wood buttons after hanging.

7 Finish-sand the assembled cabinet. Stain the cabinet (we used WOODKOTE gelled Fruitwood stain). Let the stain dry overnight before applying a clear finish.

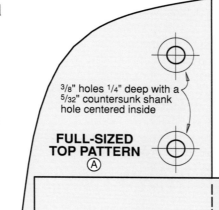

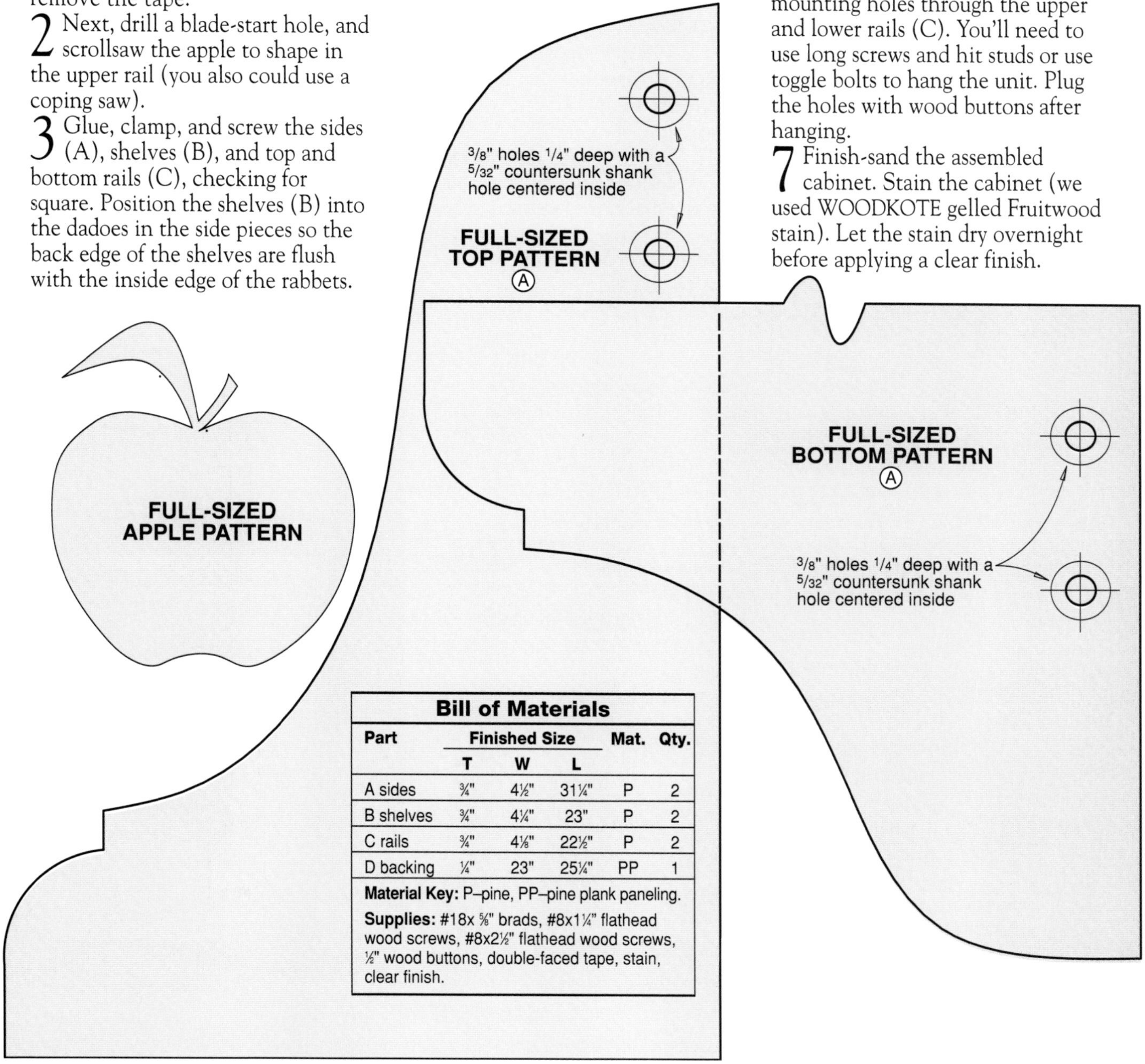

3/8" holes 1/4" deep with a 5/32" countersunk shank hole centered inside

FULL-SIZED TOP PATTERN Ⓐ

FULL-SIZED BOTTOM PATTERN Ⓐ

3/8" holes 1/4" deep with a 5/32" countersunk shank hole centered inside

FULL-SIZED APPLE PATTERN

Bill of Materials				
Part	Finished Size			Mat.	Qty.
	T	W	L		
A sides	¾"	4½"	31¼"	P	2
B shelves	¾"	4¼"	23"	P	2
C rails	¾"	4⅛"	22½"	P	2
D backing	¼"	23"	25¼"	PP	1

Material Key: P–pine, PP–pine plank paneling.

Supplies: #18x ⅝" brads, #8x1¼" flathead wood screws, #8x2½" flathead wood screws, ½" wood buttons, double-faced tape, stain, clear finish.

A Stirring Display

Showplace for special spoons

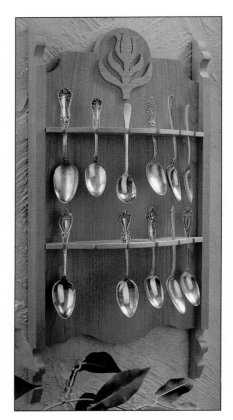

We think that collectible spoons deserve better treatment than being stashed in some drawer. Here's an easy-to-build display rack that puts teaspoons or demitasse spoons where you—and everyone else—can enjoy them.

Cut stock to the dimensions shown in the Bill of Materials. (We resawed and planed thicker material for the thin stock. For the 9"-wide Part A, we glued up two narrower pieces.)

Photocopy the half-patterns for the top and bottom profiles of the back, *opposite*. Make full patterns, and trace them onto the stock for Part A, using carbon paper or transfer paper. Bandsaw or scroll-saw Part A. Rout a keyhole hanging slot near the top center on the back face.

Transfer the full-sized patterns for the sides' top and bottom curves onto one 1¼"-wide face of one side (B). Stack the two Parts B with double-faced tape between them, placing the patterned piece on top. Bandsaw the two sides, and sand them.

Lay out the spoon holders (C) on your stock. Make two to display teaspoons, three for demitasse spoons. Stack the parts, and then bandsaw or scrollsaw them.

To form the bowl depressions, chuck a core-box router bit into your drill press. With the workpiece secured firmly, bring the bit down onto the mark deep enough to make a ⅜" diameter depression. Set the drill-press depth gauge at that point to make the rest of the depressions uniform.

After forming all of the bowl depressions, drill a ¼" hole (or one to fit your spoons, if different) in the center of each. Bandsaw or scrollsaw a ⅛"-wide slot straight in from the edge to each drilled hole. Sand the parts.

Mark the spoon-holder locations where shown on Part A, depending on your spoon size. Rout a ¼" dado ¼" deep across Part A at each location. Glue the holders into place with the bowl depressions facing up. Glue on the sides (B), placing the back edge of each flush with the back face of Part A. Sand the assembly.

Scrollsaw the decoration from ⅛" stock. Sand, and glue it to the back piece where shown. Apply a clear finish overall.

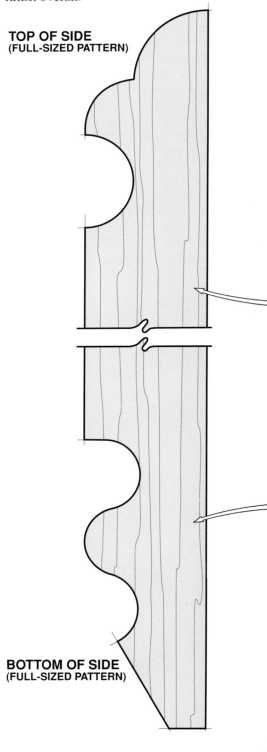

TOP OF SIDE
(FULL-SIZED PATTERN)

BOTTOM OF SIDE
(FULL-SIZED PATTERN)

Bill of Materials				
Part	Finished Size		Mat.	Qty.
	T	W	L	
A back	¾"	9"	17¼"	C	1
B sides	½"	1¼"	19⅞"	C	2
C holders	¼"	3"	9"	C	3
D decoration	⅛"	4"	5"	C	1
Material Key: C—cherry.				

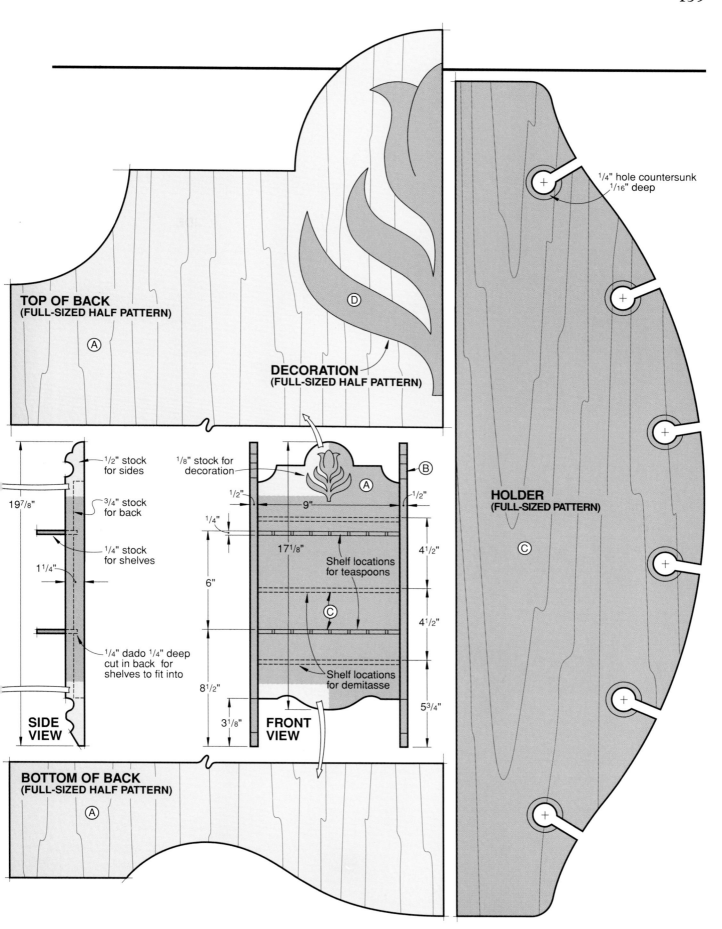

TOP OF BACK
(FULL-SIZED HALF PATTERN)

Ⓐ

DECORATION
(FULL-SIZED HALF PATTERN)

Ⓓ

¼" hole countersunk
¹⁄₁₆" deep

HOLDER
(FULL-SIZED PATTERN)

Ⓒ

½" stock
for sides

¾" stock
for back

¼" stock
for shelves

19⁷⁄₈"

1¼"

¼" dado ¼" deep
cut in back for
shelves to fit into

**SIDE
VIEW**

⅛" stock for
decoration

Ⓐ

Ⓑ

½"   9"   ½"

¼"

17⅛"

6"

Ⓒ

4½"

4½"

Shelf locations
for teaspoons

Shelf locations
for demitasse

8½"

3⅛"

5¾"

**FRONT
VIEW**

BOTTOM OF BACK
(FULL-SIZED HALF PATTERN)

Ⓐ

Acknowledgments

WRITERS

James R. Downing—High-Styled Raised Panels and Frames, pages 76–81

Larry Johnston—Down-Under Desk Clock, pages 140–141; Ring Around the Wrist Watch, pages 146–148

Bill Krier—Leaded-Glass Panels, pages 49–55

Dick Sing—Ring Around the Wrist Watch, pages 146–148

PROJECT DESIGNERS

Judith Ames—The One-and-Only Teddy Bear Chair, pages 89–95

David Ashe—© Leafy Lodging Birdhouse, pages 18–19; A Picture-Book Box, pages 130–131; A Stirring Display, pages 158–159

Barrels of Fun—Smiley the Rocking Snail, pages 108–111

Jim Boelling—Wheat-Motif Bread Box, pages 134–135

Alan Bradstreet—Projects with Porpoise, pages 142–145

Jerry Brownrigg—© Down-Under Desk Clock, pages 140–141

James R. Downing—Fun-in-the-Sun Furniture, pages 7–11; Lazy-Days Porch Rocker, pages 12–17; Craftsman-Style Wall Lantern, pages 24–27; Elegant Oak Dining Table, pages 31–37; Elegant Oak Dining Chairs, pages 38–44; Bow-Front Table, pages 65–68; Pocket-Hole Drill Guide, page 69; Down-to-Business Oak Desk, pages 70–75; High-and-Mighty Tablesaw Jig, pages 82–83, Wild Kingdom Coatrack, pages 84–87; Keep-on-Recycling Toy Box, pages 99–103; Baby's First Bed, pages 112–117; Country-Time Plate Rack, pages 155–157

Loyal Downing—The Safe-and-Simple Thin-Strip Ripper, pages 63–64

Deborah Doyle—© Jewel of a Vial, pages 149–150

Susan Evarts—© Autumn Leaves, pages 119–121

Lorenzo Freccia—One Sweetheart of a Jewelry Box, pages 151–154

Harlequin Crafts—A Welcome Sign That Says it All, pages 126–127

Larry Johnston—Little Red Tote Barn, pages 96–98; Lamination Sensation, pages 136–139

Marlen Kemmet—Craftsman-Style Wall Lantern, pages 24–27

Quality Woodcrafters/Gus Stefureac—© Choo-Choo To Go, pages 106–108

Keith Raivo—Woven-Wood Hamper, pages 56–62; High-Styled Raised Panels and Frames, pages 76–81

Schlabaugh and Sons—Echoes of Antiquity, pages 122–125; © Olympian Display, pages 128–129

Pat Schlarbaum—Seeds-and-Such Snack Shop, pages 20–23

Aaron Shaw—Keep-on-Recycling Toy Box, pages 99–103

Cary Stage—Worth-Every-Minute Wall Clock, pages 45–48

The Woodshed, B. & C. Willey—Dresser-Top Dragon, pages 104–105

Workshop Blueprint Co.—© Leafy Lodging Birdhouse, pages 18–19; A Stirring Display, pages 158–159

Bill Zaun—© Plant Hanger from Paradise, pages 28–29

PHOTOGRAPHERS

John Hetherington
Hopkins Associates
William Hopkins
Perry Struse

ILLUSTRATORS

James R. Downing

Jamie Downing
Kim Downing
Mike Henry
Brian Jensen
Bill Zaun

Enlarging gridded patterns by hand

Gridded patterns in this book that require enlargement include the statement "Each square = 1"." This means that grid squares in the drawing *must* be enlarged to the size indicated for your full-sized pattern.

To use the hand-enlargement method called transposing, you'll need cross-section graph paper (the kind with heavier lines marking off each square inch), a ruler, an eraser, and a soft-lead pencil. (If graph paper isn't available, make your own by dividing plain paper into the specified-size squares.)

Begin by marking off on your grid paper the same number of squares as indicated on the pattern grid. Next, number each vertical and horizontal grid line in the pattern. Then, number the corresponding grid lines on your graph paper the same way.

Start your pattern enlargement by finding a square on your graph paper that matches the same square on the original gridded pattern. Mark the graph paper grid square with a pencil dot in the same comparative place where a design line intersects a grid line on the original. Work only one square at a time. Continue to neighboring squares, marking each in the same way where a design line intersects a grid line.

To avoid discovering any mistakes too late, mark only part of the design, then stop and join the dots with a pencil line. For more precision, draw all of the straight lines first; then add the curved and angled lines. Once you have transposed part of the design, finish marking the rest of the squares and join those dots in the same way.

Sometimes, you'll only have a *half-pattern* to use. To duplicate a full-sized half-pattern, copy the original with a soft-lead pencil on tracing paper. Next, flip your traced pattern over and place it pencil-lines-down onto one half of the board. After aligning the pattern for position, go over the pattern lines with your pencil to imprint it on the board. Then, flop the pattern onto the second half of the board and again retrace the pattern to imprint it. This method proves faster than copying with carbon paper and doesn't mark up the original pattern.

Using a copier to enlarge a gridded pattern

A photocopier with enlargement capability enlarges a pattern faster than transposing. (Even a copier can be a little inaccurate, so always check your results with a ruler.)

To find out the enlargement percentage you'll need, use a pocket calcuator to divide the scale square size (1") by the actual size of a gridded pattern square (for example, ½"). Your resulting enlargement will need to be 200% of the original.

However, the copier you use may only have an enlargement limit of 150%. If this is the case, make a first enlargement of the original at 150%. Next, divide your desired final enlargement percentage (200) by 150. Your answer will be 133.

Then set the photocopier at 133%, and make a second enlargement of your first copy (which was made at 150%), and you'll end up with a pattern that is 200% larger than the gridded pattern. Check the final copy with a ruler to ensure it is sized correctly. If the final copy isn't exactly correct, adjust the copier up or down a percentage or two until you end up with a pattern that is the correct size.

U.S. Units to Metric Equivalents

To convert from	Multiply by	To get
Inches	25.4	Millimeters (mm)
Inches	2.54	Centimeters (cm)
Feet	30.48	Centimeters (cm)
Feet	0.3048	Meters (m)
Yards	0.9144	Meters (m)

Metric Units to U.S. Equivalents

To convert from	Multiply by	To get
Millimeters	0.0394	Inches
Centimeters	0.3937	Inches
Centimeters	0.0328	Feet
Meters	3.2808	Feet
Meters	1.0936	Yards

If you would like to order any additional copies of our books, call 1-800-678-2803 or check with your local bookstore.